CLAIRE ROBERTS

Standing Well

Claire's story is about finding your faith and believing God is good, even when life is taking everything from you.

First published by Ingramspark 2021

Copyright © 2021 by Claire Roberts

All rights reserved. No part of this publication may be reproduced, stored or transmitted in any form or by any means, electronic, mechanical, photocopying, recording, scanning, or otherwise without written permission from the publisher. It is illegal to copy this book, post it to a website, or distribute it by any other means without permission.

Claire Roberts asserts the moral right to be identified as the author of this work.

Second edition

ISBN: 9780645372793

Editing by Bronwyn Windsor
Editing by Shannon Crozier
Editing by Tracy Akerman
Cover art by Kiel Wode (photograher)

This book was professionally typeset on Reedsy.
Find out more at reedsy.com

This book is a love letter of appreciation to my Heavenly Father, no amount of words will ever be enough.

Father God, thank you for Your patience and kindness. You always found a way to pull me closer all while I was trying to push You away. You have been serious about Your commitment to me, every day. I have been a big task at times for You to work with, but none of it has been too big for You.

Contents

Foreword ... iv
Acknowledgement ... x
How to use this book ... xii

I VALLEY of DRIED BONES

1. The early years ... 3
2. More pain to come ... 19
3. Time to be honest ... 25
4. It's not fair ... 32
5. Grieving the dream ... 37
6. Wrestling with God ... 43
7. Forgive yourself ... 49
8. The choice is yours ... 57
9. In God's hands now ... 63

II I AM LOVED

10. Who you were ... 69
11. Pain has a purpose ... 76
12. Remember who calls you His ... 83
13. Trusting God ... 90
14. Sweetness of surrender ... 98
15. Warning signs ... 105

III NEW SEASON

16	You're not forgotten	113
17	Value of yesterday's	119
18	Hello to something new	125
19	Breathe	130
20	Starts with a seed	134
21	Immeasurably more	140
22	Be quiet fear	146
23	In the middle	153

IV A COURAGEOUS LIFE

24	Help!	161
25	This is your journey	166
26	Finding your brave	172
27	A courageous faith	179
28	The birth of joy	187
29	Praise is your weapon	192
30	Prepare for what's next	197
31	Your future is waiting	203

V A PROMISED LIFE

32	Miracles still happen	213
33	No shame in again	220
34	Get your hopes up, again	227
35	It's okay to ask, again	233
36	It's okay to receive, again	240
37	Keep praying	247
38	Peace lives here now	253
39	Someone needs your story	260
40	Standing Well	268

Epilogue 276
About the Author 278

Foreword

Hello pain.

It feels unnatural to welcome pain and is often the last thing any of us want to do, it feels more natural to say goodbye instead. This book is about saying goodbye to pain, but in order to farewell something, you first have to greet it. Over the years of wrestling with and fighting my pain, I learnt there is an enormous amount of value in saying 'hello pain' before I try to say my farewells. You don't walk into a room and say 'goodbye' first. No, you say 'hi' to everyone, spend some time together and then say your farewells.

What do you feel when you hear or read the word pain? What do you think of when you hear that word? What do you hear when you think or hear that word, does it have a sound?

When you go to the doctors about some sort of pain, they try to measure how much pain you're by asking you to give a number between one and ten. The problem with this is that my version, experience and perspective of '1' may be very different to yours, and to the doctor's. Pain is completely unique and personal. Sometimes it can't be explained, sometimes it can't be felt by anyone but you, and sometimes it can't be measured. Pain isn't easy to understand, manage or contain, and it's definitely hard to do life when you're in pain.

I've come to learn, understand and appreciate that pain feels and sounds different for everyone. Pain isn't just black in colour, it's a rainbow of many colours. Some are more intense and darker, while others are a little brighter.

The word very word *pain* makes most people shiver and squirm, there's nothing comfortable or comforting about being in pain. It's often easily misunderstood. It is true though, that some pain is easier than others. Some seasons of pain are easier to acknowledge and say 'hello' to, while other seasons feel like they take very last breathe you had and leave you completely broken. For years, pain made me think of punishment.

I thought my pain was my personal punishment from God. I wasn't sure what I was in trouble for, but I figured I must have done (or not done) something to deserve it. I never saw it as a gift or time of preparation. I had so many questions and yet I didn't think I was allowed to ask God any of them, I never knew that my relationship with Him meant that I was allowed to have questions and to seek understanding. For many, many years my relationship with God was strained at best. I became frustrated, and angry. I wish I knew then what I knew then, but at the time I didn't know I could ask Him for help, and *how* to ask for help.

My inability to ask for help wasn't just limited to God, it flowed into my relationships with family and friends. I had an idea of living life well, that idea was that it was up to me to fight the pain away. I thought I had to conquer it. As I've matured in my faith, I've discovered there's a difference between living life well with pain, and living with pain well: it's not about what you can do but what you *allow* God to do. Although many people knew of the pain in my life, I never felt like they really understood how much pain I was in. The ones that did know, begged me to let them in and to let go of my pain. As for everyone else, I had learnt to hide my pain and keeping people at a safe distance. Most times, it felt easier to shut people about out mainly because I wasn't ready to deal with it and sometimes, I thought they weren't ready. Silently, I was screaming for help. The best I can describe it is as if I was in a sound proof room screaming and screaming but no one could hear. When you hide your pain no one can hear you scream, no matter how loud you try or intense the pain is.

Doing this only means you remain isolated and your frustration and false belief that no one, including God, is helping grows and intensifies. I know this all too well, I became an expert tantrum thrower! Instead of inviting people in to help, I shut them out and hurt other people in the process. I truly acted like a child during my years of pain, the kind of child who yells at everyone during a tantrum.

I've rejected my pain, wrestled with it, struggled under it, mishandled it and settled in it, for years. I continued to get angry and frustrated. It's too easy to say, "but I didn't have a choice". But the truth is we do, and I definitely did back then. It's true we don't choose who our parents are, where we are born or if we are born as a man or women. But we do have the gift of the choice after that. Will the outcome of a choice be easy to walk out? Not always.

And the LORD God commanded the man, "You are free to eat from any tree in the garden, but you must not eat from the tree of knowledge" – Gen 2:16-17

No matter how long you're season of pain lasts for, there is a point where you have to grow up. I did. I ran out of excuses and people to blame, not that any of that mattered, and it was time for me to stand well. It was time to acknowledge what I was going through wasn't going to go away by me trying to ignore it or pass it on to someone else. I had a choice then and you have choice now.

Most athletes aren't automatically born Olympic gold medalists. Some are born with an incredible talent, but all of them need to make a choice. A choice to sacrifice many hours to train and stay focused when all they want to do it give up. A choice to be disciplined with their talent, and practice daily. Living a life well with pain is not much different.

I'm not a qualified professional who can give you a step-by-step program, nor am I am an expert at managing pain well all the time (my journal entries I have shared in this book will prove that!). I am simply someone who knows pain well, most of this book has been written over four decades. This book is a compilation of many journal entries and thoughts, a collection of learnings I've gathered as I walk through life. This book isn't a 'how to' or the only way to work your way through the jungle, it's just another way to consider.

In my opinion, God is the only one who can tell you how to walk through your season of pain, and get your through to the other side. This book is instead, my story of how I went from living under the heaviness of pain to standing well with pain. Being dedicated to ensuring my life still flourishes and personally find joy while in pain has been a huge part of my life. My hope is that by reading my story, your journey will be smoother or perhaps shorter than mine. It's my genuine hope that this book helps you to be kinder to yourself, and to those who are cheering you on in your journey.

The key that helped bring breakthrough into my life, was learning to surrender and allowing people in. It wasn't about me holding it together, quite the opposite actually. Real healing began when I allowed people to get close and see all my ugliness. When I was able to be grateful for the gift of pain. In the heat of pain I don't think anyone is grateful for it, but when you come out the other side of it, it's hard not see the purpose and value it had. I'm sure as Jacob wrestled God during the night, gratitude was the furthest thing from his mind. There wouldn't have been much room for gratitude during the wrestling. It was nothing short of intense, raw and brutal.

'When the man saw that he would not win the match, he touched Jacob's hip and wrenched it out of its socket. Then the man said, "Let me go, for the dawn is breaking!" But Jacob said, "I will not let you go unless you bless me."' – Genesis 32:25-26 NLT

'The sun was rising as Jacob left Peniel ["face of God"], and he was limping because of the injury to his hip.' – Genesis 32:31 MSG

There seemed to be no end in sight. With God though, there's always a sunrise after every sunset. Always. As the sun came up for Jacob, he limped away. He was bruised, tired and no doubt exhausted but instead of being mad, he was full appreciation for his pain. He knew God now. He knew God in a way he could never have without the fight and the battle, and the pain. The next time he found himself in another battle or face to face with a new pain, he knew God would be there again. Jacob knew what he was capable of, and what God was capable of. His faith was strengthened and solidified because of that wrestle and pain.

Each time I have come out of a new battle, or face to face with a new pain, my faith has been strengthened too. I wrestled and fought God a little less each time. I started to understand that I won't always understand, but that I also don't have to be defined by my pain. I thought I was the one who was strong and that's why I was still standing, but the truth was and still is, I am still standing because of God's strength. Pain doesn't have to be your end game, in actual fact it can be your starting point if you can see the value in it. This book is a story of someone who made a conscious decision a long time ago to live life well, regardless of pain, to see the glass half full no matter how empty it feels. This book is about the mix of the good and the bad, the sweet and the not-so-sweet, the hard moments and the tender moments, the beautiful and the ugly. It is a story of choosing to hope over it all, and in spite of it all.

My story, hopefully, will help you find a fresh perspective when it comes to living well with your pain. It takes practice and it takes discipline. Like I said, I am not an expert on pain but by sharing my story, I hope I can encourage you to walk through yours better than I did through mine for so long. Over the years I've had many surgeries, and each time it's hard to go about my days while recovering and still in pain. At some point the pain subsides but until then yelling at everyone because of the pain doesn't help. It took me a long time to learn that lesson and, to become responsible for my own pain, and live life well in spite of it.

By sharing my story, it's my hope I can help you be brave to share yours, as well as see the beauty within it. Yes this book was written out of pain but that's just where the story for me began, and hopefully for you too. Join with me as I share my story, my perspective and most importantly, what I think God's perspective on it all is.

Acknowledgement

For years God had asked me to write my story and for years I said "no". Without a few special people, I would never have said yes. Thank you.

PASTOR CLAIRE HEARNE

Pastor Claire, this book exists because of your words; each one of them matters. You were one of the first to say, 'you need to write your story. You need to write a book. Your mum had a brilliant mind and was a wonderful writer. Her gift is now yours; finish what she started'. Those words hit me like a lightning bolt. I never considered my story was worth telling and furthermore, that there was value in all the mess. Your words of encouragement hunted and chased me down, long after you spoke to them, and I'm so thankful.

PASTOR ANNE GRAHAM

Colour Conference 2017 will always be special for so many reasons, but the highlight was definitely joining you and your daughter for dinner. I felt so honoured. You are my Senior Pastor, meaning your time is precious and you gave it so freely that night. You listened as I shared my heart and you were the second one to see the value in my mess. You echoed, 'you need to write your story. You need to write a book'. So this book is a big thank you to you.

SHANNON & TRACY

You were the first people to ever read this book. I gave you such a mess of words but you treated every sentence and paragraph with an enormous amount of care and respect. You looked past the mistakes and muddled words. You encouraged me that this book is indeed a quality body of work that needed to be shared. The two of you were the first ones to say I was a writer and that my work was good. Thank you for helping me turn my ashes into something I can be proud of.

MY FAMILY & FRIENDS

To my friends and family who gave me the space to write, heal, cry, heal and write…thank you. Thank you for letting me go so I could rest in the hands of God and let me walk this journey the only way I knew how to. Thank you for giving the space I so desperately craved and needed to write this book. I know you are always there, arms open wide, and it hurt you at times to see me hurt. I know it didn't makes sense for me to withdraw when you were so close, but this was something only God & I could do together. Thank you for always reminding more I am so much more than my pain and beautiful in your eyes. Your love is one of my life's greatest gifts and treasures.

MY HUSBAND

I want to thank you last because you have always been the last one standing in it all. You are there when everyone else has left and you are there when no one else wants to be. Your commitment to me, our marriage and my ability has never wavered. Never. You have been unapologetic about being my biggest fan – you believe in me more than I believe in myself most days. I love you. I cherish you. I adore you.

How to use this book

This book has been written to be read differently to any other book. It's been written to feel like you and I are having a personal conversation, it's been written as if we are friends catching up and sharing our hearts. There's no judgment with this book, just love and lots of it. I purposely wrote this book to *feel* as intimate as possible and share my inner most thoughts so you might trust me with yours. Why me? It can be incredibly scary and hard to be honest with people, so practice with me first.

"we will no longer be little children, tossed by the waves and blown around by every wind of teaching, by human cunning with cleverness in the technique of deceit. But speaking the truth in love, let us grow in every way into Him who is the head – Christ." Ephesians 4:17

This book has also been written from the hope that we go from talking and into action, at some point. How any of us stand in the middle of our story matters, and who we trust determines our choices. Each of our choices have a profound impact on the outcome of our story. It is no secret that I'm a Christian but that doesn't mean you have to be. I truly think there is benefit to believing in something bigger than you and feeling connected to something. For me that's God. For you that might have a different name. I found the bible to be life changing and the bible itself has helped me not just process my pain, but actually deal with it. It's helped me make decisions, not all of them good, but the key is I made them.

Let's use swimming as an analogy for a moment, there comes a point where you *actually* have to get out to get warm. No amount of mind power is going to get you out of that pool. It's the same with pain. At some point you have to make a decision to do something. Ask for help, forgive someone, trust someone and the list goes one.

In the midst of one of my deepest seasons of pain, God very clearly said, "it's time to be responsible with this pain. It's time to grow up and grow out of the shell this pain has put you in. It breaks my heart too but this pain is not new, and you have two choices. Stand in my love and trust me or give up now". For a moment I considered giving up. But then I thought, "well it's been this hard *with* God, how much harder will it be without Him?". Whether you read all of this book, or some of it, it's my prayer that you hold one for just another day. You start to make your way to the other side. You start to believe it's not too late to start, or too late to start living a beautiful life. I pray this book is your starting point.

If you have a faith in God, can I encourage you to remember God knows where we're at, what we're willing to surrender and how much we can process or handle at any one time. In our gaps God stands and comes alive, and thankfully His mercy and grace takes care of what we can't.

I genuinely hope each time you read this book you feel encouraged, blessed and confident to move forward. I hope you feel a little stronger each week, and you treasure your tears and trust their purpose. In order to get the most out of this book, here are my personal tips:

- <u>Take your time, and rest when you need to</u>

While this book is designed to inspire you, it may also be a bit heavy in some parts and even confronting. Some chapters or sections may hit a little closer to the bone and require more time than others parts to process. Going a little faster, or slowing downing when needed are both okay. What we share between the two of us remains between us, and God if you allow. Please don't think you need to *catch up* because we haven't talked for a while. This isn't homework, this is about your life. If you need to go back and re read weeks or months – that's okay. Sometimes things in this book might trigger old thought patterns and hurts. This book is meant to be your companion for as long as you need it.

- Find a quiet spot

Consider reading this book as time is a piece of time you and on one else. It's an investment into your healing. I encourage you to put your phone away (whatever needs your attention will still be there after), and find a space where you can be completely alone. Maybe driving to the beach is your space, or in your garden - it will be different for everyone. In my experience, if you're searching for God's voice on something you need to be quiet and listen. To me, His voice is a sweet soft whisper that can get lost in the chaos and noise of this world. Wherever you choose, make it somewhere that has minimal distractions and you can be vulnerable.

- Pray & Ask God questions

Again, if you have a faith this part is applicable to you. This book isn't the only way God can be felt, experienced, heard or known. If you want Him to show you something, ask Him. My understanding may not be yours. If something doesn't sit well, or you have questions – ask God. He is the one who has all the answers. My revelations and understandings have come from my own personal experiences, your understanding may be completely different. There isn't a question too big or too uncomfortable for God, so ask away! If you have any questions or want Him to show up for you like He did me, ask Him. Pray about it and trust He will answer you in some way, at some point.

- Journal/Mark your favourite parts

Journaling isn't something everyone likes to do, but it's so beneficial.

Journaling helps you see things clearly and it can be truths you can draw back on when you've lost your way. All my favourite books I have marked or re written a paragraph that has helped me most, years later I've read those bits again and been encouraged all over again! It doesn't have to be pages long, but I do encourage you to journal while you read this book.

- Celebrate each time you read this book

This is so important! We're all experts at finding our faults and flaws, and our own worst enemy. We don't celebrate what we do well enough. Each time you read this book, pray, making a decision to do something, put the work into towards your healing, change an unhealthy behaviour or mindset, or maybe help someone else find their strength - celebrate! Your healing and restoration is worth celebrating because your reinforcing the value of your story and God's faithfulness.

I

VALLEY of DRIED BONES

Chapters one - nine

1

The early years

Like all stories there's always a start, and mine begins with my mum and me when I was just a little girl. My parents both loved me with all they had, but their marriage fell apart when I was young and they separated by my sixth birthday. My mum really struggled, both emotionally and mentally, and never really regained her hold on life after that.

While every child would love for their parents to stay together, I'm honestly thankful mine separated when I was so young. It meant their separation was just my normal, and it was what family was to me. Growing up, it's all I knew and I felt safe in the boundaries that had been put in place early. My dad remarried early, adding another dimension to our family that gave me great joy, and still does. My days with my mum and my days with my dad, however, were so incredibly different.

I didn't struggle with my mum and dad not being together; I could see how happy dad was and that made me happy. My struggle was in the going between two very different worlds. At one home, life was easy. When I visited my dad I didn't have to do the food shop, wash, iron or put the clothes away. I didn't have to make dinner and at times eat it alone. There was noise and life at one home, and not so much within the other. My mum on the other hand, was someone who needed somebody.

Mum never did life alone very well, so when it was just her and I, I knew I had to step in. I was her somebody. Unfortunately, in that process it felt like gave up my childhood. We had lots of fun together, lots, but we also had lots of days where fun was just a distant dream. Looking back, I see what helping my mum really cost me and how familiar I 'd become with pain. My earliest memory of pain is at the age of about six years, and that's when I first saw the damage it did – in a single second. In those early years, it always felt like mum and I faced the world alone.

I know that wasn't the whole reality but to the little girl back then, it really felt like it some days. My dad did all he could to help, as well as many family and friends. However the problem with feeling alone is you believe you truly are alone. Once my parents divorced, I lived with mum and saw my dad on weekends. Living with someone means you have very little space to hide things from each other, a lesson I learnt quickly as mum started finding my journals and diaries! We were incredibly close, like friends rather than mother and daughter at times. This meant that as her depression and anxiety increased, she relied on me more and more. Before either of us realised, the role of mother and daughter had swapped between us and our courses felt set in place. In order to tell my story, I have to tell hers first.

In those early years with mum, we lived in a townhouse that was part of a little community in South Brisbane. It was a two-storey house and everything was very white, matched with dark brick on the outside and bright colours on the inside. Our bedrooms were upstairs, but I remember spending most of my days downstairs in the kitchen, or out in the courtyard. My primary school was actually at the back of our complex and our front door faced towards the front of the community. I always felt safe in that little complex, until one day.

It seemed like any other day, at first. The early months of the year in Queensland are endless days of sunshine. Our summer days feel like they're on repeat for days on end, with each day competing to be brighter and warmer than the one before it. Each day is always very warm and normally incredibly humid. On this day, I was on my bike outside our townhouse when I heard the phone ring.

Instantly, I ran inside. I always felt very important answering the phone, like an important little secretary. A secretary, mind you, that dressed very casually, rode bikes around her townhouse village and rarely brushed her hair. But a secretary, nevertheless. To this day I can't tell you who it was I spoke to, but I can remember everything else about that phone call. I quickly handed the phone to mum as I was instructed and just watched. I'll never forget watching my mum in those moments. I loved watching her, she was so beautiful to me. So graceful. I wanted to be a lady just like her when I grew up, wearing red lipstick and smelling the Chanel No.5. But on that day there was no beauty, no grace – just deep sadness and anger. That's when I first saw what a broken heart looked like.

As mum took in the information that was being relayed to her over the phone, her face changed in both colour and expression. In those few short moments, I saw the effects of pain - it was paralysing and painful to watch.

The phone dropped from her hand, as if every bit of life dropped out of her along with the phone receiver. She became immovable. Silence and sadness filled our home instantly; nothing about it felt safe anymore. I picked up the phone, as any good secretary would, and tried to hand it back to her. It just kept falling out of her hands. I tried to put it up to her face, as I could hear someone still talking. Eventually, she found some strength to finish the conversation and mumbled "goodbye". Sitting still in the moments that followed felt like forever. Pain had again arrived in my mother's world, and very shortly it would also make a home in mine.

Soon I found out the phone call was to inform my mum that her sister, my Aunty Elaine, had died, by her own choice. She too was recovering from a marriage breakdown and her heart was heavy from not being a mother. I believe she would've been a wonderful mother, she loved me with so much patience and kindness. There are photos of us chatting anywhere and everywhere. Where I was, she was.

The days that followed are pretty blank to me. I was very much protected in those first few days, weeks and months after that tragedy and was (thankfully) very oblivious to what was happening. I was removed from it all. Literally. It was like at that time something had to give for mum, and that something was - me.

I believe it was the right decision to remove me from my mother's care for that time, she couldn't have looked after both herself and me. What wasn't happening though, was me being shielding from the pain. It's hard to think a child can feel pain like an adult, but I believe they can because I did. It wasn't from anyone intentionally causing it, in actual fact everyone was doing their best to shield me from it, but I too was in pain. After my aunty died, the home I knew was no longer a place I lived, and I didn't see my mum for what felt like a long time. The only thing I was told was that mum was "not well at the moment", and she was "hurting". I didn't understand why that meant I couldn't be with her, as I had been before. I suppose that's when I started to think that maybe my mum was different to other mothers, additional to me possibly being different to other kids as well. I started to wonder why other mothers weren't like mine. I wondered if everyone else's mum felt sad as much as mine, and loved to sleep as much as my mum.

During the time I spent away from my mum as she recovered from the losses, I got to experience life as a whole family. Life within a family that ate together, laughed with each other, and talked about everything and anything. I loved this new normal. I found myself feeling guilty for feeling happy while my mum was hurting with – the passing of a sister, the breakdown of her marriage and her commencement of life as a single mother. As the time grew that mum and I spent apart, I started to settle into my new life. What never left me though were my questions. I longed for 'normal', even though

I never had much experience with it. The questions never stopped.

Where mum was, and when would I see her? Why was she different to other mothers? Why wasn't she happy very often, and would she be happy again? When would she get better? Was it my fault? Could I do more, or less to help? Why were things different for me, us?

The day my mum & were reunited, I hope it was full of joy and love. I hope it was a sweet moment, and the pain of all the yesterday's weren't felt. I really wish I remembered it. What I do remember is that everything felt different after we were reunited, I know I was different. What did it feel like? Lonely is the only word I can give you. Imagine giving a child a cake mix packet so they could amuse themselves for a while but giving them no help or instruction, just "There you go. Work it out. I'll be back in 1 hour". I've heard many times my friends talk about the first day they go home with their newborn and they feel completely unprepared. They wish the hospital gave them a manual, but instead they just got a little pep talk and sent on their way home. That's what it felt like when my mum and I were reunited. Neither of us knew what to do, and so the questions started again, but they sounded different now.

Was mum going to be like all my friends mothers and look after me? Was mum still sad, or was she happy now? Was I allowed to be happy? Was I still the child or did mum still need looking after? Was my pain allowed to be talked about, or was my mum's more important?

We had no idea what to do, and now to make it harder than before, there was a heaviness to the both of us. The sense of loss hung in the air around us like a cheap perfume. We never spoke about where she'd gone or what my new life looked like while we were apart. We just transitioned into our new normal, and pretended we knew what we were doing. Before pain moved into our lives, we felt like Thelma and Louise taking on the world! Now, it just felt like it was the world against us. Mum was a single woman with a little girl not even ten years old, and a very broken heart.

I was this little girl not even ten years old who felt abandoned, confused and suddenly robbed of a childhood. I still had so many questions and more confused than ever. My mum's pain consumed her life from that point. The weight of her depression, grief, anxiety and anger felt so large during the years that followed. It felt as though we were never going to be happy again. All the light had left the room and it felt like we just adjusted to the darkness. As the years progressed her pain dictated her decisions, or lack of them. Fortunately, mum's best years were still ahead, and we just needed to get through these ones first.

My mum dealt with her pain and found her identity in not the healthiest of ways. While I think the doctors were trying to help, combined with a lack of not having the information we do now, they just made things worse. As they prescribed a range of different medications, they helped mum feel better for a while but it never lasted. The years progressed and she honestly thought she was dealing with her pain by doing this, in truth, she only intensified and complicated it all. It was a distraction more than anything. Her dependency on these medications was destructive and controlling, and it brought more darkness into our world. It took a mother away from her daughter as she increasingly become addicted. It became bigger than either of us could hide, manage or control. There's no doubt in my mind that addiction is no easy battle, regardless of what it is.

I've seen loved ones try to break free from a variety of addictions. It's hard to watch those you love to break free, like watching a fish stuck in a fishing net. The harder they try to break free, the more tired they become and as they fight to break free, they seem to get more tangled. Some people can break free and some need the help of others, someone to help rip the net apart and pull them out. For mum, she honestly didn't think she had a 'problem', and believed instead she needed them and they were helping. If I'm honest, I did love the days they made her happy and helped her keep her promises. But those moments weren't worth the cost her addiction was slowly stealing from us, especially our finances. Some weeks we had very little money left for food and fuel. My dad provided for us, but between it leaving his hands and reaching my mum's, there was often very little left for me.

We lived in extremes. There were times when going to the shops was a luxury so instead we went to the food bank, and then there were times we ate a really nice restaurants and went to the movies. We shared in the domestic duties, some weeks I did more than more than my fair share, and the food shopping was generally my job. Doing the food shopping was always my favourite, even now I still love it. However I always hated the moment I hadn't done my calculations right, and in front of everyone, told I had to choose what items I didn't want. I was so embarrassed. I still remember the faces of pity or anger from the shoppers being held up behind me. I now look back and think why didn't someone I ask if I was okay, I was only around twelve or thirteen at the time. In the mid 1990's we didn't have the internet on our phones, let alone have a mobile phone!, like we do now. Transferring money from one account to another wasn't an option, instead all I had was the cash mum had given me. Item by item, I selected which ones were least required until I had enough money.

Addictions are serious business. They encourage bad choices, complicate already complicated emotions, and keep hearts broken. From the age of six, my life was a crash-course in the reality of pain. I'd become familiar with pain, and I learnt to cope with my pain by hiding it. This pain living in my household, suffocating my mother, told me that I was now responsible for my mum. This is not the way it is ever meant to be. We moved to the Gold Coast when I was about ten years old, but a change of address didn't change our reality. I was so focused on helping my mum to heal, or get through any given day, I didn't realise pain was creeping into my life too. Eventually, I was shouldering both hers *and* mine. I remember being so alone during my teen years.

The quietness within our new Gold Coast unit was deafening. Our unit sat on the second floor with a beautiful view of the water and the lush gardens. Just like our townhouse in South Brisbane, this unit was really white inside, and as the sun filled the lounge room it somehow felt alive. But in reality there wasn't much life happening within that little unit. Some days mum wouldn't wake up for anything other than to go to the bathroom and have a drink of water. Her blinds would be closed and her room was the darkest within the unit. I'm so thankful my dad and his family decided to follow us down so he could remain close. When I say close, I mean in the same suburb! While it angered mum, it was the first time I knew God had His eye on me. Life started to feel full. There was still so much I was hiding but I didn't feel alone anymore.

My life started to take its own shape as I slotted into a great primary school and found my safe place. It was a place where I wasn't responsible for anyone but me for a majority of my daylight hours. Nor did I feel guilty about being happy. The highlight of my primary school years was the hour we had with our two religious education teachers who attended weekly. Everyone in my class loved Gerald and Sandra; they were like grandparents to us all.

Their South African accents had each of us captivated from the moment they spoke, and I'm sure our teachers were envious of how quiet and well behaved we were for our religious education teachers instead of them. That's when God came into my world and He has never left. Whenever I was around Gerald and Sandra, I felt like I was seen. I didn't want to hide. I'd found something I'd never felt before, and I wanted more. I felt joy and acceptance. For those 60 minutes I felt I was seen as a child, could act as a child and truly felt like a child. I wasn't responsible for anyone and the decisions weren't all up to me. The thought of home was never far away though, and with it my usual questions.

Did mum wake up, eat or shower today? Will mum be picking me up when she said or will I be the last left at after school care? Will I have to make dinner? Will

I be eating alone? Will I be able to tell her about my day? What was her depression like today? Did she suffer any anxiety or panic attack? Is she mad with me, or will she be happy to see me? Has she thought about something, or read something and allowed it to brew all day? How mad will she be if she has?

The main side effect to mum's medication addiction was sleep. She just wanted to go to sleep and hope when she woke up, whatever she had to face was no longer there. Not a great way to do life in my eyes but it's what she felt to be the best. My main job was often trying to wake her up. When I would try to wake her up, we had a coffee code. By the age of 14, I was a master of making instant coffee. I'd make one and leave it beside her bed for five minutes. If she didn't come out, I'd go back in and ask if she wanted it reheated. This could happen once more. I didn't go back in after the third time. I knew she wasn't going to be waking up on those days. Some days we didn't share a spoken word; it's hard to talk with someone who is asleep.

We heavily relied on communicating via written notes. Our notes let each other know what the other needed. Hers were heavy filled with her emotions reminding me she loved me, and how she was feeling, and why. Sometimes she left a note if she needed me to do something after school like a food shop, and sometimes there was a promise of pizza for dinner if I woke her up at a set time. My notes were more practical as I'd started to build walls up around my emotions in order to protect myself. My heart getting colder but there wasn't anything I could do about it, it was what I didn't in order to survive and function. My notes let her know I was going to school, going to be at the complex pool or I was heading out on a bike ride. It wasn't unusual for the note I wrote to be in the same spot, unread, waiting for me when I returned home. The best notes were the ones that said we were going to have cheese pizza and garlic bread from Pizza Hut and I would be allowed to watch Melrose Place with her!

I love surprises, whether creating them for people or receiving them. I'm better at creating them than receiving them. Generally I'm two steps ahead of the other person planning the surprise, surprises is something I do well. However, the surprise of never knowing what I was going home to was a type of surprise I never enjoyed. That was one surprise I could not plan for, nor predict - what I was going home to. Being greeted by complete silence was what I hated most. One of my editors for this book, who is a dear friend and knew me at school when all this was happening, said to me recently, "how didn't I know this was happening? How didn't anyone know? Why didn't anyone help you or your mum? I am so sorry!". For most of the years my mum and I journeyed together we hid all of our mess. How do you tell people you haven't spoken to your mum for days? Verbally at least.

How do you tell people you went home to a note informing you whether dinner was sorted or not? You don't.

You just get on with your days, smile and focus on something good in your world. - that's what I did anyway. I don't recommend or encourage lying, but in my case during those school years it felt like a necessity. While my friends shared stories of how annoying brothers were when they got home, how many questions mum asked the moment they walked in the door and how dad wouldn't let them watch TV until their homework was done. I was already desperately lonely at home; I didn't want to be lonely at school too. During lunch time banter, I simply joined in with the rehearsed stories I created or heard from someone else, and no one even knew any different.

I loved school and did everything I could to shut out everything else when I was there. At school, life was bright and vibrant, as was my life with my dad. It was a place I could just be me with no added pressure or responsibility. I loved being around my friends, and being noticed by my teachers. Everyone eagerly waited for three o'clock to hit so they could go home and get out of their uniform, I pretended to be as well but silently I begged for time to slow down. I didn't want my peers to know what my reality really was, and soon I was having to increase my lying to more and more people. What started with family, grew to my school friends and now my church family.

It sounds selfish, but I needed a break from rescuing my mum, and I needed to learn to be me. Church gave me a home, but God was the one who became my anchor. If I couldn't be at school or my dad's house, then I was at church as much as I could be. Mum and I started attending the church of my RE teachers not long after I had connected with them. Church became a safe place for both mum and I, both as a family unit and individually. I truly believe God knew I needed something to anchor myself in and showed me His love every Thursday in those primary school years through Gerald and Sandra. His anchor has held me when I've had every reason to sway.

I'm still amazed as I look back that I stayed home during my teenage years. Amazed I didn't go out and look for love or acceptance with the wrong people. I had such freedom and was really not accountable to anyone. I could've been anywhere with anyone. With all the freedom I had, even from a young girl, it never once occurred to me to be anywhere but church, home or school. It never occurred to me to try and find anything else. Even in my darkest days, God's love in my life has given me reason to believe it will be okay.

From the moment God walked into my life, I felt loved. I wasn't judged, I didn't have to lie or hide anything from Him, and I was allowed to feel happy without guilt. Hiding and portraying a different life to what was real wasn't so easy to manage at church as it was at school. Many knew what my home life really looked like as they'd seen it first-hand. I hid what I could, and deflected as many questions about mum as I could. I wanted to protect my mum. I wanted to protect myself. I felt I had to protect my mum when I wasn't with her; I wanted to protect my dad when I wasn't with him, and if I could, I tried to protect myself too.

In my efforts trying to protect everyone else, I left myself exposed and vulnerable to my first real battle of my own. Turning 16 was not as sweet as it should've been unfortunately, especially as it felt like I'd lived twice the years over by this stage. What started as a few kilograms of weight being lost due to being unwell with the flu, turned into a real war over my life. After many years of protecting and hiding, I was tired and became completely vulnerable. I didn't feel like I had any fight left in me. My eating disorder came at a time when fatigue had set in after I had given everything I had to my mum. I needed a break and what I see now is that my eating disorder was an enormous scream for help!

For my dad, that meant he became the one I wanted as 'my person' throughout this season. We'd already missed out on so much and I was desperate for him to see me. I didn't realise how much I'd pushed him away until he felt so far away. It was not easy for us to work on our relationship with mum's anger and resentment towards him. He tried, sometimes I saw it and sometimes I didn't. We can be so quick to judge others, and complain about them not being there for us, without taking the time to see the struggle within their own world. Out of my mum's hurt, she thought she was protecting me by keeping me close and away from my dad. But what it actually did was make me feel like he was building a new life without me. I wanted to be his focus and I thought being skinny would attain his love.

Can we just have a moment?

Just imagine I've just pulled a chair over to sit in front of you, so close our knees are touching, and my hands are on your shoulders. Don't look down. Look at me and hear me when I say to you, "don't try this for yourself!". If you already have and continue to, I'm pleading: "please stop!". Your life is more valuable than any number on a weighted scale will tell you. I promise you it is! No number on a piece of clothing will ever define that. No measurement will tell you the truth. I know.

"I'm fat!!!" is not a new phrase for parents of teenagers to hear. For my parents, however, it wasn't a throwaway comment, as anorexia now had a place within my world. At the time when I said I was fat I really meant it. Daily, I was indulging in a toxic cocktail of negative thoughts about myself

THE EARLY YEARS

and my life. With every negative thought, I was left more broken, alone and angry than the day before. Not eating took away the pain that I couldn't make my mum better. Not eating meant I could control how I felt about myself. I felt so empowered. The truth was, I was far from empowered and strong. As my personal battle against anorexia started, mum had begun to live better with her own pain.

Mum had started to live a vibrant life regardless of the pain she felt. She still had some dark days, weeks and months but she was doing life a little brighter each day. In the years I became weaker, my mum was becoming stronger. She'd found better doctors for herself, stopped self-medicating as much and really planted herself within church. She was sleeping less and would be awake when I got home from school. She started asking more about my school day, and made dinner more times than I did. I believe seeing me in this battle for my life meant she took her eyes off her own world and placed them onto her little girl. I never doubted her love for me. Never. I knew I was her world. I knew I was her reason for trying every day and I know she wished it was different for me. It felt overwhelming at times because she was lost when I wasn't with her, but her love is what saved me so many times! A mother's love doesn't allow her little girl to destroy her own life. There was no denying this battle scared all of us!

Some battles last decades, even a lifetime, mine lasted about three years and lingered for many more. It got a lot worse before it got any better. More bones began to show, and the lies became more consistent. I'm so thankful for every prayer said on my behalf during those years. The purpose and desire of anorexia is to kill, there's no glorifying it. Sadly, anorexia had a firm grip on me, as it has many others, and it wasn't going to let go without a fight. People have numbers for lotto and the casino, but I had one for my weight: 42 kilograms. When you're a thin-framed 5'10 woman, that is not a good number. Thankfully God, my mum and dad had other plans. Pain is the gift that allows space for people in your life to step in, or step away. Either way I think both can be a gift.

Remember when I said pain gave me the gift of gratitude? This was one of those times. God used those years to start a lifelong restoration of my heart. The second-best part? He used this traumatic time to give my dad and me another chance to build a relationship. God gave mum a second shot at life too! My anorexia gave space for my mum to step in and be a mother; and my dad to be a part of my life too. A fathers love their daughters differently to their sons I believe. Both are beautiful. My dad's love for me in those years was the perfect gift. It was consistent and practical. He made many phone calls I never knew about, appointments with the right specialists, and reminded me how much he loved me.

My healing was nothing short of a miracle. As easily as the sickness came into my world, God removed it. If God does nothing else for me, I know He set me free and I began to live again. That's enough. But God isn't a God of just enough; the Bible tells us He is a God of abundance. Mum and I hadn't much experience with abundance up until then, but my mum was about to have a life overflowing unlike any season she'd ever known before.

When my mum met her second husband, she was beyond happy. Her heart had longed to feel love again, and in 1999 she was head over heels in love like a schoolgirl! This love, however, required a passport. After months of talking over the phone and online, she decided to go and visit her new love. He was waiting at an airport in North Carolina with a single rose, and her heart was his. While she was overseas, mum and I chatted daily, with her telling me about something new and wonderful she'd seen or tasted. I was so excited as the days led up to her arrival home. We talked about going to America together, even both of us living there, if it all worked out. But her three-week holiday to Wilmington in North Carolina very quickly turned into a life established in the deep south of America, and she didn't come home.

Most kids can't wait to move out of home when they're 18, for me I was the one staying home and my mum was the one leaving.

THE EARLY YEARS

I wasn't prepared for it or ready. Mum and I had enjoyed the best year of our whole lives together only the year before, and now I was going to be alone again. I finally had my mum, and then she was gone. Over the ten years she lived in America, I visited many times and mum came back as much as she could. We were social distancing long before it was a thing, but we became distant in heart. For the first time, my mum and I were living independently of one another. She didn't need me to look after her and to be honest I felt lost. I now had to work out who I was and she was doing the same.

She had someone else to make a new 'coffee code' with, and she had to get use to a new rhythm of life with someone new. We both struggled those first few years. Her depression came back, even more intense than before because she now had loneliness to manage too. She loved her husband dearly and the life they had created, but living in two countries doesn't make maintaining relationships with friends and family easy. Are we ever really ready for what is about to happen next? I don't think so. I wasn't ready for the conversation I had with my dad in his office on June 17th, 2009.

"Your mum killed herself this morning."

They are brutal words. I can't imagine the courage it would've taken for my dad to say those words to me. That morning, at 3am, he received a phone call about my mum's death. At the time, I was working for him and to see him come in on a day he wasn't meant to be working was unusual. My nanna, his mum, was in hospital and very unwell at the time and as my dad approached me, I started to think maybe nanna wasn't in a good way. I still wonder what it felt like to be the one to press the red button of pain and watch the effects of it hit someone you had spent your life protecting.

Pain has a way of numbing everything in an instant. I look back on that day and remember not one tear falling in my dad's office. My phone calls after that were logical and practical. My mum's family needed me to step up and be in control, and I knew how to do that. My nanna needed all the support we could give her after now losing a second daughter to suicide. As a family, we needed to be in North Carolina within 24 hours. When the news came through about her passing, I thought I was prepared.

I thought I'd prepared myself for that day. Suicide wasn't new to our family and the intensity of mum's struggle was something I knew all too well. Some say suicide breeds anger but I didn't have anger, honestly I had no feeling of anything for a while. The best way I can describe it is by using the colour grey. Imagine your days only filled with the colour grey. Each day lacks the colour it once had. When mum died, I'd already prepared myself for that to be the reality I'd one day have to walk through. But nothing could prepare me for her not being on the end of the phone call, or forever there being an empty seat at every, single special occasion.

I remember it took a long time for that pain to really impact me, for me to feel her absence in my life. Each birthday meant there was always one invite left over that could never have a name on it, and a hug I could never receive or give again. There wasn't any time for tears. At the age of 26, I felt about 50 years old. I'd experienced more pain than I ever expected to feel. But now I had a choice – did I want my life to be different? The answer was YES.

I'd seen the ugliness of pain and definitely had felt it too, and I wanted more than just that. I wanted to break the mould and I was determined history would not repeat itself with me. I was desperate to turn my pain into hope. My goodness, I needed it to. I'd seen the alternative and I knew how the story ended, unfortunately I was unaware there was another pain I had yet to be introduced to before any of this could happen.

2

More pain to come

By this point, I thought I'd felt all the colours of pain. What more was there? I knew pain had a sound when I saw it firsthand with my mum on *that* phone call. I firmly believe pain had a sound to my mum when she heard the words, "your sister died overnight". Nearly 20 years later, I heard pain for myself but mine sounded a little different. Never did I think 'I'm pregnant' would be two words that could cause so much pain.

I've heard those words continually spoken by someone else, but never by me. I thought one day I'd be the one to say the words by now, not always hearing them. I've dreamt about what it would feel like to say it, and how that moment would feel when I'd break the news to my husband and family. I've wondered if I'd I say it quickly, or if I'd try to be creative and fun with the announcement. I've wondered if I'd know I was pregnant straight away or be completely oblivious for weeks. Some many times I've wondered and never known.

It isn't unusual for many couples wait, some for a few months or even years. We too expected to wait, but when we hit the five year mark with no pregnancies, the pain became pretty intense. I was struggling to pretend I was okay with us not having what everyone else had, and that I didn't want it as bad as I did.

I was struggling to pretend it didn't matter, because it did matter. I'm so glad I learnt it was okay that I wasn't okay. Like it happens for most women, I turned 30 and my fertility started ticking pretty loudly. Around the same time I was bombarded with questions, almost daily, about when we were going to have children and constantly reminded about my age. Prior to my 30th birthday, my husband and I never really had children as the focus of our lives. We knew there'd come a time when we'd probably want them, but our desire to have a family took us a little by surprise. Especially the intensity of it. We were the last couple to get married out of our friends, and now we were the last to have a family too. One after another, another friend was bringing a pram to dinner while we were always just the two of us. We assumed when we were ready, we'd be able conceive relatively easily.

When we decided to try, we soon discovered this was not going to be as easy as it was for everyone else. The first year of nothing happening was a mix of emotions. Then we hit our second year, our third, our fourth and our fifth. Nothing. I was attending baby showers that turned into first birthdays, that soon turned into first day of school and so on. We never thought for a minute that waiting for a baby would last ten years!

I often wonder if we would've still said yes to the journey if we knew it was going to be a ten year wait with the possibility of it never happening. I'm so glad fertility is something society talks about more. The silence of it is one of the hardest parts. The chats you want to have but don't know how to, the answers you want to have or be given but no one has, and the half-hearted smiles you give to tell everyone you're okay when you're not. You might be curious as to why I say 'fertility' and not 'infertility'. I didn't always and then one day I realised it was the one thing I had a little control over.

Choosing how we described our journey became a way for me to remind myself that while I might not be able, God is. It became a way to strengthen my faith and hope, especially on the dark days. Saying the word fertility instead of infertility helped me feel like I wasn't in a losing battle, no matter how it ended. There's very little control any woman has when it comes to fertility, all the control really lies in God and the doctors. For us, we never have had a medical explanation as to why we haven't been able to conceive. I've been fortunate not to have any miscarriages, but on the flip side I've never been able to fall pregnant. Saying fertility gave me some control back, control over the condition of my heart and the words I use to love, honour, care, respect and protect myself and my husband.

> **'Kind words heal and help; cutting words wound and maim.' – Proverbs 15:4 MSG**

Saying fertility doesn't take away the pain of not having a child, or mean I haven't got angry and mad. It doesn't mean my prayers are any less intense or get pushed to the front of the line for God to answer sooner (I wish it did!). It's also important to say *infertility* doesn't mean (you) I've stopped my body from falling pregnant. For me, saying 'fertility' meant I was doing my bit with my promise. I was protecting my heart, keeping my spirit strong and ultimately, being responsible with the pain. It was a choice to cultivate and nurture a healthier mindset than the one I had. Saying 'fertility' meant I was doing my bit with my promise.

I was often asked if there's was a point we had when we just accepted this isn't for us. There didn't used to be but now there is. There had to be a moment I accepted it wasn't going to happen in order to keep living and loving the life I did have. It hasn't always been easy and it doesn't mean I don't wish it turned out differently. Ultimately, it'll never be something I have complete peace with, but it doesn't own me like it used to. The pain becomes less intense, not necessarily less real. I'd like to say the pain has end date but I just don't think it ever does. All I have is the honest truth that this pain hurts. I've begged God to take the desire away and I've tried to convince myself I didn't care anymore. But I did and still do, privately.

We've been given every bit of advice – go on a holiday, get drunk, don't think about it, go to this doctor, eat this diet, pray about it, stop caring about it, and the advice goes on. When someone is pain it's hard for the person listening to sometimes understand or not try to take over with solutions and options. I've felt this struggle my friends have had when they'd ask how we were going. They just wanted to make it happen for us but all I wanted was to be heard. I just needed someone to let me release my thoughts and emotions without judgment or any more suggestions. All the well-meaning advice we've both been given has been often spoken with great love, but hurtful all the same. Not because the words are hurtful, but because it reminds us each time that was another thing that didn't work for us like everyone else.

We've gone on holidays and got drunk. That didn't work as *they* said it would, or as it did for others. We've stopped thinking about it, and we've seen as many doctors and done as many tests as we could. That didn't work as *they* said it would, or as it did for others. We've tried pregnancy diets and my goodness we have prayed about it. That still didn't work as *they* said it would, or as it did for others. Unfortunately instead of giving encouragement, those stories and suggestions can hit a nerve of frustration and anger, and leaves the one in pain with more questions of, "if it worked for them, why not us?".

As the time went on I began to withdraw and hide how much I was hurting. I actually said to my husband at one point, "why does the word *try* become such a bad word when it comes to fertility? Athletes *try* their best every day, chefs *try* to create new meals every day and dancers *try* new moves every set. But if you say you're *trying* to have family, it's a bad word. People tell you not to do it. They even get really animated about it. Why?". He had no answer, but he understood the shame that comes with that word when in reference to fertility. He also knew what I was trying to express which was such a gift in that moment. I was so ashamed people knew or thought we were *trying* that I hid it all. I didn't want anyone to know how bad I wanted it for us; that I wanted more than what we had.

I wasn't ready to be raw and exposed.

If hiding was an Olympic sport, I'd have a few gold medals by now! I used to work for a retail store located in a large shopping centre, and that's where I bought most of my pregnancy tests then. My workplace was a good hour drive from my neighbourhood which ensured there was no chance of my husband seeing me, or my family or friends. While I felt safe being unseen, I hated walking to the aisle where I knew the tests would always be. I was so familiar with that aisle I knew all the brands of pregnancy test kits and prices from memory. I think it's in our DNA as a woman to find the best bargain, but not when it comes to pregnancy tests.

I found myself wondering if the cheaper one would give me less luck than the more expensive ones, which one might give more luck, more hope, or be the one that says something I have never seen on any other test before. I always went to the bathroom straight after work. Always. Deep down, I thought it was easier for me to do this alone rather than go home and give my husband hope before crushing his heart all over again. Again, the shame of *trying* weighed heavily on my heart. I wanted to protect him where I could, just like I used to with mum. Past experiences caused me to expect what the answer would be, so I tried to protect him.

It's hard for any couple to walk this journey together, side by side. There's so much that goes unsaid and each tear has its own weight, and sometimes there are no tears for one. My tears, I'm sure, have felt different to my husband's. Different things trigger him than they do me. I hoped for a day I walked out of that cubicle with a happy heart. A joyful spirit and a smile that no one could contain. It never happened. That very cubicle over time became a place of familiarity. A place where my heart sank to the floor each time. A place where I felt pain become my friend with its arm yet again around me. A place where I struggled to open the door and 'get on' with life.

Often, I just sat in that freshly cleaned cold, isolated white and grey cubicle… and waited. I waited for the result, other times I just waited for strength to come back to my body and most times I waited until I knew I couldn't hide anymore. I never told anyone when and if I was going to do a test. I've done every test hidden and in secret. But why do we hide? Hiding didn't work for Adam and Eve, and many others in the bible, and it didn't work for my mum. Mum spent her days hiding from it, hoping it would go away if she slept. That way didn't work well for her and though I chose to hide in a different way, it didn't work well for me either.

'When they heard the sound of God strolling in the garden in the evening breeze, the Man and his Wife hid in the trees of the garden, hid from God. God called to the Man: "Where are you?" He said, "I heard you in the garden and I was afraid because I was naked. And I hid."' – Genesis 3:8-10 MSG

It says in Jeremiah 23:24 that no one can hide so well that God cannot see them, for He filled the heavens and the earth. He sees you too! Ultimately you can't hide forever, and never from God. He sees every tear, every smile and He feels every bit of your pain. He is inviting you to come out of hiding and take His hand. He will never leave you, or lead you where you will be overcome.

3

Time to be honest

Father, I don't know how to pray this out so indulge me as I write it down instead. Let my words be my prayer to You. Thank You. My feeling of hopelessness is not new nor comforting. I don't feel stronger because I am familiar with this pain, I actually feel weaker. Should I still feel it after all these years? Looking at a negative pregnancy test is nothing new. I know Your Word and yet I struggle to know You. I struggle to see Your Word be effective in my life – where is this, Your, breakthrough and answers to my prayers? I feel like yelling, 'Wake Up Lord! Wake up & just do SOMETHING! Anything! Please! Help me like You have for so many others so many times before. Why does my womb have to remain empty while others are full? Why are babies given only to be taken away again? I don't want to be the master of my own miracle or force Your will like Sarah did before You blessed her with a child. But I don't want to miss Your invitation to a miracle either. Where are You in all of this? Do we get more medical help? Do we just wait, more? Help! I am lost and my reality feels like it is swallowing me whole. Please wake up Lord. Please!
    JOURNAL ENTRY 9.07.2019 - WAKE UP

Being honest with yourself is hard, it's even harder being honest with other people, but being honest with God can be the hardest of them all. He knows our pain, and He isn't scared of it. He knows we're hurting, and He waits patiently for us to let Him in so He can help us. He isn't confrontational and demanding, He most certainly doesn't give ultimatums, deadlines or timelines for us 'to get over it'. He is patient and kind, generous in love and grace.

For me being honest with my pain wasn't the issue, but being honest with how much it hurt was. I wanted to be strong and I kept trying to convince myself I was okay I lost my mother at such a young age (and the way it happened), and I was okay with not being a mother too. I misunderstood the encouragement people gave me on how I was doing life as praise that my methods were healthy. Everyone knew me as strong and independent, and that's who I thought I had to be all the time. Instead of allowing myself to be vulnerable and honest with them, I build my walls up to hide behind and convinced myself as long as I didn't let the pain hurt me I was doing okay. In my mind I was the girl bad stuff happened to, but she always rose from the ashes again. I felt weak if I let emotion be real, and I didn't allow other people to see I wasn't okay. At some point, you have to face your pain head on, as well as be honest about how much that pain hurts. When you can look at whatever is causing you pain face-to-face and bravely admit you're in pain, you can finally start to break free. There's power in doing both not just one.

During the years of caring for my mum, I took great pride in being capable and able. I felt strong and independent, and proud I could be the one to be my mum's strength. It's been the same while journeying through our fertility struggles. I'd laugh and pretend I was great as I told myself, and other people, I was happy I could still drink champagne, eat soft cheese and cured meats, and sleep in any day I wanted. Honestly, I'd give it all up in a heartbeat to change nappies, have minimal sleep and dirty hair for a week.

"Do you have children?" is like a loaded gun for a woman without children.

For me I found it confronting not because people asked, but because my answer meant I had to be honest that I was not okay with that being my reality. The answers switched between, "no I don't", to "not yet", and "maybe soon". Part of me wanted to indulge and celebrate in the pain, and part of me wanted to push it to the side. Either way it gave me a sense of identity. Each of my responses had their own hidden meaning for me and I found myself using a different response depending on how I felt on the day. Sometimes I was okay with bravely being honest about my reality, and other days I wanted to linger in hope just a little longer and deny my pains existence. I fought hard to remain hopeful, sometimes that fight took all of me. When we hit the ten year mark of our fertility journey, I sobbed. I wasn't sure how I'd survive if we never had a child. How my husband would survive and how us as a couple would both survive.

I wondered if the world would be less colourful, and if we'd always feel as though we were missing something. I found it hard to imagine the pain would eventually fade away. Truthfully, after a decade of traveling this journey, life at times has definitely felt dull and empty. We've struggled with the open space that this unanswered prayer has left us with, but we've still created a beautiful life. We never imagined we would have a time that we decided to stop trying and not have something to show for it. As I published this book, we stopped. We knew it was time to stop. We had to. After ten years we needed to stop in order to heal and grieve. Did we do the right thing in deciding to stop? I have no idea.

I know God is able to undo any plans I make, and He can make the impossible possible. I couldn't have done it before because it felt like giving up, but now I know it's just about giving it to Him. Was there more we could have done, should;ve done? Maybe. Part of stopping is about not looking for the next sign. It's about God and I forming a true and deep relationship that isn't connected to Him doing something for me. I honestly didn't think we'd hit ten years and not be pregnant, or ever being pregnant. I'd always told myself I'd be okay being a woman without a child, and on some days I believed it. The honest truth is each time I thought about it, I broke. While I hated the long list of unanswered questions, and the endless times I caught myself counting the months of 'chances' before the last week in December arrived each year, I needed peace. Peace could only come when I got real with my pain.

The thing with my fertility journey, as with any woman, is it's not just about me. It's very much about my husband's pain, and my family's too. It's hard to be honest about your reality when it means that someone you care about very much will have their pain highlighted too. Every time I said I wasn't a mum, it was reminding my husband he wasn't a father, and our parents weren't grandparents. I couldn't pretend this didn't hurt anymore and I couldn't protect everyone anymore. I was trying to be strong for everyone, and for myself, but I was cracking. I was breaking.

Years went by before I actually found the strength to be honest with, and trust, people with my story. Most days I didn't know where to place my next step. I felt as though I was on a dirt road searching for the next sign to tell me where to go. I wish I could give you a road map out of your season of pain, but there isn't one. There are no short cuts, no direct routes and perfect paved highways. Traveling out of pain is a bit like traveling along a dirt road out in the country where there are a limited number of street signs. While we crave as much information as possible, God gives us as little as possible. I used to think He was cruel and unkind in doing so, but I've learnt in Him giving us what we need instead of what we want, is actually His greatest gift of love and kindness. If He gave us anymore we'd most probably be overwhelmed, and we would be robbed of the chance to build our faith.

I've come to understand faith is built in the days of the unknown. For me, I gained nothing from dwelling in the disappointment of being given limited signs and wonders. Focusing on finding the next sign rather than just driving and focusing on the path God was leading me on, proved only to be a great distraction and paralysed me with fear. I asked God for signs as evidence He was aware or listening to me in my season of pain. I was so hungry and desperate to see Him do *something* that I missed out on seeing Him at all. The very pursuit of those signs and wonders became a hindrance to my faith. They made God, in my eyes, small and incapable of doing anything. I left pregnancy tests out on the bed, unopened, and asked Him to physically move it so I knew whether to do a test in the morning (yup, I did that!). I even asked Him to show me a sign that proved He was worthy of my faith.

I looked for signs anywhere and everywhere, but God seemed silent. I wondered if I took a wrong turn somewhere, or if I should turn back. My road out of this particular season of pain has been bumpy and exhausting. All I wanted was something to help me know where to go next. I didn't want to end up like an old car you see on the side of the road that didn't make it, so I kept driving. As I drove, the pain hurt a little less and my faith grew a little stronger. It was messy, challenging and uncomfortable at times, but it was the beginning of my breakthrough.

'But Thomas, sometimes called the Twin, one of the Twelve, was not with them when Jesus came. The other disciples told him, "We saw the Master." But he said, "Unless I see the nail holes in his hands, put my finger in the nail holes, and stick my hand in his side, I won't believe it." Eight days later, his disciples were again in the room. This time Thomas was with them. Jesus came through the locked doors, stood among them, and said, "Peace to you." Then he focused his attention on Thomas. "Take your finger and examine my hands. Take your hand and stick it in my side. Don't be unbelieving. Believe."
Thomas said, "My Master! My God!" Jesus said, "So, you believe because you've seen with your own eyes. Even better blessings are in store for those who believe without seeing."' – John 20:24-29 MSG

I believe there's real value in being honest with your pain. When you real with it, it's hold on you starts to dissolve. The shame attached to it, and the fear of being exposed starts no longer has a hold.

There's a fine line between being real with and allowing it to dictate your reality. The reality for Thomas, one of the disciples, was that Jesus was dead. That's what my reality looked like for many years too, or did it just appear to be?

The disciples thought Jesus was dead. They'd seen Him tortured and hung on the cross, with their own eyes. They saw Him take His last breath, felt the weight of His death on their hearts. Their reality seemed bleak and done. All their days with Him they begged for signs so they could be sure that Jesus was who He said He was, and now He performed the most significant sign of all; and He was met with more disbelief! Thomas, after his encounter with the risen Jesus, presumably didn't question who Jesus is ever again. I've learnt a lot from Thomas and from his weaknesses. What eventually gave Thomas freedom from His doubt, I believe, was God's truth. It broke him free of the doubt, and it can break you free of yours too.

For my husband and I, it is true our home's silence can be heavy and too loud to bear sometimes. It is true our home has empty rooms I wish were filled with conversations, and laughter. It is true our home has a dining table to sit six, but only two occupy it's seats.

God's truth has allowed my perspective on it all to change, allowing me to live with peace rather than fear and anger. Our home is a place where we stay sensitive to God's truth, regardless of my reality. Our home's silence is a gift of refuge to those who need to escape the chaos of life. Our home's empty rooms give space to anyone who needs it without question. Our home's dining table has become a place where my husband & I talk and build our marriage.

'Yet there are those who yield to their weakness' – Psalm 16:4 TPT

When I started to be honest with my pain, I grew up. I matured. I didn't live the same way over and over again. Our response has so much value. He knows it hurts, He isn't asking us to deny that. He is just asking us to trust Him no matter what. My reality is I have never been a mother and don't think I ever will be. It really hurts that I am not, but I have hope in God who is well able. I have joy in the strength God gives me to do every day well, and I have peace in a God who will always finish what He started. Being honest with your pain will often mean you have to be honest with what you're lacking. Whatever we lack though, God does not. There really isn't much value in staying hidden in your pain, or trying to deny its existence. Pain is part of life and so easy weeping, even Jesus wept.

It's okay if you cry, like really ugly cry. I have, many times. Nothing about this journey is meant or expected to be easy or quick. There was no chance after not being able to conceive a baby for ten years that my journey was going to be quick or easy. The same applied to when my mum committed suicide, along with her two sisters (my other aunty died in 2021 just as this book was being finished). Nothing about healing from that was going to be easy or quick. It takes time, it takes a lots of little decisions and it takes courage.

Each day you will be able to be a little more honest with yourself, God and those who love you. And each day you will be able to look at your pain a little longer in the eye and speak the truth of who God is, in spite of your pain.

4

It's not fair

It's probably not. Good, we've got that out of the way.

> 'And so I'm not keeping one bit of this quiet, I'm laying it all out on the table; my complaining to high heaven is bitter, but honest. Are you going to put a muzzle on me, the way you quiet the sea and still the storm? If I say, 'I'm going to bed, then I'll feel better. A little nap will lift my spirits,' You come and so scare me with nightmares and frighten me with ghosts. That I'd rather strangle in the sheets than face this kind of life any longer. I hate this life! Who needs any more of this? Let me alone! There's nothing to my life – it's nothing but smoke.' – Job 7:11-16 MSG

I've been the poster child for 'it's not fair' for years. Another pregnancy announcement was guaranteed to set off an instant tantrum inside my heart. Envy, anger, disappointment, denial and judgment exploded within seconds. I'd feel everything within me burn, my heart beating faster than normal race, and before I could stop the words, "it's not fair!" would be shouted. Internally acted like a brat for years. I was angry, and I let my anger control me instead of fuel my hunger for breakthrough and more of God. Each time I stated something was fair, or not, I gave more volume to fear, resentment, rejection, doubt and pain. I hadn't considered pain was a necessary tool

God was using for my good.

We all have a different understanding of what is good and what is bad, what's yours? Shouldn't good things happen to good people? But what is good person'?

Most people would say a good person tithes every week if they went to church, served in their local community, helps strangers in the street, wouldn't litter, and is nice and kind to all. A good person doesn't swear, well maybe only a little. So then, why do bad things happen to a good person? Life just doesn't seem to be fair! At times, it seems to be harder for good people than others. I've thought I was a 'good' person. A 'good' person who throws the occasional temper tantrum. But seriously, what is fair?

Does it mean the people who do good are the only ones who get good things? Does it mean that when someone stops being bad and turns into a good person, only good things happen to them thereafter? Does it mean I get to be the boss of what's fair and what's not, what's good and what's bad? Does it mean only bad people get bad things? Does living a good life make you a good person or does it only require moments of being good? Are you a bad person because you made a handful of bad decisions or because you lived a life never doing anything good?

PSALM 73
'God is indeed good to Israel, to the pure in heart'
'Did I purify my heart and wash my hands in innocence for nothing'
'But as for me, God's presence is my good. I have made the Lord God my refuge'

Oh my goodness I've struggled with God being good, as well as in my opinion at times, very little good things happening in my life. I've complained and compared my life to others, accusing God of forgetting about me over and over again. I've done it all more times than I'd actually like to admit and I've treated God like a genie in a bottle. I've said…"I'm tired of being the one who has to do everything God, where are you in all of this? Why don't you do what I can't do? It's not fair everyone gets what they want, and I don't!". I've played judge more times than I ever should've; determining what is good and bad by my own personal measuring stick. There are plenty of flaws in that attitude, travel with me as I share my thoughts for a moment.

'You didn't think, did you, that just by pointing your finger at others you would distract God from seeing all your misdoings and from coming down on you hard? Or did you think that because he's such a nice God, he'd let you off the hook? Better think this one through from the beginning. God is kind, but he's not soft. In kindness he takes us firmly by the hand and leads us into a radical life-change.' - Romans 2:3-4 MSG

I simply love the whole chapter of Romans 2, it talks about good and bad so beautifully. I highly recommend you take some time to read it for yourself and don't just take my revelation from these two scriptures. As I read this chapter I'm always convicted of my own actions and behaviours. If I correct someone for judging others, and then judge them myself, then am I too considered bad? And if I am bad, then do I only deserve bad things? It would be highly unlikely anyone would disagree that it's bad to murder someone, to cheat on your spouse, or intentionally hurt another person. But what if we haven't done any of those things but we tell a white lie, swear once in a while or skip a weeks tithe? Are any of us considered *bad* then? Welcome to a whole lot of grey area and a very deep rabbit hole! The only true judge of it all is God.

For a long time I thought it was unfair I lost my mum, and my family was broken. I thought it was unfair that on top of that I battled anorexia, and had to look after my mum. And then to put more on the list, I couldn't get pregnant, and my first business failed. None of those things were about it being fair or not. If it was, then the very foundation God has built His love on would be a sham. It's a lot I know, stay with me - *please!*

'For it is by grace you have been saved, through faith – and this is not from yourselves, it is the gift of God – not by works, so that no one can boast.' – Ephesians 2:8-9 NIV

Just like the 'good' person described in the opening of this chapter, I've serve in my church and have for years, given financially to big and small causes, helped strangers where I could and so on. We should all do those things because we want to or God has given us the means to be able to, not because we want Him to do more for us in return. If God worked that way, we could never do enough. Does it seem fair that in my lifetime pain has been constant, while almost non-existent in others? No it doesn't. Not by a long shot.

'No test or temptation that comes your way is beyond the course of what others have had to face. All you need to remember is that God will never let you down; he'll never let you be pushed past your limit; he'll always be there to help you come through it.' – 1 Corinthians 10:13 MSG

This analogy is for my fitness people. When I lift weights it hurts at the time, but it makes me stronger afterwards. While I appreciate my seasons of pain now, and the purpose it's served (I'll share how I got from there to here in the next few chapters!), it doesn't mean I did then or am excited for more of it. What I'm thankful for is the greater understanding I now have because of my pain. God has used pain in my life to build steps upwards, upwards to Him. When stand on top of a mountain you get a clearer view of the valleys below. It's the same when you stand next to God viewing your pain, it all seems to pale into insignificance in comparison. Sometimes, it will not be fair. Sometimes it won't seem right and sometimes things definitely won't seem good, either in our eyes or in general.

Is it fair some women conceive easily and some don't? *Probably not.* Is it fair your business fell apart while everyone around you succeeds? *Probably not.* Is it fair you work harder and for longer hours and the co-worker who is younger than you and does less work than you got the promotion and you didn't? *Probably not.* Only God knows.

When I really understood that only God knows what is fair and what isn't, and I started to be less interested in if it was or wasn't, pain started to loosen its grip. For a long time my situations didn't change, but something inside my spirit, mind and body did. I became physically healthier, I became nicer to people and was more enjoyable to be around, and my relationship with God really started to take shape. I invited Jesus in more and allowed the Holy Spirit to guide me more. I was released from the lie that I was the judge of all things.

It might not have been 'fair' for my childhood to be what it was, but if it wasn't I wouldn't be able to write this book. It might not have been 'fair' to have battled an eating disorder as well as everything else, but without it I wouldn't have known my true worth. It might not have been 'fair' for my life to be filled with so much pain, but if it wasn't I wouldn't have realised what my gifting was or been able to use my gift to help others. It might not have been 'fair' for my life to be filled with so much pain, but if it wasn't I wouldn't have learnt to lean on God when everything else crumbled beneath me. Without my pain, I wouldn't know what true joy feels like.

It might not be 'fair' that I still have to live with pain, but without it I wouldn't have learnt how to live a life well with pain. Pain has been a gift. A gift that has equipped me to help others, deepen my relationship with God and rebuild hope in my heart.

'When I tried to understand all this, it seemed hopeless until I entered God's sanctuary' – Psalm 73:16-17

5

Grieving the dream

Grieving the dream, or letting go, is a term I heard many years ago. Since then, I've heard many counselors use it and have come to understand the value of it.

Just like me, there are people in the world living lives they didn't think would be their reality. They had a dream, some had an idea of life, some had a painted picture in their mind, and some had a vision board loaded with goals they hoped to achieve by a set time frame. I too had a vision for what I thought my life would look like by now. I didn't think I'd be a 40 year old woman without children, and I definitely didn't think I would have been able to call myself a published author! This wasn't what my dream looked like. Not at all.

> *Dear womb, promised children, my heart,*
> *I thought by now I would have wrestled with sleepless nights and begged you to go to sleep, I would have wondered why I wanted this life so bad on those days you wouldn't stop crying or drive me crazy I thought by now I'd be one of those women who tell the young ones to enjoy the time they have while they have it and having a shower by yourself. By now, I thought I'd be 37 and be a mother. By now I thought*

Mother's Day would give me a reason to celebrate rather than mourn, it would be a day I didn't have to find that extra bit of strength and 'put on' a smile to prove to everyone I am okay.

Today, I thought I'd be receiving a badly made gift from you made at school and pretending it really was the best thing I ever did see. By now, I thought I'd know what a mother's love felt like and what my mum felt for me. A love that drives you more than anything else. By now, I thought I'd have a reason to give thanks to the Lord rather than of asking Him to help through another year of doubt, confusion and mystery. By now, I thought my friends wouldn't have to tip toe around my emotions. By now, I thought my name wouldn't have a question mark next to it on the invite list to another baby shower because they didn't want to hurt me, or I'd be the one text or phone call someone had to make before publicly announcing their good news.

By now, I thought I would have given up and become bitter. I thought by now I would have no room or strength left for hope and yet here I am...desperate for you. Desperate to see your dad hold you, kiss you and just look at you. Desperate for your grandparents to fuss over you and spoil you with kisses and sweet treats. Desperate to see God's word stand true. By now, I thought I'd have no more prayers and no more tears. And yet I feel like I am full of both of them. By now, I thought I would have seen God make His name glorious through you. But He hasn't and in some crazy way, that's completely okay.

JOURNAL ENTRY: *Mother's Day 2019*

It took me a long time to understand that grieving the dream, laying it down, resting in Him or letting God have control, didn't mean saying goodbye to His promises - just the pain of it. It just meant I was placing it in God's hands, and giving it to God to hold instead of me. For me, grieving has always been a continual and repetitive process. It isn't a one-time thing. It's a continual action to let something or someone go. In moments where I've felt, and possibly will again, overwhelmed, angry, distraught and broken, it was and will be a choice to grieve again.

When my mum died, I grieved her for years, and still do. I grieved her when I couldn't call her to tell her Craig had just proposed and asked me to be his forever, and when she wasn't there on my wedding day. I've grieved her every time I left another doctor's appointment, specialists office or my periods came every month. I just wanted to talk and cry with my mum. I used to dread the day I'd be pregnant because it'd be another day I couldn't share with her.

Have you thought something should happen by now? You are not alone. I didn't just grieve my dream of being a mum once; I did it month after month.

Mother's Day after Mother's Day. Christmas after Christmas. Birthday after birthday. When I thought, 'this is the month', only to discover it wasn't, I had to let the fresh tears flow. As each tear fell, I had to grieve every thought and feeling to make room for what God had to say about it all, again. Not to argue or debate, I'd done that for years and all I got was bruises and a tired spirit, but to listen. Lay it down. Very honestly, those three words have filled me with so much dread, and rebellion. I didn't want to lay it down, say goodbye and I definitely wasn't ready for all hope to be taken away. I've learnt the outcome isn't for us to give our concern too, we're just asked to be obedient to His lead. He doesn't despise our tears and He is patient with us in our grief.

I truly believe grieving is a gift from God.

I'm not sure anything about grief was ever supposed to be quick or clean. In western society we underestimate the value of grieving, giving a few hours of one day for someone to grieve a lost one. In many other cultures, grieving goes for a week and it's encouraged for you to take your time. Grief is a process that's different for everyone. For me, when mum died it took nearly ten years for the grief to no longer have a significant impact on my life. In the deepest moments of my grieving, none of it was pretty or controlled. A grief like that has an audible sound that comes from something deep within you that can no longer settle for what is. There is a release, a groan, calling out again. Right there is the true definition of grieving a dream, any dream, it becomes something physically feels like a moment of complete release. It's gritty and it takes all you got. When you're in the heat of grieving, you want it all gone then and there.

'But, I keep calling out to You, Yahweh! I know You will bend down to listen to me.' – Psalm 69:13 TPT

I love how descriptive this small piece of scripture is, showing us the word *again* is one of comfort and discomfort. No matter how messy our grief is, and how many times we call out; He will bend down to wherever we are and listen. We all have our own version of *calling*. For some of you it won't be so gritty and intense, for others it will be. Over the years mine has changed between the two, but I kept calling because I knew that it all mattered to God. It still does now. He bends down and listens to each of us every time. You might not always feel it, but that's where the gift of His Word comes in. When our grief is the only thing we feel and He seems distant, His Word tells us He isn't.

I believe nothing is a coincidence with God, nothing happens by chance or because 'we' got lucky'. His hand is over everything in our lives and this world. Therefore my seasons of pain, and yours, all have a purpose to them. I knew there had to be a purpose why my life was coloured with different seasons of hardship and pain. I wasn't just chosen to suffer, it didn't line up to who God was. However, that purpose could only be found once I grieved the pain each season brought. It was an opportunity to see the gift each season brought with it. When I look at the stories of Job, Joseph and Paul in particular, there's much purpose in their seasons of pain. Their hardship became their story and built their foundations in God, made His glory brighter and built their own personal character. No matter how many times I've had to cry *again*, forgive *again* and heal *again*, I know it's been worth it. I made a decision a long time ago I didn't want any of my life, or season I walked though, to be a waste. I always wanted each situation to bear fruit and be used in some way.

While doing research for this chapter I did some reading on fruit trees and gardening in general. I discovered there can only be fruit on a tree once the dead branches have been cut away. To me, grieving any dream is like cutting off the dead branches and allowing new fruit to grow. Fruits of kindness and forgiveness, fruits of love and tenderness.

'And so also is my word. I send it out, and it always produces fruit. It shall accomplish all I want it to and prosper everywhere I send it. You will live in joy and peace. The mountains and hills, the trees of the field—all the world around you—will rejoice. Where once were thorns, fir trees will grow; where briars grew, the myrtle trees will sprout up. This miracle will make the Lord's name very great and be an everlasting sign of God's power and love.'– Isaiah 55:11-13 TLB

I discovered *laying it* down isn't declaring God has wiped His hands of the promise and the case was closed, it simply means it's in His hands now. He is still able and He stands by His Word. Laying it down and grieving what I thought life would look like by now meant I had to do some personal gardening on my heart. It was time to trim away the dead branches and allow new ones to grow. It's my heart's desire to be known for my faith and for my hope in Him, rather than the pain I battle through. I don't want to be seen as a tree with dead branches.

'True, the grass withers and the wildflowers fade, but our God's Word stands firm and forever.' – Isaiah 40:8 MSG

And yet, grieving felt like failure. It felt unnatural and it felt like I was being weak. I'm glad I now know what it feels like and what it actually is are to totally different things. Grieving then and still is, far from giving up. It definitely didn't mean then or does now mean I'm a failure - nor are you! Very much the opposite. It's an invitation to trust God with our tears and heart. When we grieve and release it to Him, He can give us more. More love, more kindness and more mercy where there was pain, doubt and confusion. Each time you grieve a dream, it turns the light. When we turn the light out at night, it's easy to think darkness has the final say. It never does.

Grieving your dream, or what you thought life would look like by now, makes space for something new.

A full bucket of water cannot fit fresh water in it unless some of the old water is released. Grieving and trust go hand in hand with God. When you grieve what hasn't been, or what was, you are in turn saying 'yes' to a God who is able. Everything attached to Jesus has life. He wants 'new' to be something that becomes more familiar than the old. He only wants to be part of our lives and help us do life well. When it's in God's hands and not ours, it doesn't mean it's finished, it just means it's still a work in progress.

He wants to give each of us a new normal, He knows how much the grief hurts, and He knows how much it took for us to give it to Him.

6

Wrestling with God

"What if I fail? Oh my darling, what if you fly?"

I love this quote! I just wish I could really believe it too! Unfortunately, I have to repeat it to myself every time I'm confronted with old fears of failing. It surprises some because of my gift to encourage and have hope, but success isn't a natural mindset for me. It's something I work very hard to have for myself, it's a real fight some days. I haven't been naturally lucky or necessarily fortunate, though compared to some I'm sure I have been, but it really has felt as though the success or breakthroughs I've had have been fought and worked for. I'm not a big thinker by nature, I like to measure the risks and be prepared. The truth is, none of us will ever be ready for what God has for us, so we might as well just do it anyway. Easy to say, less easy to do I know! Automatically I assume the worst will happen, or that it won't work for me. I hate that pain has left me with that scar. Oh but what it would be like to fly, and just trust you could!

Flying, to me, evokes thoughts of freedom and peace. When you fly, you are above it all. Nothing can reach you and you still have some control, like choosing when and where you land. During the editing process of this book, I saw something different hidden within the opening quote. I love how the Holy Spirit just flips the script on you sometimes! The last word I expected to be connected with that quote was gravesite, and yet that is the word that wouldn't leave me I sat with that quote and wrote this chapter. Shortly after, a question came to my attention, "What gravesite are you revisiting? Who's doing the talking – are you listening to the gravesite of what was or are you reminding that very gravesite of who you are and the future ahead of you?". I'll do my best to link it all together.

"What if I fail? Oh my darling, what if you fly?"

Wouldn't it be wonderful to just win at everything, accomplish every project or never have to deal with pain or rejection again?! There will be times when each of us is held back, or have been because of what if questions. Often what if questions are centred on fear and failure, and can be truly debilitating. For me, what if questions have felt as though God and I have gone a few rounds in a boxing match. I'd love it if I just became victorious! But victory doesn't just happen, it comes from being dedicated and focused. Boxing matches are fought for in the ring, but they're won in the months of training beforehand. My understanding of being victorious is twofold – it is a gift from Heaven, and it's a decision to act like it.

Whether you like it or believe it, or not, we all have talents and gifts. Some of us are confident in them, and some of us struggle to own them and put them on show for others to see. Privately, I know I can speak well and connect with people, but I rarely act like I can. All too often, I let fear steal my opportunities to operate in that ability. The Bible tells us that the Creator of the Universe dwells within us, and that He Himself is victorious over all, so by default so must we be. He works in the business of wonders and miracles and He alone makes all things possible. For years and years though, I lived defeated.

I lived completely overcome by doctors' appraisals of my eggs, my age, my body, my temperature or lack of and so much more. To be honest, that part was hard to write. My idea of victory in this area has looked a certain way for a long time, but the victory He has given has started to look very different. I may not be victorious the way I wanted or thought I'd be (holding a baby), but I am victorious because His love has restored my broken heart and given me joy for the rest of my life; whatever that looks like. Yes, His name is higher than any word doctors speak over me. Yes, He is still at work and in the business of wonders and miracles and He makes all things possible. Does His victory in this look the same as what I envisaged? Maybe, maybe not. I don't think the victory is in if I hold a baby or not; I think it is if His will is done.

'So, what do you think? With God on our side like this, how can we lose? If God didn't hesitate to put everything on the line for us, embracing our condition and exposing himself to the worst by sending his own Son, is there anything else he wouldn't gladly and freely do for us? And who would dare tangle with God by messing with one of God's chosen? Who would dare even to point a finger?' - Romans 8:31-34 MSG

The key, I've found, to living with a victorious mindset is to stop wrestling with God in order to have full control and understanding, and put my what if questions to the grave. This isn't anything new, the story of Esther is one many know and love. She had her own what if questions to silence when it was her time for her to step into the victory had prepared for her. She became queen at a time when a whole population of people were depending on her voice and courage to speak up. I used to think she was automatically courageous and fearless, assuming it was in her DNA and that she knew no different way to be. That she just had something in her that made her bold and secure. But it wasn't something she just was, it was something she chose to be.

Being courageous doesn't mean you don't feel fear or have doubt, it just means you do what you are called to do in spite of it. You manage your fear, and don't let it conquer you or steal your blessing. Esther knew she had

God's hand on her life – that was already evident. But for her to really be who she was called to be, she now needed to act like it. She needed to truly believe in God's victory over her life and all that He called her to be part of. Can we just talk about the start of Esther's story for a moment. Before it all worked out and she became the queen we talk about all these years later, Esther was taken against her will - the bible says Esther was *brought* (taken against her will) to her king.

'As a result of the king's decree, Esther, along with many other young women, was brought to the king's harem at the fortress of Susa and placed in Hegai's care.' – Esther 2:8 NLT

'Well, the king loved Esther more than any of the other girls. He was so delighted with her that he set the royal crown on her head and declared her queen instead of Vashti.' - Esther 2:17 TLB

I'm very confident in my assumption she would've had questions, concerns and doubts. I'm sure in the private moments of her day she wrestled with why God allowed this to happen to her and what the point to it all was. While the story ends well, she didn't know that at the time. She didn't know she'd become queen, and she didn't know her relationship with the king would be more special than just an arrangement. What she didn't know then was that a whole nation's life was depending on her to silence her what if questions and doubts.

What if I try to escape, will life be better or worse? What if the king doesn't like me as much as the other girls? What if I don't like the king and can't pretend that I do? What if the other girls don't like me, or I don't like them? What if my parents hadn't died; what would my life look like now?

Maybe they were some of the questions that went through her mind and maybe not, I can only guess. Regardless, no answers to any of those questions would bring peace, joy or strength. In fact, quite the opposite. They only led to more questions and more confusion, anger and resentment. I wonder if she reflected upon her journey years after and thought the greatest what if over her life would affect so many others, *"What if I hadn't become queen and trusted God?".*

Just like Esther, many of us can only see the right now. God doesn't allow us to see everything all laid out so we can obediently follow knowing all the details, picking and choosing as we go. He asks us to trust Him in the unknown and the unseen. He asks us to act victorious when we don't understand how we have any right to be in the midst of all the chaos.

'But I'll take the hand of those who don't know the way, who can't see where they're going. I'll be a personal guide to them, directing them through unknown country. I'll be right there to show them what roads to take, make sure they don't fall into the ditch. These are the things I'll be doing for them – sticking with them, not leaving them for a minute.' – Isaiah 42:16 MSG

The reality is, there'll be things that happen in all our lives that we don't like or haven't liked. Most what if questions either have no answers or too many, leaving you in a state of confusion and panic. You can't move forward if your feet are tied up, all you can do is wriggle around stuck in the same spot. Breaking free of what if questions is like breaking that very rope around your feet and running forward.

Some on my what if questions sounded like what if....
   mum never knew I truly loved her, needed or liked her even?
   mum thought I was disappointed or angry with her?
   I went to America straight after school, would she still be alive?
   I went to America straight after school, what would life look like now?
   I different decisions with my first business?
   my parents stayed together?
   my mum got better sooner?

Maybe some yours sound like what if I'd...
   never married, or had married someone else?
   taken that job you said no to, or didn't even apply for?
   gone on that holiday with your friend, or didn't?
   said something different in the heat of the moment, or said nothing at all?
   just apologised, or let them apologise to you?
   booked that flight earlier, or had never gone at all?
   gone to the doctor sooner, or never made that first appointment?
   tried one round of fertility treatment, or tried at least once?

I used to think it was wrong to have so many questions. I used to think my questions were too big and uncomfortable for God to answer. They definitely felt too big and uncomfortable for me. Jamie Kern Lima's shared how she also struggled with her faith once in her book BELIEVE IT. In one particular therapy session, she told her therapist about her struggle with her faith. I love her therapists response, "Ask God to show you. If He is as big as you believe Him to be, ask Him to show you". Talk about a mic drop moment!

So that's what I did. I asked some pretty big questions and got real with my fears. He wasn't scared of those big questions, nor of the wrestle. At some point in any wrestling match there comes a point when you need to surrender, someone needs to *tap out*. Wrestling with God is no different.

There comes a time when each of us need to stop fighting Him at every corner and every hour of every day. Our faith has to come alive at some point, even our deepest seasons of pain. I'm sure Esther's heart was hurting greatly when her parents died and also when taken to live with the king. I can imagine she felt abandoned, scared and fearful. The bible doesn't tell us of her internal struggle but at some point she made the decision to align her eyesight to Heaven's way of thinking. She focused less on the lack of, and instead allowed God to have the final say.

7

Forgive yourself

Ever wanted something to work so bad you'll do anything to make it happen? I did and it was all bad! You need to know something about this particular chapter before you read any more - I have *never* been this open to anyone about this part of my life because I carry so much shame around about it. Yup, even now. I never shared this with my family. No one knew apart from my husband and one other person. Shame is really uncomfortable feeling. Out of the all 40 chapters, this has been one of the hardest to write and not delete.

In 2011 I opened my first business that sold gift favours for special events as well as designing lolly buffets. It was created for a few different reasons. The first was after our wedding I noticed there as gap in the market of someone what I did myself, and well. The trend was already gaining momentum in America and slowly gaining traction here. I though then was great time to get a head of the trend. The second reason was because I desperate to discover my purpose, and thirdly, I was tired of waiting to fall pregnant and thought making something to distract me would be a good thing to do. I was basically telling God that He was doing terribly at His job of making my life beautiful so I would take over from here. It was going to get worse before it got better.

This business was a business I ran by myself from home and heavily centered within the wedding industry. What does everyone spend money on? Weddings, babies and funeral - I thought I was sitting on a goldmine of an idea! Although my husband wasn't part of it directly, he was affected by it. Soon our home was filled with glass jars, styling props, anything wedding related, meters upon meters of ribbon, and so much double sided tape. While he loved to sample all sweet treats or eat the leftovers from wedding expo displays, I'm sure there were days he wish he could of seen less ribbon pink everywhere! Try all I did, that business never took flight. There were moments of success, but never consistent and all were short lived.

In order to get the dream happening, I sold my car, left my job and put everything I had into it. I'm an all in or all out kinda girl, never just slowly working it out. Each morning I was up early and going to bed late. I went to every networking event I could afford to buy a ticket to, lived on social media every day and sent hundreds of emails out. Keep that dream alive cost us dearly. Soon the savings I had ran out and the few sales that were coming in quickly got swallowed up in fees and operating expenses. It's fair to say living on one wage while trying to build a business started to take it's toll. I fought for five years to keep it alive, and then I had nothing left. I finally ran out of the strength and will to keep going. My husband had asked me to do it a few times before but honestly, my pride stopped me. I couldn't be the woman who wasn't pregnant and failed at running a business. I didn;t want to be the woman who had nothing. I just wanted something to work! Although closing the business was a huge relief, the stain of regret and the mountain of 'what if' questions I was left with was hard to process.

Goodbye
I am alive and I am well. How are you? For my new fans, I am Claire and I've been the owner of JLTG (Just Love to Give) for over five years.

I haven't been on this page for a while and to be really honest, it's been refreshing. I started a new full-time job which I am loving. I wanted to make a clear & conscious decision about what I was doing with this page before I said anything publicly, as well as the people I've connected with and the name of Just Love to Give. I have been torn as to whether I keep going this business going, do I just keep the page open to encourage people, do I turn it into a blog, do I say goodbye completely or do I just keep a bit of myself here I some form.

The question has always been - does it serve you (my customers) in a positive & meaningful way?

The answer - yes and no. I have felt obligated to keep the page open and to do a blog but I wasn't excited about it. I didn't want to give you something because I had to. I want to give you everything & anything I have because I desire to. Being completely raw & honest with you has been my priority, as well as what I do next. My greatest desire is to help and give what I can to people, hence the name, but that isn't always a good a to run a business I've learnt. So I've decided to close this business. I want to thank my absolutely wonderful husband who has stood beside, in front and behind me. Your patience and belief in me will never go unfelt. I am sure there will be another adventure to take you on in the future! But for now, it's time to appreciate all the good in my life - our kindhearted dog, loving family & friends are huge blessings I fail to recognise most days.

I have loved & hated this business over the last five years, and saying goodbye is so much more than just not being a business owner. I have learnt great lessons, anyone with a business can say amen to that! You have all been wonderful. Truly you have. Thank you to my suppliers for your support. I wish you all wonderful days ahead and hopefully we cross paths again soon!

Claire, owner of Just Love to Give, August 15th, 2015

As I mentioned I wrestled with closing that business for a long time, and while I felt complete peace over my decision when I did, I still felt as though

I was a failure. It was just another thing that didn't work, another prayer that wasn't answered and another thing I tried that failed. After that, I truly believed I didn't deserve anything good to happen to me. I truly believed my life was one that wasn't going to be like the others, I was destined to live a life of struggle and heartache, and I just need to settle in that. That's a hard place to come out of.

While I am proud of the work I produced and reputation I created, I am not proud of what I did to make it all happen. Closing that business was the best thing I did for us financially and as a couple, as well as me personally. After selling my car, I thought I'd have enough money to sustain me and the business until I got some clients. My husband and I never expected we'd need more money. We honestly though we'd done our maths correctly and soon the business would just take off anyway. I had so much to learn, and the hard way! As month after month passed, and I wasn't falling pregnant, I made less smart and healthy decisions. As I look back writing about it, I was repeating some of the same decisions my mum had made when I was a little girl (and I knew that didn't end well). I figured if I wasn't pregnant than my business was what God wanted me to focus on – I've learnt there's a difference between focusing and obsessing. My business became my obsession and my distraction, not just from not being a mum but from not having my mum as well. Mum died two years prior to opening the business, so to say I was very lost and confused during this would also be accurate.

As the months turned into years, my pain grew too. What didn't go was the bank balance of the business. Perosnally, I hid behind fake smiles and told everyone it was all great. What I was really doing was withdrawing from the truth and painful reality and did what I'd always done, I started to hide again. I hid my pain behind smiles, told people what I thought I should be telling them and suffered alone. I tried to copy what my competitors were doing, and in the process I lost myself and found myself constantly chasing other people. It all had a price, and one I couldn't afford. Buying the latest and greatest stock doesn't come cheap, and it became harder and harder to pay our personal bills. I once borrowed money from family and truly believed if I could just get a bit more cash than that would mean I would be okay. It was a losing battle, in more ways than one. I would've been better at trying my luck at a pokie (slot) machine each week. In the end I just paid that money back with money I borrowed and I was lost in losing cycle.

During those years our marriage suffered, trust had been broken and resentment set in badly. None this helped the whole fertility journey by the way, distracting yourself from the pain is never a good idea! Fast forward to 2019 and I had new dream, yup another business. This one felt even bigger than the first. I never thought of my myself as a writer, I mean knew I could write a fairly good card and journal entry but anything more than that seemed too big. I didn't study writing, struggled through English at school, labelled dyslexic and still miss words and rearrange sentences unknowingly in my texts most days (as you've probably seen in this book to be honest!), and yet God kept asking me to write. After the pain and devastation from my last dream, I was hesitant and and extremely scared to try again. Honestly, I was petrified. Petrified of trusting God again, trusting myself again and asking my husband to trust me again. What if this too didn't work? What if this too was going to be hard and lead to more struggle? So I just pretended I didn't hear the question God was asking, until it got too loud to ignore!

Before I could start something new I had to finally deal with the scars of closing my first business. Physically closing the business was easy, processing the mountain of regret and unanswered questions was the hard bit. I didn't realised how much guilt I still carried over myself until I spoke to my husband about my dream to write a book, become a professional author and create a small range of handmade gifts. I never want to go back to being someone my husband couldn't trust or treat as his equal, someone he didn't respect and admire. And honestly, I wasn't sure if I wanted to be that reliant on God again, if I could trust Him again. The thing is, this wasn't just my pain and it was breaking my husband's heart as much as mine. I didn't want to hide anything anymore, and I definitely didn't want to feel that much shame again. But I knew there was something special waiting for me if I I processes this and took hold of this new invitation, so I finally said yes and began writing. First I had to forgive myself, and that took a few years to be honest. I love that God knew that and so while the goal was big, He knew the little steps along the way matter. He didn't ask me to pick up a pen straight away, first He just asked me to dream with Him again. To think about what my life could look like and what gave me joy. That in itself was a struggle. There were days where I had to, and still do to be honest, forgive myself all over again or believe I deserve anything more than the crumbs that fall on the floor while others are feasting at the banquet table. Discovering my self worth has been a long journey!

The forgiveness process was intense and each time I blamed myself for something I did wrong, it felt like fresh alcohol being poured over a wound that had just begun to heal. I remember years after I closed the business, someone asked a question that brought to life all my regret and shame. It really did feel as though each question was a drop of alcohol that found a way into the wound I thought had healed only to discover there was more healing that needed to be done. Often it stung just as much as the first time, and in an instant, the pain felt very real again. The Bible is very clear that the Lord hates robbery and wrongdoing, and He LOVES justice!

'Instead of shame and dishonour, you shall have a double portion of prosperity and everlasting joy. For I, the Lord, love justice; I hate robbery and wrong. I will faithfully reward my people for their suffering and make an everlasting covenant with them.'
- Isaiah 61:7-8 NLT

When you truly forgive yourself, the questions and accusations Satan tries to throw at you don't hold you back anymore. His lies used to rob me of the chance to live with hope and joy, and hindered me from living with expectation. Forgiveness drives the enemy crazy mad because he knows what freedom is hidden within it.

God, You are the God of the suddenly. I have a decision to make – when You speak, do I stay in the war that was happening in my mind or I drop my weapons in full trust you have got me?

You have gone before me. I have spent many of my days verbalising every 'what if' scenario in my head with many different people, leaving me more confused and twisted. Teach me to keep what we share together in our secret place, what I hold onto no matter what. I never want to stop being surprised by You, or trying to understand everything about You. I want to allow myself to be surprised by You. But to be surprised means I jump when I don't see what I am landing on. It means sending my 'what if' questions to the grave. Never taking any gift or blessing for granted. When I don't see it God, there is a plan. A reason why some things need to happen at all or before other things. Instead of grumbling my way through the process I want to praise. I want to take my grumbles, my what if, my questions to understand and reason with you to the grave. I have so many times buried my hope, my joy, and my patience instead of my bad attitude, my frustration and anger. When I've lost my faith, I've retraced my steps back to where I lost it. But instead I acknowledge my weakness and ask for Your help to make me strong.

Lord, let today be a funeral for my 'what if' questions. No more wonder that doesn't keep You lifted up and held in awe. I make a pledge to turn my 'what if' to instead of. Be with me. Stay with me.

JOURNAL ENTRY 2.12.2019 - SECRET PLACES

No matter how often you have to forgive yourself, it's always worth it.

No one can do it for you, not even Jesus. I'm beyond thankful He was so patient with me during this time and still is. I wrestled and argued until I had no more fear or doubt left. Honestly it felt like I didn't have much of anything left really. I started to see this new dream didn't have end in failure like all my other dreams had. I was excited I was discovering my purpose and my gifts, I was excited to wake up each day again! Finally it felt like I was given the missing piece to my life and it fit perfectly! No longer was I trying to put a square sized wooden block into a space that would only hold a circular shaped piece.

Jesus died for you because He forgives you. If you're a Christian than you will believe that Jesus died for you because He forgives you. I have often said that without letting it really sink in. If He can forgive you, then you can forgive yourself. I think He needs us to. Forgiving yourself doesn't wipe away the bad choices you made, undo the hurt you caused or change situations you were in. In short it doesn't change the past, but it does change your future. Why would you spend each day wearing a 100 kilogram lead jacket, when you don't have to? Forgive yourself. The King of Kings, Lord of Lords, Creator of the Universe, your Father in Heaven and the Alpha and Omega has.

'Because of the sacrifice of the Messiah, his blood poured out on the altar of the Cross, we're a free people—free of penalties and punishments chalked up by all our misdeeds. And not just barely free, either. *Abundantly* free!' Ephesians 1:7 MSG

8

The choice is yours

My mum was born in Manchester, England. I loved visiting her home town when I was young girl and eating jam sandwiches after dinner. I didn't like going to bed when the sun was still shining brightly though, it just didn't feel right. My mum moved over to Australia with my nanna & granddad, and her siblings she was nine years old. At the time the only way to relocate affordably was via ship, and even then it was expensive for a large family. My mum told me that each child was allowed to take a limited number of possessions with them on the ship, mum chose her favourite teddy.

One day my aunty, my mum's younger sister Elaine, decided she was too old for teddies and she needed to let go of it. Elaine told mum for days that big girls don't have teddies, but mum wasn't ready to let go. To her, that teddy was the only thing she had that was familiar and safe. One particular day, as the familiar argument played out between the girls, Elaine decided she would *make* mum let go of her teddy. She didn't care if she was she was ready or willing, and just to be clear - mum was very much not ready! In the heat of the moment, the story my mum told me was Elaine grabbed mum's teddy and threw it overboard into the big ocean. I'm sure Elaine had a different version - ah sisters! Mum used to tell me how sad she felt in the days after. She was mad and she felt so alone. Every time mum told that story, or I relive it now, I too feel immense sadness. I could imagine her as a young girl standing there, unable to move, looking into the ocean staring at her teddy. I'm so glad that God doesn't rip from us so violently, even if it feels as though He does.

As I look back, I too have had moments where I thought God did indeed rip something from me. It's helpful to take a breath if you feel like this too and assess your mindset. For me, often my mind was reacting to what I was feeling rather than the reality of what was happening. When loved ones leave us, it can feel like they were ripped from us, and the same can be said when a child loses the stability of a home with two parents. When we don't have the control of situations and we are the ones left behind, it definitely can feel as though God has ripped things from our life. But while that's what I have felt I know it not to be true. I just know that God is kind and gentle, and while He is asking you to let go, it's your choice whether you do or not.

While I definitely don't condone my aunt's actions in taking my mum's teddy from her so cruelly and causing her so much pain, I want to suggest that we all need to give up our teddies at some point. Sometimes sooner than we think. Sometimes *letting go* simply means an unhealthy mindset or doing things the way you've always done them. If you've chosen to keep holding onto your teddy, there's a good chance you're no longer reading this book. I hope you still are with me and maybe starting to feel a little brave. Maybe even loosening your grip over whatever you've been holding onto for so long. This is your (gentle!) eviction notice to move into the new days. Moving from what's familiar to the very unknown is anything but easy or comforting

Moving days are hard work and often full of stress, hiccups and complications. I moved a lot when I was younger and even into my early years of dating my now husband. Moving often involves long days, little rest and it seems like it will never end. The key to successful move is careful preparation. There are removalists to book, power companies to contact, cleaning to do and boxes to pack. Lots of boxes. Some boxes you unpack straight away, some you leave for another day, some you don't know what to do with, and some you know you don't want to open. I still have boxes completely untouched in my storage cupboard from the last time we moved!

The bible talks a lot about moving, God is incredibly passionate about it. Whether it's moving off your beggar's mat, or a place of comfort you've built in a hard season – it's time to move forward. Even the devil knows how powerful it is to move. Why do you think he whispers so much fear into situations you face that are going to bring you success, blessings, breakthrough, provision and healing? He knows if you remain still and immobile, you'll eventually stay there. Ever tried to start a car after it's been sitting in the one place for a while? It's not easy, often you need to try and few times, and sometimes it just doesn't even start at all ever again.

The story of David and Goliath is one many either know well or have heard of briefly. David went from being the young boy who tended sheep alone to being seen by the king. That's a big jump and really what made it possible was his time of preparation. The time David spent tending to sheep, alone, was time God used to build him. I could imagine David grumbled through some of those days and wondered why he couldn't be with his brothers doing the really good stuff. I can imagine there were days he could see any value in the endless days he spent alone and isolated. However, when no one else was able to stand against Goliath, David knew he could. David knew he could defeat Goliath not because of his own strength, but because of the foundation in God. A young unknown shepherd doesn't just beat a giant, he was preparing for the moment years before. In those days David spent alone, he learnt to rely on God for protection and wisdom. David learnt to talk with God and trust His Word, and David knew God's voice intimately because he was surrounded by every other voice. In those days David spent alone, he learnt how to lead a flock, care for them, make decisions for their good and provide for them.

David was cast aside and rejected by his brothers. I don't care what anyone says, rejection stings and it definitely hurts. It's something that can cripple you in a second, everyone wants to be loved and accepted. In a moment, David had to overcome self-doubt in order to move into the new life God had prepared for him. The story makes it all sound like it happened so easily, but I doubt that was the reality of that day. There was a lot happening and many voices speaking. In amongst it all, David had to stand up against it all. He could've said no and gone back to what he knew, tending for the sheep as he had every other day. He could've procrastinated and made up a million reasons why he could do this, just Moses did and so many others in times before. Someone who knew about procrastination was definitely Moses, he had a long list of excuses for God!

And that's how things stood when God next spoke to Moses in Egypt. God addressed Moses, saying, "I am God. Tell Pharaoh king of Egypt everything I say to you." And Moses answered, "Look at me. I stutter. Why would Pharaoh listen to me?" - Exodus 6:28-30 MSG

God wanted Moses to go to Pharaoh and ask him to release the Israelites from slavery. This was no small request, and it's safe to say Moses panicked with fear. Moses was well aware of his limitations but what's highlighted most in this story to me is that he failed to recognise who God is. No king, no pharaoh and no other power position is ever a threat to the name of God. Finally Moses said yes and the story continues. After Pharaoh released the Israelites, the wondered for 40 long years before they entered the Promised Land! The story doesn't end there and the rest of their days weren't about drinking cocktails under the shade of a palm tree in the warm sun.

Although Moses was no longer with them, it's the next move the Israelites had to walk that really speaks to me, and I want to focus in on it for a few moments. Here is where the Walls of Jericho come back into the story, and here is where this mighty was awaiting them. Of the 600,000-plus Israelites that many historians believe entered the Promised Land, I'm sure a few decided they didn't want to keep moving or have to go through *another* battle or hard thing. Maybe this time, they really felt what God was asking of them was too big! I'm not exaggerating when I saw the Walls of Jericho were HUGE.

'Then he told the people, "Set out! March around the city. Have the armed guard march before the Chest of God."' – Joshua 6:7 MSG

In 2007 I stood outside the now destroyed World Trade Centre in NYC and felt so small in comparison. I remember as I looked up, I felt as though my whole body went horizontal. I'd never seen anything as big and tall. I was completely overwhelmed and felt so insignificant. I imagine the walls of Jericho had a similar effect for the Israelites. Those Walls of Jericho were considered immovable, set there as the ultimate protection, it would've felt so daunting to see those walls.

I wonder if they felt like I did outside the World Trade Centre. All the Israelites had as weapons to fight against these impenetrable walls were some rusty old trumpets. If they weren't procrastinating before, I'm sure they were then! I'm always encouraged, and in awe of, by their faith in God. Armed with only trumpets and their praise, they chose to trust. Their faith in God wasn't in what they couldn't see with their own eyes, but in who He said He'd be with them once more, as He had all along. No matter how long ago this stories happened, I truly believe reading them are so important for our faith. This particular story reminds us that sometimes we need to put footsteps to our voice and a voice to our footsteps to bring the walls down. During my various battles of struggle and seasons of waiting, I've learnt this to be true, one can't be effective without the other. God has never asked me to move, nor will He ever ask me to do anything He hasn't first blessed and given me the strength for. It's the same for you. We all have our own Walls of Jericho to walk around, Pharaoh's to meet, teddy to let go of, or beggars mats to step away from.

Moving requires trust, and normally lots of it. God knows how much of us it takes to trust Him and put movement to that trust.

God doesn't want to just rip what you've been holding onto and leave you empty handed, and feeling abandoned. He is inviting you to trust Him with what you've been holding onto and use His strength to release it, not your own strength. His love is all you need to cause chaos and cracks in the devil's plans. Just like it was for Moses and Joshua, we have no idea how why God chooses us other than because He believes in us. He is with us always and with Him we can do all things. Life has a way of not being anything like we planned, and maybe that's been the plan all along.

When God asks us to move, we don't know how long it will take, and to be honest, it doesn't really matter, just our obedience does.

9

In God's hands now

I'll never forget the day a friend said to me, "it's not over, it's just in God's hands completely now". While letting go of your dream into God's hands, or what you thought life would look like by now, makes space for something new - it doesn't make it any easier. Just like a full bucket of water cannot fit fresh water in it unless some of the old water is released, I truly believe grieving and trusting God go hand in hand. Again, I didn't ay anything about it is easy.

'For I know the plans I have for you," declares the LORD, "plans to prosper you and not to harm you, plans to give you hope and a future. Then you will call on me and come and pray to me, and I will listen to you. You will seek me and find me when you seek me with all your heart. 14 I will be found by you," declares the LORD' - Jeremiah 29:11-14

If you allow it, this scripture can be a life vest for you in the painful season on life you find yourself in. Instead of declaring, "I'm done!", this scripture flips it to letting God say "when". God knows the perfect time to say, "when". *When* the time is perfect, *when* you're well equipped, and *when* you'll be most blessed - that is when God will move and not a moment before. That

I have learnt many times over! Will you let God say *when* over your life and circumstance?

The story of Moses and Sarah failing to have a child until their very old age is familiar to many. Sarah tried to make her baby promise happen on her time, but all that did was add to her pain. God, however, had a perfect *when* moment. This moment wasn't just for Sarah and Abraham, but for Isaac their son and for Israel. Another story that is based on this is the Walls of Jericho. Those incredibly BIG walls didn't fall because of the Israelites strength, but because they placed the whole situation in God's hands. When it came time to shout, they shouted with all they had.

> **'Don't shout. In fact, don't even speak – not so much as a whisper until you hear Me say, "Shout!"' – Joshua 6:10 MSG**

God told the Israelites to first march. Just march, not make a noise. Just put their faith into motion. Imagine the sounds coming from each person marching around those walls, the stomping and pounding. I'm sure it wasn't easy to just march. It wouldn't by a far stretch of the imagination to think God would've been bombarded with quietly whispered fears, doubts and silent concerns with every step. They had to hand over any control they thought they had and trust God, completely. Allowing God to have control is hard, but when we try to control the situation the truth is we make it harder because we're working against God's work and plans. When the footsteps weren't enough anymore; God told them to make a noise. There needed to be a declaration and so confident and sure it shook the very foundations of those fortified walls. God wanted them to see when they place their trust in Him, He can make even the strongest walls come crumbling down. Nothing and no one is a match for Him.

So often cracks resemble ruin, brokenness and weakness, but in this case, the cracks were showing God's strength. Each crack showed those Israelites, and even us today, God's ability to do the impossible. His ability was on full display for all to see that day, along with His strength, might and power. This was seen and heard in every crack and sound. I love to think about what the sound on the other side would've sounded like. On one side of the wall there was silence, only rivaled by the marching steps. Marching steps coupled with faith, confidence, assurance, hope, and then praise and joy. On the other side however, there was a city of people going about their days. Above all the noise, a large city heard there was another sound slowly rising. As the marching got louder, so did the uncertainty, fear, doubt, confusion, hopelessness and even arrogance within the city. We all have our own Walls of Jericho. We all have a situation that looks immovable and unbreakable, but the key word is *looks*.

Nothing for God is immovable or unbreakable. For some of us it's fertility, for others it might sickness, divorce, financial loss, death and being single. Just like the Israelites did, and like I did & do every day, you too have a choice about what side of the wall you'll walk on. One side holds God accountable to His nature and Word over it all, marching with faith, hope and confidence. The other side is closed in by fear, resentment, doubt and confusion. The problem with being on that side is there's no way out, the walls have got nowhere to go but to crumble on top of you.

Imagine being the people within the Walls of Jericho and seeing the cracks appear. Maybe they heard the cracks first and dismissed it in disbelief. They dismissed the sound and continued to go to work, take their children to school and meet up with their friends. This city was their safe place. But then, crack after crack, the wall began to crumble. With each crack it started to become a little less safe. As the walls finally fell, people were buried and dreams were completely destroyed. I'm sure there are miracles yet to be seen in your life, as there are in mine, all God is asking is for you trust Him with the unseen.

'So we look not at the things which are seen, but at the things which are unseen; for the things which are visible are temporal [just brief and fleeting], but the things which are invisible are everlasting *and* **imperishable.' - 2 Corinthians 4:18 AMP**

Don't let the delay of a promise fuel more fear, disappointment, and discouragement. Instead let your heart be grateful for more time God is taking to do what He needs to in the days ahead of you. God sees you. God hears you. God loves you. If He said He would do it, then He will. For ten years I walked around my own walls, walls of fertility. I yearned for those very cracks to appear. I was desperate to hear the sound of those cracks. When the time came to shout, I thought it was going to sound different. I thought I had God figured out as well as the rest of His plan, turns out He had a better plan and sound to shout. There will come a time when you're asked to shout too. Shout with everything you have, with every tear and breath. There'll come a time when the former things will be but a distant memory and my eyes are focused on what's ahead.

'the wall collapsed; so everyone charged straight in, and they took the city' - Joshua 6:20 NIV

The truth is God doesn't *need* us. He has never needed us, and He will never need us to do anything, but He *wants* us to be part of the journey. There lies the challenge and key to it all. To be part of it, not to do it all. After all, they're His plans, and in His hands our life could be no safer.

II

I AM LOVED

Chapters ten - fifteen

10

Who you were

You can't hide when you've got the spotlight on you. Not one bit. When I go to musicals, I often find myself looking to the side of the stage to where all the unseen people are, otherwise known as stage hands. Just a little note on if you're ever curious about what you're passionate, pay attention to what excites you or you do without thinking about it and you'll be close. I know what it's like to feel unseen and forgotten about, it's my daily mission to make sure no one feels that. Anyway back to my story. Stage hands often wear black as it makes it easier for them to stay hidden and unseen. I used to live my life like those very stage hands, choose to remain in the darkness. I choose to be someone ruled by shame and fear. The more we choose to keep myself ourselves hidden, the more space we give the devil to have his fun. That was who I was.

The honest and uncomfortable truth is I was hiding because I didn't believe God was big enough to pull me into His spotlight. How wrong I was. What I've learnt since is most times it's up to us whether we step into God's light or not. His spotlight, His love and grace, is always on our life, He never turns it away to make someone else brighter for a moment. When we step into the spotlight, that's when I believe we truly shine. Just like a diamond reflects the light, or a light bulb shines the power within it, we too shine when we allow God's light to be our source that shines through us. The beautiful thing about a diamond's light is that it doesn't just reflect one ray of light but multiple, and our life is no different. When we live in God's spotlight, His love shines through us helping us to reach not just one life but many. Before I realised this beautiful truth, I was spiralling down quickly and taking every chance I could to hide from life. Thankfully, God stepped in and my transformation of who I was into who I am began, again.

I look at myself now and I'm amazed I got here, for many reasons, especially physically.

When I weighed my lightest, 42.5 kilograms, my dad asked me, "what would happen if you weighed 45 kilograms?". I can't remember my answer but I can remember how I felt. I remember feeling so shocked he asked me that. I was disgusted and scared. He then said, "I'd love to see you weigh 65kg one day". At that point I was just mad! Every father wants to see his daughter healthy and happy. Who I was then was breaking his heart. I can proudly say today I weigh about 65 kilograms and I love it! Eating disorders are very much centred around what you feel, what you think look like, what you think people think and after all that there isn't much room left for anyone else. I selfish during those years and I was very self centered. I couldn't hear the words of those who loved me and I'm pretty sure that's why God has to work in mysterious ways, because we don't make it easy. While it's been a painful battle to overcome, I'm so thankful anorexia is part of my story now. Without it I wouldn't have discovered my true identity, it took some time for that to be the case.

In the deepest part of my anorexia, the mirror was my best friend and mortal enemy. Mum wanted to cover every mirror, or surface that reflected my image because she knew I wasn't seeing the truth. She knew it was adding to my pain and giving me more reasons to hide. Each day I was absorbed into a fake reality as each reflection of what I saw fuelled my life threatening thoughts of myself. Those reflections were how I measured my value and worth every morning and night, my eyes hunting down every flaw like an eagle who hunts for rabbits in the hills of Tibet. I was consumed to the point of obsession, to find everything I thought was wrong about me instead of acknowledging anything good. For me, my greatest focus was how flat my stomach was. If my belly was flatter than normal it was a good day, but if it was bloated then it was going to be a rough day.

Mirror, Mirror on the wall…when will my belly be flat?
　Mirror, Mirror on the wall…when will I be attractive?
　Mirror, Mirror on the wall…when will I look as good as everyone else?
　Mirror, Mirror on the wall…when will you be truthful to me? *Never*

How I looked determined how I felt about myself, my life as a whole, and it heavily dictated my emotions. To me, I was incomplete, imperfect and broken, I was fat and far from anything beautiful. I saw a girl who'd been rejected, believed was unlovable and undeserving of anything more than what she had. What God saw however, was His little girl who He adored so much. He saw her being lied to on a daily, even hourly, basis and His heart was breaking like mine. God saw His little girl breaking in front of Him. I didn't understand then, but what I know now is He knew that in the breaking was where I'd find more of Him. The breaking was necessary, the breaking held so much value.

In the breaking He knew my old identity was loosening its grip, my new identity would be found, and in the breaking He knew my old ways of thinking were finally being stripped away. In the breaking He knew my new thinking was being formed on His truth and love alone and where relationships were broken and fractured, they'd be restored.

In the breaking God finally become real to me.

Think of an earthquake, or shaking something that's been broken. If it wasn't for the breaking, things wouldn't be loosened off. There's rarely anything easy, fun or comfortable about a season of breaking. Like you have or might be thinking, I too considered giving up. But then I thought, "well it's been this hard *with* God, how much harder will it be without Him?". Life is hard at times, it's a struggle and life is not pretty at times. For a moment, imagine how much harder it could be, and how ugly it could be if not for God. No season is a waste, not even the short ones. Each has value and purpose, helping you to do life better the next time a storm comes your way.

After I received healing from my anorexia physically, the mental healing was the one that took me by surprise. I'd put in the work to match God's faithfulness as He set me free, I never missed a meal and always ate something every meal time, even if was just something small. Not eating wasn't an option anymore. God was the one who healed me, but I had to be the one to protect that healing and be responsible with it. It wouldn't be for many years until I really learnt that lesson. I naively thought because I'd been healed from my eating disorder, physically, I was indeed completely healed. When we began hoping to be parents, I discovered how fragile my mental state was and in a cruel twist, instead of desiring my belly to be flat, I welcomed the bloating. I started to long for the round, full shape I used to hide from.

A good work had begun in those 15 years prior, but I was far from a finished work. I've come to know God well enough to know He doesn't do things by halves. He isn't happy with half healed, half set free, half blessed and half happy. He's an all-in kind of God. Slowly I found myself becoming self-reliant and self-focussed again. Again, God went to my identity. As each month passed us by and we had no positive pregnancy tests in our hands, I found it harder and harder to tell let people in. I found it harder to show to not find comfort in safety of who I used to be, and I found really hard to let God in again.

After all I'd been through and the truth God had got me to see and understand about myself, it was all dissolving very quickly. Just like it did all those years ago, all that mattered was what I saw in that mirror. I look back now and wonder how I allowed myself to forget who I was. After all the breaking and pain I went through the first time, you'd think I'd never forget. But we all do forget. I forgot because I believed my own abilities were the reason why I was still standing – not God's. I put my trust and hope in my own strength. The problem with that is that my strength and abilities are limited. I can only do so much, but God can do all.

Just like I was thankful for my season of with anorexia, I'm also thankful for my fertility battle. Without it I wouldn't have discovered my true identity, and my true healing would never have occurred without those days. However, it took some time for that to be the case.

Mirror, Mirror on the wall…when will my belly be round and filled with a child?

I tried everything from bargaining with the mirror, sweet talking it, ignoring it, yelling at it, and even begging for it to show me something different. When you give something your focus, it consumes you and my mirror was no different. It almost felt real, with its own personality and choices. But my mirror, any mirror for that matter, is just an object that has no heartbeat or personality. It doesn't have a soul, and it definitely doesn't have the right to judge you. It can't make its own decisions and it definitely doesn't care about you. It was time once and for all to silence the voice of that one-dimensional piece of material and allow Jesus to have the final say. Have you let Jesus have the say over your life, your identity and your worth?

Please know if you have or do struggle with your outward appearance, your outward appearance doesn't determine your value. Heaven doesn't erupt with praise because we're a certain size, if our belly is flat, or our new outfit looks better than someone else's. There isn't a panel of angels holding up score cards confirming if we're good enough because of how we look in the mirror, validating our worth and value. When I looked in the mirror and believed I was the sum of what I saw, I gave the devil an open door to judge me, humiliate me, discourage me and lie to me. I was the one that agreed with him for too long though.

What do you see? What do you want to see?

Now when I look in the mirror and find another flaw or discover another imperfection, God is says, "Yeah I see that and I love it. Remember I made you and formed you. Nothing was a mistake. I love you", and I believe Him! He wants us to see all the amazing qualities He has given us. He carefully considered and crafted you when He formed you. Nothing was left out and nothing of too much was put in by accident. You are perfect to Him. Absolutely.

The difference between Jesus and a mirror is that Jesus has a heartbeat and a personality. His heart truly cares about you and me. The next time the devil tries to judge you, humiliate you, lie to you, and discourage you, get right up in his face and tell him some truths (in the process you will remind yourself too)! Remind him that God is the ultimate judge and each of His decisions are final, and that God's promises stand true every day of the week. Remind him that God has a desire for you to live extraordinary lives.

'My heart is confident in You, O God, no wonder I sing Your praises.' – Psalm 108:1 NLT

'He forgives *all* my sins and heals *all* my diseases. He ransoms me from death and surrounds me with love and tender mercies.' – Psalm 103:3-4 NLT

'Not one of all the Lord's good promises to Israel failed; everyone was fulfilled.' – Joshua 21:45 NIV

Before I knew who I was, I had to say goodbye to who I was.

WHO YOU WERE

God used the pain in my life to build resilience, to build strength, to build wisdom in His name, not my own. My identity is found in who God says I am, not a single other thing. Looking back now, it's an interesting thought to think I was ill prepared to stand in front a mirror all those years ago. I let everything else have the power to tell me who I was rather than ask Him. I am firm believer that sometimes we'd do better in life if we spent less time in front of the mirror and more in His Word. It's there that we discover who we really are.

11

Pain has a purpose

This whole book is about this simple fact – pain has a purpose.

I was sitting with someone dear to me while writing this book and they said, "I'm so sorry I'm telling you all this. The last thing I want to do is bring up old memories or give your more to carry than you already have". Was it comfortable to hear them share how they were struggling? Definitely not. Were there a lot of old feelings and thoughts that resurfaced? There definitely were.

But my pain, the days I've walked through up until that point, gave me a seat at their table. It meant my words had impact, my thoughts could be trusted and my heart was known to be true. The thing about pain is it can add value to your life or strip everything away from it, you choose which it does. I became curious about what does God have to say about pain. Of course, I don't know His thoughts precisely, but I think His Word shows us His heart about it.

'Happy are those who are strong in the Lord, who want above all else to follow your steps. When they walk through the Valley of Weeping, it will become a place of springs where pools of blessing and refreshment collect after rains!' - Psalm 84:5-6 TLB

What a beautiful image. I love the thought that my past and future seasons of weeping have been, and could be, made into refreshing springs. That my journey so far, and the different valleys I've walked through, wouldn't be wasted. Instead turned into something that blesses me and those around me. The very thing that tried to hurt and destroy me, is the very thing God will use to bless my life abundantly. The very water, the tears, that fell from my eyes in my season of pure sadness is the water that will now be a place of refreshment.

The scripture doesn't say could be, should be or would be. It says will be. I love the idea of purpose and nothing being wasted. The notion of purpose is something I cannot ignore; it underlies everything in my life. Even when it's caused me to get wound up in knots of questions about why, I still think purpose is a beautiful thing. It's given me a rod of clear direction and thinking to cling onto, when nothing else makes sense. Psalm 84 isn't of a question of maybe, but a definite. I encourage you to trust the tears you're shedding now are the ones that will rehydrate you and bring life back to you, just like they have for me. I have such comfort and value in allowing my tears to fall now.

I'm no longer fighting them back and trying to hide them, feeling embarrassed by them or ashamed of them. If anything, at times, I ask for them to come. When I first started to grieve, they felt like razor blades falling down my cheeks. But as I started to see that my pain and tears had purpose, I began to respect them and even treasure them. Something shifted when I gave my tears special attention and saw them as worthy of high regard.

My attitude changed with how I treated them, thought about them, spoke about them and even how I let them fall. As I reflect back on my life, with this new understanding, I wonder if I hadn't had learnt to release my tears where would my spring of refreshing form from? A pool doesn't fill up by itself, it needs a source of water to fill it up. During our summer, the days are very humid and our pool water evaporates almost daily. We have to keep filling it up with our backyard hose, I think now, my tears have acted in the same way to my own refreshing springs. My new understanding causes me to ask, if I didn't release and trust every tear had a purpose, then what source would fill up my refreshing spring when I came through my valley?

I just love thinking about that refreshing spring. I'm sure you and I have a different image of a refreshing spring in our mind, and that's completely okay. My spring is like a lagoon. Never ending clear waters with a hint of blues and greens. The kind that as the sun hits the still waters it's turquoise colours glisten against the beige sandy bottom. Oh and my lagoon has no rocks, no seaweed, or weird grass on the bottom to freak me out as it touches my leg. My lagoon does have a few colourful fish, not a lot, swimming around. All different sizes and shapes. Above all, it's a body of water that's calm and warm to touch. What's yours look like?

Like many millions of people, I love watching David Attenborough's nature documentaries, they're just stunning. I feel complete awe when I see a lion, a hippopotamus and a gazelle all drinking from the same water. It seems illogical and impossible they'd all rest and be renewed by the same source at the same time, while their defenses are down. There seems to be an unspoken truce between all of them in that moment. Whatever their differences or grievances are, they don't matter at that moment. They not only allow themselves to be next to each other, but it's as if it they welcome one another – we as a human race could learn a lot from them but that is a whole other book!

Back to what I was trying to say, imagine if each of our refreshing springs would be an oasis for someone else. Just like the water is a place of refreshment and restoration for the lion, it is too for the hippopotamus and the gazelle. A refreshing spring is a place where all people can feel safe. A place they can release their tears, be refreshed by the touch of God and begin to heal. A place where they can begin filling up their refreshing spring for the season of joy and abundance that awaits them. I'm so encouraged by this Holy Spirit given thought alone. Pain has had a fierce grip on my soul at times, but with God's gift of the Holy Spirit, I've come to lean into the sweet whisper of His truth along the way. His help has meant I now view pain differently to the way the world says we should.

When I say I love God it doesn't just mean I love the idea of Him, but who He is. I'm ashamed to say I used to just love the idea of Him, I didn't respect Him, and I definitely didn't hold Him and His ways in high regard for many years. I didn't trust His intentions towards me were good or kind. Thankfully that's changed. I started to understand that being responsible with my pain meant I needed to reassess my relationship with Him. To love Him was not just to love the idea of Him, but also respecting who He was and His nature. Only then could I then begin to respect my pain. Since those days, I've come to see His purpose in my pain and the gift that it is.

Travelling through your own season/s of pain, you too may have felt the same way I used to about God. I'm not shaming or judging you, and I wouldn't blame you if you wanted to shut this book right now and not read any further. I get it. I've been pretty open so far about how I used to think I deserved to deal with, endure, handle or suffer through different seasons of pain (and we're only getting started!). For years, I struggled to respected it or see purpose in it. I even thought, in some super weird and extraordinary way, that God liked to see me in pain. I'm forever grateful Psalm 84 helped me realised that wasn't the truth.

'For the Lord God is brighter than the brilliance of a sunrise! Wrapping Himself around me like a shield, He is so generous with his gifts of grace and glory. Those who walk along His paths with integrity will never lack one thing they need, for He provides it all!' - Psalm 84:11

God doesn't like pain, but like most things, He uses it to bring out the best for us and in us. The devil does like pain, he likes to inflict it and see the damage it causes. He knows the power pain has and uses it to hurt us, limit us, restrict us and hopefully destroy us. God on the other hand uses pain to show how much bigger He is compared to it, to help us strengthen our faith, and to help us discover our life's full potential. I like to think God uses pain as a launch pad, and the devils tries to make it our gravesite.

> **'As far as I am concerned, God turned into good what you meant for evil, for he brought me to this high position I have today so that I could save the lives of many people.'**
> **- Gen 50:20 TLB**

> **'He offers a resting place for me in His luxurious love. His tracks take me to an oasis of peace near the quiet brook of bliss. That's where He restores and revives my life. He opens before me the right path and leads me along in His footsteps of righteousness so that I can bring honour to His name.' - Psalm 23:2-3 TPT**

There is no question God often leads us beside still waters and gives us all the generous gift of peace, but what about when He doesn't? What about when He leads us to waters that are not so calm and peaceful? Just like when Jesus knew the disciples were going to encounter a storm and He still took them out into the sea. Nothing that happens under God's watch, whether in our lives or in this world, is a coincidence or by chance, or luck. Everything answers to God, even the storm we find ourselves facing in life at times.

His Word says there's a time for everything, and there's a time when He leads us to face the stormy seas. I know for me personally, my faith has been strengthened in the storm more than the days where I laid beside still waters. My faith has been built when God was my only chance for survival, when He was the only one that I could trust and rely on. My faith has been built when everything felt unsteady except for His love and grace. My faith has been built on the days I stepped out on the waves and met Him in the middle of the chaos.

PAIN HAS A PURPOSE

Then when God led me to the still waters, where I rested and He renewed my soul. We can easily see obstacles and rocky seas as a sign of God's absence. Sometimes we forget how fierce, strong and powerful God is. I know I did, I got too comfortable and familiar with His peace. Sometimes He leads you through the rough seas on the way to the still waters. God is the Almighty King, the Creator of the universe, the Maker of all things and the Judge of the world. He is also a loving and kind father, a friend and a provider. His nature is good, extravagant, creative, bold, insightful and kind.

He knows what fruit your pain can produce if you allow it, the beauty this pain will add to your story, the strength this pain will give your faith. I've learnt to see my pain through this viewpoint. What I know and understand now is that God withholds at times because He knows what He's doing. It's at this point you can see pain as a gift - a gift that can help you reach others, and a gift that deepens your relationship with God. A gift that rebuilds hope in your heart.

The plan for my life has always been bigger than just a story of pain and striving to survive. God's always had something better planned, it just took me a while to see it. He knew I'd only understand and see the other side of the story by first being exposed to one side. My vision became clearer and began to understand that God withholds at times because He loves the other people involved in your story too. The season of pain you find yourself in isn't just about you a lot of the time.

Before I finish this chapter, let me use my fertility as an example.

The pain of not falling pregnant flowed into my husband's life, our parents and very close friends. It helped me respect my pain better because I started to see there was more involved than just how I felt. It was if my eyes were finally being opened and I saw the greater impact it had on others, not just my heart and in my life. The pain you're in has a purpose, and you need to know God is not only working in your life but others too. The whole time I thought was about God withholding was instead about planning, designing, preparing, creating, building and putting into place all the pieces to make the miracle so, miraculous! I have a strong feeling it's the same for you too. Fully respecting my pain meant I had to respect the outcome too. If my parents let me eat chocolate every morning for breakfast and ice cream for dinner, I'd have long-standing health issues and probably no teeth! At the time I probably didn't respect any of it, but I do now, and I respect them because of it. The same goes for our relationship with God.

My perspective on pain and heartache started to move from believing I somehow deserved to suffer, to believing it had nothing to do with what I deserved or not. None of us deserve the perfect amount of love or care God puts into every detail of our life. When I started to understand, appreciate and respect this, I could process my pain in a healthier way. Sometimes you won't know the specific purpose while you're in your season of pain, I never did, but that doesn't mean it doesn't have one.

Nothing God does is by chance or coincidence, and that is the same for you and every part of your life. Just because it doesn't make sense now doesn't mean it won't. Hold on.

12

Remember who calls you His

> *In worship at church tonight, I melted. For the first time I saw that God has always been there. Tonight, He was completely focused on making sure I understood He has been in every fire I faced and it broke His heart to see me struggle. I may have been fire, but I've never been burnt. Why? Because He has always been there. While I have felt alone and abandoned, I never was. Ever. Tonight I saw my life from His perspective. Tonight was the moment I truly first allowed myself to cry since mum's died. I've held it in for so long and I just couldn't contain the weight of my tears any longer. And He was there to catch every tear tonight.*
>
> *But it went further than that tonight. It was like He took me on journey to show me where He has always been. He has been in every empty toilet cubicle and looked at the same negative pregnancy test I was looking at. He's been there in every doctor's appointment when we heard over & over again that there is nothing that could be done to help our situation. He's been there when the shower was washing away the tears I was hiding from everyone else. He was with me when someone I loved deeply pushed me aside and rejected me, He's been with me in the car as I drove to work reluctantly full of anxiety. He's been with me in it.*

> *He has shed tears. I finally understood how He could be a loving Father and see His child suffer so much. Because as I suffered, He suffered, He took my pain in each of those moments and tried to give me peace. A Father that will do anything to protect His little girl – no one is ever going to hurt her.*
> JOURNAL ENTRY 27.10.2019 - WITH YOU IN THE FIRE

That entry has never left me, nor have these words - there was another in the fire standing next to me | there was another in the waters holding back the seas | and should I ever need reminding of how I've been set free | there is a cross that bears the burden where another died for me | there is another in the fire | - Hillsong, *Another in the Fire*

There are certain questions I've been asked many times but no matter the question the answer is always the same, "because of God". *Because of God* I'm still smiling, standing, I still believe God is good, and I still wake up each day desperate to find the beauty hidden in the mess. I have lots reasons to not smile, or see that life isn't beautiful, to disagree God is good, and to struggle to see the good in each day. Most days I don't but some not all. I have my moments where it's a struggle to do any of those things, where I wrestled with God and I'm so angry I think I might explode. I still have those moments, I just don't stayed in those moments for as long. I've come to learn there's a different in sitting in your pain and staying in it. The key for me is remembering who calls you His despite it all. Pain is temporary but God is permanent.

Some life lessons take longer to learn than others. I used to be think I would always be alone. I thought God had forgotten about me. My childhood wasn't horribly violent or full of abuse, it was just very isolating.

When you're an only child of a single parent, life can be pretty lonely. There wasn't anyone to converse with, to fight with, to sit with, or really do much with. Buying me board games for Christmas or my birthday was useless.

To fill the void I had imaginary friends (who I knew were completely in my imagination but it gave me comfort thinking there was someone with me) who walked with me to school, sat with me at the dinner table, or swam with me in the pool on afternoons after school. I watched a lot of TV and found company in the stories of fictional characters. Mum wasn't always asleep and we had some wonderful times together. Being alone was something that was very normal for me regardless.

During my teenage years, I walked to and from school alone, often ate meals alone, did the food shop alone, went for bike rides alone, watched TV alone and swam in our complex's pool alone. When I was younger, the silence was something I hated. I always had the TV on for noise or to feel like someone else was in the house with me. I wasn't okay with being alone. I was desperate for company, not attention. I wanted to feel connected to someone.

Now as an adult, I still spend a lot of time alone but it doesn't feel the same. When I was alone as a young girl I had no sense of connection to anyone and *alone* felt like another word for abandoned. I now enjoy my alone time because of the healing God has done in my heart over the years. I know He is with me even when no one else is. I know I'm loved, seen and I know I'm heard. In the stillness of being alone, God reminds me He calls me His. It's taken many years to get to this point, many years.

Two things that have been the hardest alone are spending weekends alone, and doing a pregnancy test. Weekends are hard because that's when I'm reminded we don't have a family and it's a space that's very hard to fill. The other is taking each pregnancy test. I still remember each one, there's been more than a few! The result of doing life alone is you become fiercely private and independent, sometimes to the point where your loved ones feel rejected or hurt because you keep them at arm's length. The real reason I've kept everyone at arm's length is because I thought I was protecting them, when really I was trying to protect myself.

In the movies, husband's sit outside the door waiting with a hug or a hand to hold as we watch the line/s appear, or a best friend is waiting outside with a glass of wine waiting excitedly for the outcome, or ready to comfort me. That's not how it played out for me, it's always been me and God only. Except for once - I once sat in my doctor's office after doing a test, only to see him thrown the test in the bin after it came up negative, along with the hope any other result could be possible, disregarded. I've already touched on this earlier, but I feel it's important to say that this isn't because my husband hasn't wanted to, or wouldn't. Many times, he knew or sensed I did one because of my mood. Sometimes he heard the opening of the packet. No matter what, he has always had a beautiful dose of love available for me and knew me well enough to know I would tell him when I was able to. It's a weird feeling in that moment because you want to be comforted, but you also just need some space to breathe.

How are you still smiling? How are you still standing? How do you still believe God is good? How do you keep finding the will to wake up each day and find the beauty hidden in it?

Because of Shadrach, Meshach, and Abednego's story.

'Shadrach, Meshach, and Abednego fell into the fire. They were tied up very tightly. Then King Nebuchadnezzar jumped to his feet. He was very surprised and he asked his advisors, "We tied only three men, and we threw only three men into the fire. Is that right?" His advisors said, "Yes, King." The king said, "Look! I see four men walking around in the fire. They are not tied up and they are not burned. The fourth man looks like an angel." – Daniel 3:23-25

Just like in the story of these three men, God has been in every fire I have faced. He's been in all yours too. While the flames felt like they were engulfing me and the heat became more intense, so did His protection and love for me. Not one flame has ever touched a hair on my head when it should've and not one part of my skin has a burn mark. That night I shared in my the journal entry at the start of the chapter was a true turning point in my relationship with God.

While my mum's suicide wasn't unexpected, it still left me with many big questions that only added to the ever increasing fractures of my already fragile faith at that point. I didn't understand how a God who loved me so much and saw how abandoned I felt, allowed for another person to leave me. When my mum left, the loneliness I'd felt only intensified. Why didn't she knew I still needed her? Why didn't God?

In my mum's final moment on earth, Jesus was in the fire with both of us. That night i share about in my journal entry has been to date, one of the most supernatural experiences of my life. A moment held in time. I was there in church *and* I was in North Carolina, in the lounge room where my mum was making her decision. When my mum took her last breath, Jesus vividly showed me His hand outstretched, like a parent reaching out their arm to a child learning to swim or walk, to my mum.

He wasn't mad at her and He wasn't disappointed. He just wanted to lead her home. But in this vision, it's the best way I know how to describe it, He didn't have both hands outstretched though, just one. As my mum was being welcomed home to heaven, His second hand was embracing me. Never were either of us alone, He was with both of us. But with me it was more than a hand that was outstretched, it was His whole arm ready to hold me close as the impact of what just occurred would soon hit me. He knew that moment was going to knock me off my feet and I was going to need someone to hold me for a while. His chest was turned towards me and I could feel His whole arm wrap around me. His heart and His embrace was His gift to me for He knew I was going to need all of Him in the days, weeks, months and years ahead.

As this vision and moment continued, I felt His tears fall with mine. I felt His heartbreaking and while I still had hours to know what had happened, His embrace was still holding me while He whispered He wished there could be another way. What I remember very clearly about that whole experience was how strong, intentional and protective His embrace was, nothing was going to break it. Up until that moment I questioned, almost daily, if Jesus saw my pain or if He could see I needed Him. I wondered if He knew I even existed, but I've never had those questions since 27th October 2019. Never. I've had many other questions, but not what I mean to Him. I know I'm His and I know He is with me, always. That same truth is the same for you too. I promise you, there is another next to you in the fire.

'Nebuchadnezzar went to the door of the roaring furnace and called in, "Shadrach, Meshach, and Abednego, servants of the High God, come out here!". Shadrach, Meshach, and Abednego walked out of the fire. All the important people, the government leaders and king's counsellors, gathered around to examine them and discovered that the fire hadn't so much as touched the three men – not a hair singed, not a scorch mark on their clothes, not even the smell of fire on them! Nebuchadnezzar said, "Blessed be the God of Shadrach, Meshach, and Abednego! He sent his angel and rescued his servants who trusted in him! They ignored the king's orders and laid their bodies on the line rather than serve or worship any god but their own."' – Daniel 3:26-29 MSG

**'Is anyone crying for help? God is listening, ready to rescue you. If your heart is broken, you'll find God right there; if you're kicked in the gut, he'll help you catch your breath.'
– Psalm 34:17-19 MSG**

God's been there to wipe away every tear, and He'll be there to wipe the tears that fall in my days ahead, as He will with you. With every test I thought I took alone, He has been there.

He was the One holding my hand and waiting for me outside the door. I thought I was looking at the back of a cubicle door, when really I was looking at Him and He was looking at me. He was holding my hands as they held each test.

His heart knew my pain and He wasn't gloating in it. He wasn't mocking me or punishing me from His judgment throne above. He wasn't distant anymore. He was right there. I now know His promises aren't dead, I haven't missed it and that I'm enough. I used to think I was alone, but that was a complete lie. A really well-told lie. He has been there with His hand on my shoulder every moment of every day. Don't miss your own whispers from heaven, they are so precious. They are our life support.

> *My love will always be greater than your burden – always! It is ok to voice your pain; it is ok to hurt and give that hurt a voice. But don't hold on to it. Don't let it determine what you think of yourself or what you think I think of you. My love will be with you regardless of whether you see it or feel it. My love will be the unknown hug holding you tightly, shielding you from the arrows and absorbing your tears, your pain and your anguish. You are so loved and I love YOU so much more than you will ever comprehend, possibly appreciate.*
> JOURNAL ENTRY 14.08.2014 – ANOTHER IN THE FIRE

13

Trusting God

'I chose you before I gave you life, and before you were born, I selected you to be a prophet to the nations.' – Jeremiah 1:5 GNT

I'm not sure my brain will ever fully comprehend that God knew me, and He knew you before anyone knew your name. He still does. I'm amazed that God knew everything about all of us, and He still decided to go ahead with our creation. He knew everything we'd do to disappoint Him, to hurt Him intentionally and unintentionally. He knew we'd reject Him. He knew every sin we'd commit and He still chose us. He still loves us. He knew every good word we'd speak and deed we'd do. He knew every decision we'd or wouldn't. He knew when and how we'd turn our backs to Him. He knew we might blame Him when we couldn't make sense of it all. He knew we'd call upon Him in our darkest hour and He knew some of us would never come back to Him. He knew all of this and yet God *still* created you and me. He still chooses to love us, and continues to choose to love us every minute of every day. He still loves us and gives us a chance anyway.

'After he had said this, Jesus was troubled in spirit and testified, "Very truly I tell you, one of you is going to betray me."' - John 13:21 NIV

I wonder how much it hurts His heart knowing many of us aren't happy with what we look like. I often think about why some people have certain colour hair, why some have freckles, some have bigger noses than others, some have more hair than others and some are taller than others. It amazes me how He knew we'd try to alter ourselves in some way to change our outward appearance and He still created us in hope we'd see His perfection in us. He knew some of us would look in the mirror and miss His reflection, choosing instead to believe a false reality or a lie. I don't know why our bodies aren't all perfectly shaped and proportioned. The truth that sometimes gets blurred is that we weren't made to be perfect in this life, but were made with a perfect love from a perfect Father.

One thing is definitely not perfect is our hearts after a few years of life. It starts to feel a little battered and bruised. Unfortunately our hearts don't always heal instantly. It's fact that sometimes we come up short more times than we'd like to admit. But God doesn't see that, instead He sees someone He's spent an enormous amount of time and effort on. Nothing about any of us is an afterthought, a throw in or casual addition. His days are spent thinking about us, finding ways to bless us and pour out His love upon us. The truth is I've spent a large part of my life worried about what others might see in me, or how I value myself, rather than understanding the above truths.

What does God see when He looks at me?

It's a question that's been stirring in my heart for a few years now. Trusting God has been one of the hardest lessons in life I've had to learn if I'm honest. I'm still learning and where I struggle to trust God was most was with provision. He has just simply felt distant. I understand how hard it's for people on the outside to see how God is alive in a messy situation because I struggled to understand too. I do truly believe God always sees opportunity in everything.

Many people have questioned how I can have a hope or faith in God when all they see is so many unanswered prayers and heartache. In the first seven years of our fertility story I had very little hope or trust in Him. By the day it felt like it was disappearing rather than strengthening. I didn't appreciate the time I had well. I was so envious and desperate to have sleepless nights and everything else that goes with having a child that I couldn't see what I had. I didn't see, value or look after my gift of time well. I didn't the see women who I wanted to be look at me and be envious of the time I had. My heart was cold. Something happened when I started to write this book though.

On the 27th of Feb 2019, chains started to break and the hardness started to dissolve. Word by word I felt something I hadn't felt before be birthed in my heart and spirit – gratitude for time. The time I would've spent nursing a baby, has instead been given to writing this book. The very time I would've dedicated to making new memories with a growing child, has been spent developing my craft to write and create beautiful pieces of encouragement. This unanswered prayer has become one of God's greatest gifts to me. Would I still like to have had this *and* a baby? Yup. What does God see when He looks at me *now*? I hope God sees something different. Hopefully my trust in Him is evident. It's still a little dented I will admit but where He used to see resentment and anger, I hope He sees joy and gratitude.

Time used to feel like nothing more than torment & punishment, now it feels like a gift of opportunity. A gift bless our lives financially by building a strong business, as well as our marriage, and relationships with those we love and care about. We learnt early we needed to keep communication front and centre in our marriage. It took time and practice to not be scared to have the big conversations and pray about all things. Maybe if we'd been given a child, our time wouldn't be focused on building and strengthening the foundation of our marriage and friendships. Time is something we have learnt to respect, and protect.

What do others see when He looks at me *now*, especially on the hard days? I wonder if people will always see a woman with no mum on Mother's Day to be in pain on that day? Could there be opportunity for them to see something else?

For me, the days that actually hurt most are the ones that have no significant meaning. Days like Mother's Day can still hurt but they're also a day for celebration. In the absence of my own mum, God brought me several amazing women to guide me and love me. In the absence of my mum, my relationship with my dad was able to be restored and gave us space to navigate our way back to each other. The void my mum left meant my lean into God has been much more than if I had her here too. Where I might have turned to her, I've instead turned to God. Over time I've learnt trusting God means looking at things with His perspective, not my own.

When I saw mess, He saw something else. I think He always sees opportunity. God is a big God who sees it all, every battle and hardship and isn't fazed by any of it. He doesn't care how messy things seem and He doesn't care how loud the lions are roaring. He isn't intimated, scared or fearful. He doesn't close the door on situations that seem to complex and hard, like a parent does hoping of their teenagers room will go away if they close door. Not at all, He is the One who opens the door, mess and all; it us who are the ones that close it!

'For all of our faults and flaws are in full view to you. Everything we want to hide, you search out and expose by the radiance of your face.'
– Psalm 90:8 TPT

Does it matter what others see? Does it matter what we see, or does it matter more what we want to see? Or does it matter, ultimately, what God sees?

Let me share another story before I answer those questions. A few years ago I read a beautiful story of a hidden wall. The story mentioned how the wall was almost covered completely by dirt, ivy, moss, assorted weeds and how it was broken off in bits. Passers-by had no idea of the beauty and treasure that lay beneath the dirt and assorted weeds. All they saw was an awful sight walked past each day. As I read that story, I thought of our lives and what God sees.

Often, we too, can't see past the moss, the dirt, ivy, assorted weeds and even the broken bits of our life. We have no idea how God could either. We think we need to clean ourselves up before we let God see us, use us and love us. The moss and dirt in our lives sounds a little more like pride, doubt, resentment, rejection, fear and anger. We see a wall that cannot be saved and has no hope, but God sees a beautiful wall, full of character and uniqueness. Then God asks us to trust Him. He knows trusting Him often means taking little bites at a time, prayer by prayer, hope after hope, and forgiveness after forgiveness.

Maybe it's been different for you, but for me my trust in God has grown a little more each day. It's never been a whole hearted thing all at once, I wish it was. Just like the wall is cleaned by first removing the weeds, then the ivy, then the moss and finally the dirt, so are our lives are cleaned when we put our trust in Him. What I love the most in this story isn't that there was a beautiful wall underneath the mess all along (I mean that's great too!), it's the gardener who made the choice to maintain the wall. The gardener reminds me of Jesus. I love how Jesus deals with one pain at a time. He knows we're all dealing with something and need His love and grace to get us through. He knows it takes time. The ivy will most probably try to creep back into the familiar crevices, sneaking around as if no one will see them. The weeds will most likely poke their heads up again, as if daring anyone to remove them or pretending to be small enough that they don't matter. The dirt will come again and so will the moss. This is the best bit - so will God! Trusting God is an invitation to see your situation the way He does, not the way you used to. That's where the power in the story really is.

The story of the 'Woman at the Well' is another beautiful example of how our vision is naturally so different to God's but trusting Him only ends well for us. With His grace and wisdom, He shows the woman what He sees. He saw a chance for redemption when she only saw rejection. He saw a chance to start again when all she saw was no hope. He saw a chance for her to live instead of hiding.

'A woman, a Samaritan, came to draw water. Jesus said, "Would you give me a drink of water. The Samaritan woman, taken aback, asked, "How come you, a Jew, are asking me, a Samaritan woman, for a drink?" (Jews in those days wouldn't be caught dead talking to Samaritans.) - John 4:7-9 MSG

'The Samaritan woman, taken aback, asked, "How come you, a Jew, are asking me, a Samaritan woman, for a drink?" (Jews in those days wouldn't be caught dead talking to Samaritans.). Jesus answered, "If you knew the generosity of God and who I am, you would be asking *me* for a drink, and I would give you fresh, living water". The woman said, "Sir, you don't even have a bucket to draw with, and this well is deep. So how are you going to get this 'living water'? Are you a better man than our ancestor Jacob, who dug this well and drank from it, he and his sons and livestock, and passed it down to us?". Jesus said, "Everyone who drinks this water will get thirsty again and again. Anyone who drinks the water I give will never thirst—not ever. The water I give will be an artesian spring within, gushing fountains of endless life.". The woman said, "Sir, give me this water so I won't ever get thirsty, won't ever have to come back to this well again!'. He said, "Go call your husband and then come back". "I have no husband," she said. "That's nicely put: 'I have no husband.' You've had five husbands, and the man you're living with now isn't even your husband. You spoke the truth there, sure enough.". "Oh, so you're a prophet! Well, tell me this: Our ancestors worshiped God at this mountain, but you Jews insist that Jerusalem is the only place for worship, right?".

"Believe me, woman, the time is coming when you Samaritans will worship the Father neither here at this mountain nor there in Jerusalem. You worship guessing in the dark; we Jews worship in the clear light of day. God's way of salvation is made available through the Jews. But the time is coming—it has, in fact, come—when what you're called will not matter and where you go to worship will not matter. "It's who you are and the way you live that count before God. Your worship must engage your spirit in the pursuit of truth. That's the kind of people the Father is out looking for: those who are simply and honestly *themselves* before him in their worship. God is sheer being itself—Spirit. Those who worship him must do it out of their very being, their spirits, their true selves, in adoration.". The woman said, "I don't know about that. I do know that the Messiah is coming. When he arrives, we'll get the whole story". "I am he," said Jesus. "You don't have to wait any longer or look any further.". Just then his disciples came back. They were shocked. They couldn't believe he was talking with that kind of a woman. No one said what they were all thinking, but their faces showed it. The woman took the hint and left. In her confusion she left her water pot. Back in the village she told the people, "Come see a man who knew all about the things I did, who knows me inside and out. Do you think this could be the Messiah?" And they went out to see for themselves.' – John 4:9-34
NLT

Does it matter what we see of ourselves, or what we want others to see of us? Does it matter what we see and the lens we put our pain through? Or does it matter, ultimately, what God sees? After all that, yes I think it all matters.

I believe it all effects the condition of our heart, our attitude towards God, and it definitely effects our trust in His name. Trusting God doesn't give us all the answers and we can't protect God from people questioning Him (spoiler alert – He doesn't need us to!). I've come to understand the true value of putting my trust in God. When I put my trust in Him, it's a beautiful opportunity to let me story be a gift of hope and encouragement the someone else. Our response to the not-so-pleasant things happening in life is where the power of your story begins.

When the Samaritan woman went back to her village she had the chance to put her trust in God and let her story have value. It's the same for us today. She chose to show God off in the midst her mess and confusion. She showed God was kind and loving and in full control. It didn't wipe away her past or instantly change her reality, but she influenced the name of God in the minds of those who may never have trusted Him otherwise. Most importantly, she knew she could trust her God. Always.

14

Sweetness of surrender

Lord, I don't know how to pray without this pain remaining deep in my heart. Without me having a reason to reach up to You.

I don't know how to live without this pain as much as I want it gone. It takes up so much space in my heart and mind and requires so much time to care for. I have spent so much time wrapping You around this pain rather than trusting you with it. It just seems too big. I feel like I have been carrying it around, caring for it even, for so long and in an instant, I am expected to just give it away. Like a mother handing over a brand-new baby. I am expected to just release it You. I have almost dedicated my life to this pain. But You want to take it from me. You want me to surrender it to You. How do I do that without looking back at where I left it? I don't know how to worship You without desiring this pain to leave and the answer to come. How do I praise You and sing with joy when my heart has felt so heavy for so long and I find more comfort in sadness than joy?

I don't know how to remain hopeful, to look forward, to be ok with it and to be responsible with this pain. I don't what else to do – see more doctors, see less, talk about it more or be distracted with other things, try more treatments or do nothing, keep going out for prayer or know

You've heard me by now and will move if You want to move. I don't know how to not think about it, how to not over think every moment, I've forgotten how to dream about it. I don't know. Did I miss You in amongst the pain, were You there and I couldn't see You? What does my life look like if this prayer is never answered or answered in a different way? I could handle not being a mum if you God, weren't involved. I could possibly find peace. But when the Creator of the world is able to give me all I desire, because He gave me the desires of my heart, I struggle to find peace. I struggle to let it go and surrender. I struggle not to fight. I struggle not to want it all.

I struggle not to let my faith die. What does my marriage look and feel like for me and my husband if it never happens? What words will go forever unsaid or start to become quieter because of the vacancy in our hearts. How do I surrender all this and leave it with You?

JOURNAL ENTRY 26.10.2018 - PERSONAL PRAYER

According to the Oxford Dictionary the act of surrender is to stop resisting, to submit to a powerful authority/ influence, to give up or to hand over. The Cambridge Dictionary says it is to admit defeat. Admit defeat? That one stopped me in my tracks. Did it mean defeat as in that's it, finished? All over? Travelling along our fertility journey, we tried to do everything, nothing, and then everything and nothing all at once. For the main part, many of those years I thought it was all on me to make it happen because it's my body and the action happens within me. What I've come to learn now that we have reached the other side is that in fact, Jesus is the one who really has the control. My goodness it's been a fight in itself to try and not wrestle Him for it. When I think about admitting defeat, or even surrendering in general, I am full of questions about Moses' mum as told in Exodus 2:1-3 in the New International translation.

'Now a man of the tribe of Levi married a Levite woman, and she became pregnant and gave birth to a son. When she saw that he was a fine child, she hid him for three months. But when she could hide

him no longer, she got a papyrus basket for him and coated it with tar and pitch. Then she placed the child in it and put it among the reeds along the bank of the Nile.' Exodux 2:1-3 MSG

Did she wrestle with God about what had to happen? Did she try to think of another way? Did she try and chase the basket down the river as soon as she placed it in the water? Did Moses cry as he floated away from her, or was he asleep? Was she consumed with grief? When did the tears turn into peace? Was the act of surrender a daily choice she had to make like it has been for me? So many questions!

It took me ten years to get to that point myself, putting my dream to be a mother completely in God's hands. Until that tenth year, I couldn't. Over the years, my hope of becoming a mother became like carry a tonne of bricks with me everywhere. It was no longer a joy, it no longer blessed my relationship with God and or anyone else. And yet for years, I couldn't let go. The very thought of letting it go was too much. The thought of letting go seemed so much harder than enduring with it. Before Moses' mum actually put Moses in the water, there came a point where she had to admit defeat in doing it her own way. She knew keeping him meant death, and while she wasn't sure of the outcome by putting him in the river, her releasing him actually meant he lived.

Sometimes we can hold onto something for too long. I do believe, because I've felt it in my own life, there's a grace to carry what God has equipped you to carry. It's not necessarily easy, but you can do it because in your weakness His strength becomes what carries you through. And then there's a time when that grace lifts and I believe the act of surrender becomes your greatest gift, to you and to God. A long time ago, I had to admit I didn't know best when it came to becoming pregnant. I'd tried to do everything in my own strength and ability, but ultimately the impossible was always going to be out of reach. I had to let God be God.

Surrender will only ever be a nine letter word and never truly work unless we truly trust God to let Him be God. Have you ever done the trust exercise in a team building conference and you're blindfolded? If not, it's an exercise where you're paired up with someone else and told to trust them as they walk you around an obstacle course. I think surrendering to God feels the same. We depend on Him for His guidance, and where to place our next step. Often there comes a point in the activity where you struggle to trust and surrender your will to know best. The person guiding you becoming frustrated, which makes me wonder if God feels the same sometimes when we don't trust Him.

What is your pain? Are you ready to surrender? Are you ready to admit defeat and let God take control again?

They aren't easy questions to answer. Some days I've boldly said "yes" to the last question, and then in the early moments of the next day, I've run ahead trying to see what God will do and even get involved again. Nothing about surrender is easy. It's not always simple and it's not always quick, but it is worth it. I'd love to know the timeline of this story at the start of Exodus 2. Imagine giving away the one thing you loved the most, feeling complete devastation, only to have it come back with a double portion of blessing! Not only did Moses' mum get her son back, but she got paid too!

There are many journal entries I've written like the one I opened this chapter with. Some are more hopeful; some are angrier and some are kind towards God, and some are just ugly. Some have been more like a dumping ground of emotion, a justification for my disobedience and frustrations. Some journal entries are a gravesite for my brokenness. There are pages that are pure fuel to my pain, like adding gasoline to a bonfire. There's plenty of defeat within the pages. Just not much surrender.

Sometimes you have to get real with yourself and give your face a good old-fashioned (metaphorical!) slap. I've had to do it many times and I don't think I've felt the end of them. As humans, we love to self-indulge in our emotions and think the world is about us. We don't bother to see anyone else's reality unless we are feeling good. When you are in the midst of your pain it's easy to *feel* dead.

I once sat and read through the pages of one of my journals, highlighting how many times I wrote 'I have'. There were a lot! I've tried to outwit, outplay, out talk, out pray, out say, out do, out sing, and out give God. All with the best intentions, but with a misguiding understanding of how He works.

There's was a lot more striving in those pages rather than surrender. I realised I wanted to trade, not surrender. I didn't want my pain to be gone without the gift of something else to place it with, maybe a child Yes, God gives us so much more than we ever were holding onto when we surrender, but that isn't the heart of why we should want to surrender. There are ones where I really did surrender, I love finding those ones! Places where I had enough strength to raise my own personal hallelujah and found complete peace in His perfect works. I can almost feel the freedom of that moment of pure surrender; it's as though it's soaked in the pages. There's something different about them to the other entries. The handwriting is mine and the ink colour is the same as the ones full of hurt but there's something that glistens on the page.

I wish I could give you a five-step program to follow to make the act of surrender easier, but to be honest with you if I did you'd miss out on the most valuable part. Don't discount the wrestle and fight as you do your best to give your pain to God. Surrender will always be worth it. I can only tell you my story and how I wrestled and fought it, and even resisted it. The act of surrender is only powerful when we do it to purely give Him what we have, the good and the bad, because we trust Him with it.

> *I raise a Hallelujah*
>
> *I raise a Hallelujah in the presence of my enemies and louder than my unbelief*
>
> *I raise a Hallelujah louder than the unbelief that I won't be a mum*
>
> *I raise a Hallelujah louder than the unbelief that I won't be effective for God*
>
> *I raise a Hallelujah louder than the unbelief that I won't live to see God's miracles*
>
> *I am so thankful, that when all I have is a whisper, Heaven comes to fight for me*
>
> *I raise a Hallelujah*
>
> *I will watch the darkness flee. Greed, darkness, disease, unforgiveness, arrogance and*
>
> *pride, addiction, separation, judgement, resentment, rebellion, guilt, pain, accusations,*
>
> *revenge, lies, pure evil & cruelty from our families, workplaces, government and nation.*
>
> *I raise a Hallelujah*
>
> *In the middle of the mystery (of it all) - fear, you've lost your hold on me*
>
> *I raise a Hallelujah*
>
> *JOURNAL ENTRY 9.05.2019 - I RAISE A HALLELUJAH*

To be honest, surrender for me has been easier with my eyes open. The Holy Spirit a long time ago told me to "keep my eyes open" because He knew what would bless me best. He knows I'm someone who loves direction and clear pathways, so he shared, "I need you know where I am leading you. The obstacles to avoid, when to lay down my battles that are set as a distraction and who to look to in it all". I haven't forgotten that. One morning while I was praying in my secret place I remember opening my eyes. My gaze fell upon a sign I hung very intentionally many years ago in our vacant (nursery) room 'ALL THINGS ARE POSSIBLE'.

I definitely can't make all things possible and as soon as I realised that, surrender became easier. I was able to move, one step in front of the other, with my eyes open so I could see Him and where He is leading me. My battles have been large and in each one there's been very little control for me to have. But maybe that's the point, because it has meant there's been plenty of room for surrender. And rest.

What's left now once you finally surrender? So much more!

15

Warning signs

It's okay to say no.
  It's okay to say yes.
  It's okay to say maybe.
  It's okay to change your mind.
  It's okay to say you need to think about it.

What does the word *warning* make you think or feel? Does it make you feel safe, scared, restricted, free, limited, loved? They make me feel all of those things, but mainly I think of the word boundaries, and I honestly think God is a big fan of boundaries. What Eve saw as a restriction, we know now was a boundary set in place by a loving Father who wanted to the best for her. It's easy to believe the lie that God wants to limit us, but His boundaries come from a place of deep love and care for us.

Moving forward is exciting and fun. There's a sense of freedom about moving forward into open spaces. I LOVE going to theme parks, and always went every chance I got during the school holidays when I was younger. I loved being early and being one of the first in line. When those gates opened, I ran in and every time was overwhelmed with all the choices. I didn't know what ride to go on first, what treat to taste first or what show to watch first. I was just so excited!

Not much has changed when it comes to theme parks if I'm honest, I just run a little slower and eat more treats! In those younger years each time I ran in, I wasn't looking at my next step, and I often tripped over things I didn't see in front of me. Pain can feel like tripping over a hazard you missed from running too fast.

In a moment, your plans come to a sudden halt. Everything had momentum, there was progress in motion, excitement, your path seemed clear and the destination near. Then you stub your toe or trip over and the sudden stop takes you by surprise. Isn't that life to a tee though? Everything is wonderful when it's all going smoothly and you're all smiles. It's easy to be happy with life, and God even, when life is good. When everything just falls into place. It's easy to say 'yes' to God in those seasons. But what about when it hurts? What about when there seems to be no end to the pain and nothing makes sense? What about when we experience a blown tyre moment or we hit the wall of a boundary?

What about when your husband loses his job or the promotion/pay rise he was promised never happens? You get sick or hurt yourself. Your friend accuses you of a wrongdoing. Your child makes a bad decision. Someone suddenly dies. Have you ever blown a tyre while driving?

Talking about bringing everything to a stop. Usually you can drive for a while with a blown tyre but eventually you stop. Until that stop happens, normally the drive is uncomfortable and pretty bumpy. While writing about my story so far I found I kept asking myself, "Was there a warning sign, or even a few, that somehow got missed?". Maybe it wasn't that there was a sign that was missed, but purposely ignored.

To warn, according to the Oxford Dictionary, is to advise so someone can take certain action. Children can change their behaviour, and sometimes not for the better, when they start hanging out with a new friend at school. Often it's not a big change, just little ones here and there. Slowly what might've slipped past the parents as a 'passing phase' soon becomes a fight to keep their child in line as decisions affect their life in a negative way.

Aren't we all guilty of being *those* parents with our own pain in life? I know I am. If I'm honest, there were warning lights when I was 16. The reason my anorexia felt like a blown tyre, and a sudden blow to my parents' hearts, was because we all chose not to see the warning signs. They were there all along but I kept going instead of pulling over. Day by day, I ate a little less than the day before, and the words I used to talk about life and myself changed. The warning signs were brightly shining and we all kept driving. What started off as something small or manageable, turned into something that took hold of every part of my life. By ignoring the signs, my pain had a ripple effect into the lives around me too. What should've been confined to a physical fight, became an emotional and spiritual one.

Driving with a blown tyre is really not recommended, and generally you don't get too far before you need to stop again. A perfectly well maintained and working car starts to deteriorate really quickly when one tyre is blown. The pressure starts to build on the other tyres and they eventually start to wear down, while the suspension becomes unbalanced as it tries to support the whole weight of the car, and the rims bend. The car become a hazard to anyone else on the road. Not dealing with pain is like this; it is a hazard to everyone around you.

If I was a car when I was 16, when I weighed 42.5 kilograms, I severely damaged my suspension. I was not balanced. I had a significant blown tyre, and the car was warning me of more danger ahead if it wasn't tended to, but I kept driving. As I drove, the other tyres started to give under the strain as they took on the extra load and work, and my panels were dented and bent from the rough driving conditions. I treated my heart and my body like an old car that nobody loved. I drove around with a blown tyre for years. I tried to just get on with life, tried to cover it up and push the pain to the side. When I did finally stop, there was much more damage to tend to.

There's no denying moments of pain still require effort, just like changing a tyre, but it's less than what's required if you keep driving. Once a tyre blows, it will never be the same. Yes it can be repaired in some cases but even then, there's a part of it that's forever changed. The warning signs help us to possibly save that tyre from being lost or destroyed.

Have you ever tried to ignore a warning light in your car, or drive with a blown tyre? Or in a loved one's life, or maybe your own?

Warning lights are only effective if you listen to them. Ignoring the signs can be intentional and unintentional, but either way the outcome is often the same. Most cars need a service each 10,000 kilometers. As the time comes close to the next 10,000 km interval, the warning lights on the starts to warn the driver so the driver has time to call a mechanic and get it serviced. If the driver ignores the warning signal, the car will soon stop working. Home smoke alarms warn us of impending fire danger, but what if we ignored the warning sound of the smoke alarm when the battery needs changing? When we need the alarm to work because there's a fire in our home while we're sleeping, ignoring the warning sign weeks ago could cost us everything. If we don't react to the warning signs, there could be dire consequences. Dealing with our pain is the same, our reaction impacts the outcome greatly.

I saw the warning lights with mum, I just didn't react quick enough. It was a busy time at work but I knew mum was sick and hurting, more than usual. I knew she needed help. I knew I needed to be there. I knew the warning signs well enough to know she was in a dark place and I still chose to ignore them. Quite literally, my phone rang at times late in the night and I didn't pick up. We had journeyed so much together and I was tired. It felt like 'the boy who cried wolf' moment again. I didn't know how to help her anymore. I tried everything I knew – I was kind, loving, and forgiving, and when that didn't work, I was cold, anger and stern. Nothing seemed to hold. I find myself wondering if I should have gone to be with her after I graduated from high school when she first offered. As tempting as it was to live where all my favourite shows were (*90210, Dawsons Creek, One Tree Hill*), it wasn't as tempting as having some space and starting to live my own life. Privately, I felt as lost in her pain as she did.

This was different. Normally I knew what to do, but this time she was in another country and all we could do was talk on the phone. I couldn't take a coffee into her room, write her a note, do the food shop for her, call the doctor or drive her where she needed to go. She was in the greatest battle of her life and for once I couldn't fix it or be in control. So, I turned the volume down on the phones ring tone. I don't have many regrets in life, but this is my greatest regret in life.

The morning I found out she took her life, I'd told my husband I was going to over to see her and send some time with her. An hour later, I found out I would indeed be going to America but I won't be sending time with her. I was on the next plane out the following morning. I missed every warning sign and now all I had was a blown tyre, a tyre shredded to pieces. A heart in a million pieces. Nothing felt the same again. June 17th 2008, I realised how important warning signs were.

'A prudent person with insight foresees danger coming and prepares himself for it. But the senseless rush blindly forward and suffer the consequences.' – Proverbs 22:3 TPT

When mum died, I did what I had done all my life: tend to everyone else's need first.

I placed everyone else's oxygen mask on before putting my own on. I remember people checking in with me, asking me to stop for a while. I assured everyone I was fine and went about my days. Maybe they could see the warning signs of an impending crash ahead, I surely didn't. I'm not sure I would've listened if they told me anyway as I was in complete denial. Shortly after coming home from her funeral held in North Carolina, I still didn't pull over or see the warning signs that I needed to stop. My husband and I continued with our plans to move to central Queensland for a job he had waiting for him. Moving meant we were both way from anyone we knew or could lean on. It was a move we'd already planned before mum died and instead of stopping, I just kept going. It honestly didn't occur to me this was going to be a silly idea. But it was. One day, I did stop. My tyre finally blew.

After weeks of walking every block in the town, applying for every job and cleaning our unit every day, I eventually ran out things to keep myself busy. BANG! I just remember coming completely undone. I cried and journalled for hours. I cried some more, and I finally pulled over. I couldn't move any further without help. I needed to address the damage and make some repairs before I started a new trip and entered my new season. We moved back home and a new season of healing began.

III

NEW SEASON

Chapters sixteen - twenty three

16

You're not forgotten

Have you ever been told you need to rest? I have, and I've ignored that advice many times. Rest is something I treasure and protect *now*, but it never used to come easily for me because I thought it meant God had forgotten about me.

I thought if rest meant to do nothing and if did nothing, nothing would happen. I loved the idea of rest though. It felt as if I was almost hunting for it at times, and yet when it is given, I pushed it away. Resting felt like I wasn't in control of the situation I was in and my chances of something happening, changing, were slipping away. I always felt like I should be doing something to help make the situation better, or make a contribution towards it. In preparation for this chapter, I felt the sweet whisper, "Rest doesn't mean you have been forgotten. Rest doesn't mean nothing will happen. Rest doesn't mean I am too busy. Rest is just means rest. It means do what you can and let me do the rest. It's not all on you to make it happen. There are only some things you can do, and there'll be a time where I need you ready to go into something bigger. Now is not that time. Now is for rest because there are wounds I still want to heal and strength I want give you. You are not forgotten." I'll give you one guess who that whisper came from…you, our loving Father in Heaven.

The thing with pain is, and life in general, most of us are not in control of much except for how we respond to it and handle it.

Spoiler alert – there's no control as to when pain happens, or how long it lasts. Most pain causes you to stop at some point, purely because it's too much. It causes you to pause, to rest at some point, sometimes longer than you thought. A marathon runner can't just keep running when they get a cramp in their body, or their lungs run out of air. They need to rest for a moment and assess the damage. When pain hits our lives, it's very similar. At some point it causes you to be inactive, it interrupts what you're doing, stops you or hinders you from continuing. It might even add weight to your journey. You don't get to choose when the cramp occurs, but you can choose if you rest to assess the damage.

'Just rest' is something most of us have said at one point or another to a friend who's hurting, and it's definitely in every doctor's vocabulary. When you're sick, it's the first words doctors say. When your mum knows you're unwell and run down, or your boss sends you home early from work…they tell you to rest. Be still. Let the body heal and become strong again. Easier said than done for most of us, as it was for myself. Some pain doesn't give you the choice to rest. Sometimes it's so strong you literally cannot move, and in that case being still is your only option.

When Snow White was put to sleep, that was the ultimate act of rest.

She had no choice and simply could not move. She had to surrender to the power of the poisoned apple, and rest. The dwarfs and everyone else thought her story was over, and she would never wake up. It was when she rested that the impossible happened. While she rested, the Prince went to work. It took both of them to do what was required of them for the story to be told. She wouldn't have woken up without the Prince, but the Prince wouldn't have known he could wake her up if she didn't rest. Our rest in God is the same. When we rest in who He is in all that we face, He goes to work while we build up our strength. In places of complete emptiness, He works at His best.

And just like with Snow White, one touch from God in our seasons of rest and we are rejuvenated and brought back to life. I don't believe God arranges bad things to happen to us, but I do believe He uses them for good.

'You intended to harm me, but God intended it for good to accomplish what is now being done, the saving of many lives.' Gen 50:20 NIV

I believe He uses painful seasons or times in our lives as opportunities to create something beautiful. I really believe He loves working in the realm of impossibility. In my life, He's turned many of my 'poisoned apple' moments into an opportunity for me to regain my strength, take a breath and rest. Let me use the analogy of young children. They fight their parents when it's bedtime, declare they aren't tired and keep fighting on, and their mood often takes a turn for the worse. I've been that very child at times when God is giving me a gift of rest.

For me, valleys have actually become my places of rest, I used to think valleys were just places of struggle and abandonment, but I've discovered they can be so much more if we allow them to be. They can be places where we can rest and take a breath. Places where we sit under a tree to cool down and allow God to show us where our next steps are. They don't have to be places where we stop and everything dies. This revelation came years after I'd kept trying to power through another valley when God was inviting me to rest. I burnt out and I had nothing left. I was in a complete state of unrest.

I wasn't dreaming anymore. I wasn't finishing anything, let alone starting anything new anymore. I wasn't moving forward or backward anymore. I wasn't writing in my journal anymore. I wasn't praying anymore. I wasn't feeling passionate about life anymore. I wasn't really living, for the now.

Everything felt like a chore, rather than something that brought me joy, and everything felt hard and required so much effort. If rest is considered being harmonious work of the heart, will, imagination, creativity and conscience with God, then I was definitely not resting. When I looked into the meaning of rest I found many different definitions, but what each one highlighted was true rest equates to doing something without force or striving. For me, resting is baking, reading, writing, washing my car with the radio on, making candles and being creative; and making lists. There's an ease to those things for me, there's no struggle in those activities or routines. They are my true places of physical rest, but they also give me deep mental rest. I feel rejuvenated and fresh after I do these things.

Before I understood what resting was, I thought I was resting. In hindsight, it made sense that people kept telling me I needed to rest because my unrest was obvious to everyone but me. In my mind, I didn't understand the difference between resting/pausing and stopping. I thought if I rested, nothing would happen. If I wasn't working, then God wasn't working. In actual fact, I wasn't giving God any room to work because I was too busy trying to do it all for Him (not very well might I add!). I thought I was the battery God needed to power my dreams to fruition. Yes, I have a part to play as we all do, but not at the expense of God.

> *What is rest?*
>
> *Yes it's a time of quiet and refreshing, a time to abstain or give yourself relief from doing too much. But could it be more? When I looked up what resting means I was hit with some interesting perspectives. One definition says that rest is to be supported or placed so as to stay in a specific position. Maybe just maybe, the valley I am in is perfectly part of God's plan and I'm not lacking or missing a single thing. It also says rests is a state of motionless or inactivity. Maybe just maybe, I have been stilled to give my body physical rest.*
>
> *This morning I listened to audio from WW II, when the war ended and*

> within minutes the gunshots and horror of war was instantly replaced by the chirping of birds and whistles of wind through the long grass and leaves in the trees. This makes me think of the other definition, that rest is an interval of silence for a set duration. Maybe just maybe, the silence I am hearing is only set for a duration and has a reason to it. Maybe just maybe, the silence allows me to hear things I haven't been able to hear before.
>
> Could rest mean I am being renewed and things are being restored? Could rest mean I am being revived, and the old is being replaced with the new?
>
> It's not secret that resting, and waiting, have been something I've truly struggled with while on my fertility adventure. I don't feel God has said it's over, so it's a road of life not the denial of life or dead ends. I found Holy Spirit guiding me to Hebrews 3 & 4 this morning and Him asking me, "if rest is doing life with ease, then the opposite of that is working, striving and struggling...yes? So then, have you thought about what hinders you from resting? What hinders you from trusting God to do the work, and what makes you think you have to do this life in your own strength?"
>
> Today I can see I have some resting to do. I don't have to fight my lack of faith, but instead rest. My faith will be built as I lean into His opinions and knowledge more than my own. I am certain of this one thing, waiting and resting are not about inactivity at all. JOURNAL ENTRY 12 & 13.10.2019

Waiting and resting are not about sitting around expecting things to magically happen – with or without prayer.

When Jesus was on the cross, the pain He was in physically is something I don't know if I will ever truly understand or appreciate. Humanity can be cruel and that was a dark time in humanity when we treated people like that. In those moments of waiting for God, Jesus prayed. He didn't have the luxury of a quiet space, air conditioning, quality worship music or a comfy chair. He was often interrupted, people mocked Him, He was uncomfortable and in pain, and it was dirty. Yet He prayed as He waited. Resting while waiting is not about letting life pass by like a bus at a bus stop. Bus after bus, whizzing past.

It makes me wonder, isn't there more we can do than just sit around and wait? Can we still do something that brings life while we are resting? I think we can, it's up to you whether you accept God's gift of rest. We know now resting doesn't mean nothing happens, it just means you let God do the heavy lifting. Let's finish with these questions and imagine rest is a bus…

Can you talk to the person beside you, or even offer a warm smile? Can you pray for the bus driver while he drives you to your next destination? Can you engage your mind and let ideas flow from your heart and mind onto paper so you're ready to go when God says it's time to get off now? Can you make a call or send a text of encouragement to someone outside the bus? Can you just sit still and appreciate the gift of stillness God is giving to you in that moment?

'Do you still want to argue with the Almighty? You are God's critic but do you have the answers?' – Job 40:1 NLT

Resting, waiting, pausing, I've come to discover it's all linked back to surrender and nothing to do with any of us being forgotten.

God sees you and He sees all your next days. And you know what, there are some people you don't even realise who see you too. They're inspired and encouraged by you, and when you rest, it helps them trust in the process of rest too. This life was never meant to be a competition of how busy we can and fast we can live every day. Look at Jesus, He rested a lot *and* did a lot! He had the benefit of knowing why, where and when He needed rest. We, however, only have the ability to see now and sometimes rest can seem pointless and a waste, it's far from that.

17

Value of yesterday's

'The wilderness becomes a lush pasture, and the hillside blossoms with joy.' – Psalm 65:12 NLT

I agree with the saying that preparation is the key, and while most times I think it's true, there times when life is all about pure grit. There are times when no matter how much planning you've done will make it easier and you just have to roll your sleeves up and get dirty. Let me use boxing to explain what I'm trying to say. Boxing was never meant to be easy, delicate or kind. It is raw, intense and intentional. You can put in long days of preparation, practice all the greatest punches and plan to show off your best moves, but when you're in that ring and the punches are flying, it's just about pure grit. There's nothing pretty about it, and there's definitely nothing pleasant about it.

When we hit our season of pain with fertility, I thought I was prepared for the fight because of the different seasons of pain I had already trudged through. I thought *I had this*, and it wouldn't consume me like pain had in the past. All my preparation went out the window though, and most days it was about pure grit just to survive them. I was nowhere near ready or prepared for the fight. A boxer doesn't face the same opponent time after time. Each time they defeat one opponent, they face someone new and that's when the value of their yesterday is understood. Because of yesterday, the way they fight next time will surely be different. They'll move their feet differently, they'll change the way they punch, and maybe they'll be more verbal than the way they were with the last opponent. Each fight is different. If they kept fighting the same way, they'd lose pretty quickly. I realised I had to change the way I fought this round of pain.

Fertility was different to the other battles I had fought, it definitely felt different. It moved in my life differently and it definitely hit differently. Unfortunately I kept getting knocked around because it took me quite a few years to learn I couldn't just keep doing things as I had always done. I didn't see the value in my previous seasons of pain, I didn't take the opportunity to learn from those seasons so I could do this one well. Instead, I just thought God was punishing me some more. Nothing made sense and instead of asking Him, I accused Him, waiting wasn't a well-developed skill of mine.

Although waiting had now become almost ordinary to me, part of my everyday routine, it was something I struggled with for many years. My waiting to become a mother became almost as normal and routine as the everyday things I do without thinking about – waiting for the traffic to move, waiting for your coffee, waiting for lunch to come and waiting for work to finish for the day. For a very long time I never saw the value in the waiting because it was something I did every day.

> 'Take your everyday, ordinary life – your sleeping, eating, going-to-work and walking-around life – and place it before God as an offering. Embracing what God does for you [*or doesn't!*] is the best thing you can do for Him.' – Rom 12:1 MSG

Waiting, for me, really was another word for worry. Waiting meant I worried and tried to regain control over the situation. The longer I waited, the longer I worried that God was running out of time and that I was running out of time. As I 'waited' aka worried, all I was doing was making life harder for me, and I was becoming more frustrated as my situation wasn't changing. I despised each day that went past because I saw no value in them. I saw them as lost opportunities and prayers that were unheard. I didn't see that they were valuable and were crucial for my future days.

As I was putting this chapter together, I remember a time when I hit a writers block. I just sat for a few moments and looked outside the window searching for the words I needed and a butterfly caught my attention. It just sat outside my window and that's when God spoke to me about waiting and the value of yesterday's. Butterflies aren't just born beautiful, elegant and able to fly. Without the days of it first being a seemingly boring caterpillar, they simply wouldn't exist. Our yesterday's matter, without them there'd be no today's or tomorrow's. Without a caterpillar a butterfly wouldn't be, but that doesn't mean the caterpillars exchange of life to be a butterfly is easy.

Caterpillars aren't often talked about or even thought about. They can't fly, there isn't anything graceful or elegant about them, and they aren't gorgeous to look at. However, without the *boring* old caterpillar, the butterfly just wouldn't be. The creation and the purpose of both has its perfect time. Can you imagine changing from a caterpillar to a butterfly? No doubt there's struggle and probably even resistance in the process. Imagine what would happen if the caterpillar resisted the process, struggled against what was supposed to happen and there was no butterfly. Learning to value our yesterday's, I think, is just like the story of a caterpillar becoming a butterfly. At some point the former things will fade away to make room for the new, but they're vital to the story and the process. At some point your pain will fade away just like a caterpillar will become a butterfly at some point.

Understanding this helped me appreciate the transformation process of my own life and that my yesterday's aren't just grave sites of pain and lack. I started to value the days behind me and see them as places where I could see where God was faithful. I started to see that God didn't just taking away but He was exchanging my pain for hope, my tears for joy, my weary heart for strength and my doubt for faith. I started to see the value of waiting. As I learnt how to wait better, I saw there was purpose to it. While seemingly insignificant changes were happening on the outside, there were very significant things happening within me.

Our transformation doesn't always mean the changes are visible on the outside. As the caterpillar starts to exchange its life to be transformed into a beautiful butterfly, a lot of changes happen without being seen. Our transformation isn't any different, we just don't end up with wings of colour or the ability to fly at the end of it (or maybe we do!). The changes are often subtle but they are deeply impacting.

Just like a caterpillar begins to fly instead of crawl, so do we. I started to think differently, act differently, move differently, relate to other creatures differently and communicate differently. I started to see my seasons before this one as gifts to learn from and draw strength from, instead of despise. They weren't adding weight to my days anymore but actually helping them to be lighter. Just like the boxer we talked about at the start, I started to fight differently because I was learning from days behind me. Transforming into a butterfly wasn't just about an outward appearance, it was about becoming different from my spirit out. It was about being equipped to handle the struggle and transformation.

'God brings the best out of you, develops well-formed maturity in you.' – Romans 12:2 MSG

God has equipped you, and me, with all we need to allow our own personal transformation to take place. He has given you and me the ability to walk, so why are we on the ground crawling? There's waiting and then there is waiting well.

'God has given each of us the ability to do certain things well…Take the responsibility seriously.' – Romans 12:6, 8 NLT

'Don't copy the behaviour and customs of this world, but let God transform you into a new person by changing the way you think.' – Romans 12:2 NLT

'Then we will no longer be like children, forever changing our minds about what we believe because some has told us something different or someone has cleverly lied to us and made the lie sound like the truth.' – Ephesians 4:14 NLT

Waiting well, living life well, creating a beautiful life, standing well, handling pain – they're all learnt behaviours. Again let's talk about our boxer. A boxer learns new ways to react and behave in their days of preparation. Yes it's all about grit and determination when they enter the ring, but that very grit and determination is built on decisions made with intention and discipline. It doesn't mean it won't hurt or that we won't struggle, or have tears to cry.

If I'd never waited, I know I wouldn't have come to know God like I do now. I wouldn't be able to sit alongside others in their season of waiting, and be a voice of hope and encouragement. I wouldn't be able to appreciate who I am like I do now, and I wouldn't be able to see the potential butterfly in anyone else. If I had never waited, I know I wouldn't be able to live out my purpose like I am now.

As a caterpillar, I despised the waiting. As a butterfly, I'm so thankful for it and see the value in it. As a butterfly I learned to fight differently. Through the waiting, God has brought me out of the worst seasons of my life and created pure beauty. Through the waiting, God has brought out the best in me for all to see. It's a choice to be responsive to His invitation of waiting, resting and surrendering. It's a choice to resist the devil, say NO to his lies and align my thoughts to God's truth. I am so thankful God taught me how to fight each season of pain differently, through my season of waiting, because that's where I started to fly.

'Summing it all up, friends, I'd say you'll do best by filling your minds and meditating on things true, noble, reputable, authentic, compelling, gracious – the best, not the worst; the beautiful, not the ugly; things to praise, not things to curse. Put into practice what you learned from me, what you heard and saw and realized. Do that, and God, who makes everything work together, will work you into his most excellent harmonies.' – Philippians 4:8 MSG

18

Hello to something new

'I am doing something brand new, something unheard of. Even now it sprouts and grows and matures. Don't you perceive it? I will make a way in the wilderness and open up flowing streams in the desert.' – Isaiah 43:19 TPT

A new thing. A new thing is when there's an exchange where new replaces the old - that only happens when one yields and lets the other become more prominent. I love the analogy Holy Spirit gave me for this chapter, a new thing is like opening all the windows of your home after a huge storm passes. There's something about letting the fresh air touch the carpet, your clothes, your kitchen bench and everything in your home. It's refreshing and rejuvenating. Allowing the new to replace the old is not much different.

In the last last chapter I shared how I lived life and walked through a lot of my pain breathing old air, old ways, and old mindsets. When I think of the words 'new thing' I think of moving. The word 'move' is a doing word, a word that commands action. It's not always a peaceful word and it can imply that things happen quickly. Chances are you've moved home once in your life, and I'm sure you can agree there's nothing quick about moving house. Sure there's an excitement when you move into a new home. Suddenly the four walls you once called home feel old and unfamiliar, and it's replaced with a new familiar that awaits. I love that first feeling when you walk into a new home, everything is empty and fresh and new. But relocating can be hard too.

We haven't moved for about twelve years and when we moved into this home, I became very I was putting things where I'd put them in my old home. I stacked the cans of food the same way, hung the same group of clothes next to each other, and placed the couch cushions as they were before. I began to wonder if I'd really relocated if I had just put everything where it was before, carrying one atmosphere from one physical dwelling place to another. It's an interesting thought.

God seems to love moving day, well maybe just 'moving' is more accurate. Sometimes God's version of moving days are big and bold like when the Israelites crossed the Jordan or moved past the crumbled walls of Jericho. They were big days! I mean, the sea was split right down the middle and they walked on dry land where they should've only been able to swim! Thankfully some moving days aren't so big. When it comes to pain and relocation, turning pain into hope, it makes me think God is fan of moving days, or as I said 'moving' is maybe more accurate. I think He loves to move big things to show us nothing is impossible for Him, and that moving is a physical way for the new to replace the old.

> *God,*
>
> *I'm scared to move from where I am & I still have questions. My anger still feels very real. My doubt still feels more real to me than Your Word. My pain still feels as though it's my identity, and my confusion still rules my prayers. My prayers feel more like accusations if I am honest. I don't want to stay where I am, but I don't know how to not be this person. As another year comes, a new year, I don't feel like much is new.*
>
> JOURNAL ENTRY Jan 1st 2021

> **'Our God spoke to us: "You've stayed long enough at this mountain. On your way now. Get moving... Look, I've given you this land. Now go in and take it. It's the land God promised to give your ancestors Abraham, Isaac, and Jacob and their children after them." – Deuteronomy 1:6-8 MSG**

One of the things I love about God is He always gives everyone the choice to move, and He gives you a place to move to.

When you're a child, you don't really get the choice as to where you move to. Until your name is on the mortgage documents, you don't get to choose. You go wherever mum and dad go. Maybe you were like me, and you relocated often. Moving from one home to the next, most times without a choice. But God gives you a choice. He gives you a choice if you even want to relocate or not. It's never forced. I used to think that moving into a new space or season meant I never had to deal with what was behind me anymore, writing this book definitely proved that theory wrong! Sometimes as you're transitioning to a new place, there's a season of to-and-fro between the two places. The place you're leaving and the place you're going to, reminded of what was as well as what is yet to be. It's hard to move away from what has been so familiar and move towards what is so unknown.

Moving away from the pain I knew how to manage and was all too familiar, was actually very hard to leave behind. As much as I wanted to be free of my current situation, whichever one it was, the thought of tackling a new and unknown pain was daunting. Just because I knew pain, didn't mean I was going to know more. It's the same for you.

Some of us expect pain will be waiting for us in the new place God has prepared for us because it's what we've become familiar with. But there isn't always more pain. I thought moving into a new season of never being a mother was certainly to be filled with even more pain. It's not easy, or even always enjoyable, but there's always a lot of good about this season that isn't even close to feeling painful. There's more joy than pain, and there's more hope than despair, and more peace than anger. When God first asked me to take His hand into this season, I pulled my hand back. When He asked again, the answer was a little 'yes'. Little by little. Closer and closer. Trip by trip. Box by box. I started to let the transformation begin. It wasn't done in one trip. There were too many boxes to carry in just one trip. Each trip was like carrying one box at a time. It was done over time.

First I unpacked, with God, the box that came from my mum and dad separating. Then, as I got stronger, I unpacked each box after that. One after another. Some took a little longer to unpack and deal with. True transformation is making a decision not to keep being who you have been, not to think the way you have thought before, and do what it the way you had before. Transformation is based of every thought and action that asks, "do I want the old to remain, or do I want something new?".

For me, sometimes that choice was daily, sometimes hourly and sometimes weekly. A choice not to rehash old questions, or rerun old situations and scenarios over and over again. Those thoughts became like unwanted friends trying to take reformed alcoholics or drug users back to places where they used to hang. None of it was good. To be honest, my transformation will never truly end until the day I enter heaven's gates. Neither will yours, if you say yes to the new. Little by little. Choice by choice.

Please don't beat yourself up if you find yourself like me, remember transformation takes time.

I can't tell you how many times a new face or familiar situation has brought up old memories. It was like opening that box up all over again, just as painful as the first time. Welcome them. They're God's way of showing you there's more healing to take place there. He will hold your hand through it all. You're not a failure if you find yourself here. Pain will come and go, just like people in your life. Some will be in your life every step of the way and some will only be there for certain times. That's all part of it. I don't think I could've appreciated or felt God's love for me if He wasn't the only constant thing in my life.

'Move your heart closer and closer to God, and he will come even closer to you. But make sure you cleanse your life, you sinners, and keep your heart pure and stop doubting.' – James 4:8 TPT

19

Breathe

'God, the Master, told the dry bones, "Watch this: I'm bringing the breath of life to you and you'll come to life. I'll attach sinews to you, put meat on your bones, cover you with skin, and breathe life into you. You'll come alive and you'll realize that I am God!" I prophesied just as I'd been commanded. As I prophesied, there was a sound and, oh, rustling! The bones moved and came together, bone to bone. I kept watching. Sinews formed, then muscles on the bones, then skin stretched over them. But they had no breath in them.' – Ezekiel 37:5-8 MSG

This book has travelled internationally even before it's been read by anyone else other than me. This specific chapter was written while my husband and I were holidaying in New Zealand. New Zealand is a country that does its utmost to steal your breath away. I understand nothing can ever steal our breath but God, however, the scenery of that beautiful country did come close to doing so. New Zealand has the cutest sheep you'll ever see, colours of green I never knew existed painted the hills, and then there's the nature, the wine, the cheese, the clear water and the culture and so much more! What I really noticed that was different to home was the air.

As soon as I got off the plane, the crispness of the air hit my lungs like a knife cutting sharply through a four layered cake. At first it was confronting, soon gave way to an obsession to get as much of the fresh air as possible. The air was cool, but it was how it tasted and felt that captured me. Every where we drove we had the windows down, we were addicted to the air. It was easy to breathe in the air, but in the most painful peaks of my pain, I've found breathing one of the hardest things to do.

Nurses and doctors tell women in labour to 'breathe', and parents tell their children to 'just breathe' while they tend to their wounds. There's something about breathing your way through pain that seems to be important. Once I tried magnesium pools; the cold pools definitely takes your breath away! Magnesium pools are great for your muscles as you alternate between the cold and hot pools a few times. As I sat in the cold pool first, I felt like every breath was racing out of my body. I'd never felt anything like it physically before, but I've felt it emotionally.

When it hurts to inhale or exhale, you tend to shorten your breaths. This unfortunately leaves you feeling confused and gives fear a chance to take hold. Before you feel like you have any control, you're overwhelmed. I've found being in pain to be very similar. It's hard to find peace. It takes longer to get into worship and prayer is a struggle. The mind is focused on everything else happening. New Zealand, in a little town called Kai Tieri Tieri, is where I learnt how to breathe again.

The thing about breathing is, it requires something from you. While it happens for all of us without much thought, breathing doesn't just happen. Pinch your nose and see what I mean (don't actually!). If any of us really wanted to, we could make ourselves stop breathing (again I don't recommend or encourage you to try!). Breathing does require some effort on your part, and it can't work if we just inhale or just exhale. We need to do both. Breathing first starts with each of us. It may sound a bit odd but I thinking of breathing much like driving to dinner and then home.

Whenever my husband and I go on a dinner date, we first make the decision on where to go. After enjoying our meal and time together, we return home. We leave home, and we return home. We breathe in and we breathe out. There's a rhythm to what we do, we didn't just magically arrive to dinner on a flying carpet and click our fingers to be back home. No, we made a decision and we put action to that decision. And in it all, God was with us in the car and at the dinner table. He listened to us share our hearts with one another and laughed as we shared jokes. He blessed our food and ensured we returned safely from our travels.

In the most intense parts of my pain, I've wanted to do nothing. I didn't think I should've had to do anything. I was the one in the pain, I was the victim. God is the one who is big and almighty one, isn't He? God is the one who was responsible for getting me out. Right? Not always. Actually, not ever. It was never His responsibility to save me, or even His obligation - it was His promise.

'For no matter how many promises God has made, they are "Yes" in Christ. And so through him the "Amen" is spoken by us to the glory of God.' – 2 Corinthians 1:20 NIV

It's His delight. Because of His love, He saved me time and time again from my own mess, as well as the mess I found myself in from no fault of my own. God has given each of us this beautiful and frustrating gift of life, along with the added bonus of free will. He never has, nor never will, force Himself on us. He never will make someone else smaller just to make us bigger, hide when we seek Him or guilt us into loving Him. He waits. He looks on. He continues to love. He continues to keep working behind the scenes on our miracles and promises. He misses us and longs for us. He ensures the Holy Spirit is always with us even when we don't choose to acknowledge Him.

Let's connect this to breathing. Breathing is formed by two actions – exhaling and inhaling. Both depend on one another, equally.

Our relationship with God is no different. We need Him as much as He desires us, but God only gets involved when we invite Him to be part of our lives. He was drawing me to invite Him to be part of my pain, to help me and guide my steps. When I made the choice to inhale His goodness, His forgiveness, His mercy and His love, that's when I was breathing fresh air in. Inhaling isn't just about breathing air in anymore, it's about inhaling all of God in every breath. Just like when I stepped off the plane in New Zealand, each breath brings instant life. Understanding the importance of inhaling allowed me to gain fresh perspective, fresh hope and fresh life. Inhaling. It's more than just the action of breathing air in. It's becoming mindful of what we allow to enter our minds and hearts.

Imagine if Jesus was in every breathe you inhaled. Stay with me on this, I know it's a little strange. As you inhale, He helps you love yourself and/or another. As you inhale, He helps you forgive yourself and/or another, He helps you see another who everyone else passes by, and He becomes your strength. As you inhale, He becomes your joy, your peace, your comfort and provision.

Exhaling is every time we read His Word, again. Exhaling is making the decision to pray, to trust, to hope, to love and forgive, again. Exhaling is laughing in the face of fear, doing it scared, reaching out and turning up the volume to our praise and worship, again. In every exhale, He will be there in the exhale with us. When you take a deep breath in, notice that your breath out is as long and deep. In both the inhale and the exhale, He is with us. Take a few moments before you go to the next chapter to inhale, exhale with God.

'Then the Lord God formed the man of dust from the ground and breathed into his nostrils the breath of life, and the man became a living creature.' – Genesis 2:7

20

Starts with a seed

We all have a part to play when it comes to dealing with pain, it isn't all on God. I know this sounds a little harsh, but it's almost as if we need to grow up a little. You can stay the victim in this moment, or you can get your fight and warrior cry on. There's a point where parents stop feeding their children because they can do it on their own. They don't stop giving their children food, but they don't do everything for them anymore. There comes a point when we need to play our part in it all too. Growing up in God, just means we learn to listen to Him *and* obey.

Before the walls of Jericho came down, God was very clear for them *not* to shout. Not to even say a word until He said so. He didn't want them to mess with the promise. Their part to play in the miracle was very clear, and so was God's. Each had their part for this to happen. I thought about my moments of shouting, and my role to play in pain. Did I shout when He needed me not to? Did I stay quiet when it was time to shout? When I was young and immature in my faith, I shouted at the wrong times and stayed quiet that wrong times. I wanted God to hand feed me every day, but God wanted me to grow. And thank goodness I finally did. My maturity has helped me to respect His ways, His timing and His will. Growing up also means you pray.

I used to see prayer as a chore, now it's my anchor to God. Even though a child grows up and can eventually feed itself, walk and talk independently, they'll always go back to their parents when they need help or advice. In some form or another, children still need their parents. They still need to ask for help, accept help and learn. Prayers are our way to stay connected to God. They can be easily disregarded in seasons of pain, and I can understand why people lose faith in them, I did. On the flip side, others rely too heavily on them and refuse to do their part.

There's many things I am unsure about, but one thing I am very sure on, is that prayers matter.

Prayers are seeds - seeds of hope. I truly believe these kind of prayers that bear much fruit. What does fruit start as? A seed. Seeds, maybe because of their size and lack of flair, they don't seem to ever be that special. They can be disregarded as nothing. They just don't seem to be valued as much as a big tree or beautiful flower. Their size makes them seem insignificant. Most times, the value of the seed is more about the harvest it yields. I'm no green thumb and will freely admit that I don't see much value in seeds. My husband, however, loves to grow new things and loves seeds. He is patient where I'm not, and he takes care of the seed, when often I leave it be and neglect it.

I don't think God uses the analogy of seeds in the Bible by chance, they're such a strong visual to help us understand the power of faith and the power of right now, today is all we have. Yesterday is gone and tomorrow might be, but what matters is what we do today with what each of us have been given to plant right here, right now. The devil knows the value of the seed, maybe better than most of us. I am convinced he is more fixated on the seed than the harvest sometimes. Without a seed, the devil knows the possibility of a harvest isn't a reality. Nothing can be celebrated if it first wasn't sown. He knew the value of the seed when he planted a single thought into Eve's ear.

He knew the value of a single seed when he planted a seemingly innocent question in her heart, it robbed her and the rest of us of an incredible harvest. He tried to plant a seed with Jesus in the wilderness, only to be cast aside. He is patient and is happy to spend his energy going after what we think is insignificant, small and of no value. Single seeds. While we're so busy fighting for the harvest, we often leave our seeds unprotected and undervalued. I truly believe each seed has a name, and for each of us it's different. For some of us it's hope, joy, or peace, and for others rest. I found my seeds have yielded the best harvest when I learnt to surrender the control, not the seed.

If a farmer leaves his seeds in his corn field unattended, his chances of a harvest would be pretty minimal. He can't control the weather and maybe other elements, but he can control what he has authority over. He needs to know when and where to plant his seeds. Some seeds are best harvested in the winter and some in the summer, so it's vital to know when to plant the right seeds so they have the best chance of flourishing. The farmer keeps a watchful eye over his seeds, watering them, using the right machinery and ensuring the seeds are protected from anything harmful. We're never out of sight from God, just like each seed isn't unseen by a farmer.

'I'm an open book to you; even from a distance, you know what I'm thinking. You know when I leave and when I get back; I'm never out of your sight. You know everything I'm going to say before I start the first sentence. I look behind me and you're there, then up ahead and you're there, too, your reassuring presence, coming and going.'
– Psalm 139:1-6 MSG

If seeds are simply another word for prayers, then that would suggest we need to be mindful of when and what we pray for. We can't control the outcome of a prayer, but we can control how we care for it. I'm saying this again because I truly believe seeds yield the best harvest when we learn to surrender the control, not the seed.

What we speak over our seeds have a deep impact over the potential harvest. Have you ever said - *"I could never do that! It will never work! I don't think I'll ever be pregnant. My body can't conceive. I don't think I'll have a successful business. I try everything and nothing works. I don't think I'll ever feel good again. I am always sick and my body feels so tired"*? I have. Watering and protecting your seed is almost the most important thing any of us can do.

'A sower went out to sow his seed. As he sowed, some seed fell along the path; it was trampled on, and the birds of the sky devoured it. Other seed fell on the rock; when it grew up, it withered away, since it lacked moisture. Other seed fell among the thorns, the thorns grew up and choked it. Still other seed fell on good ground; when it grew up, it produced fruit, a hundred times what was sown.' – Luke 8:5-8 AMP

Watching what we speak over our promise truly matters I believe. And so does God.

'Words kill, words give life; they're either poison or fruit – you choose.' – Proverbs 18:21 MSG

All seeds soon start to grow roots and attach themselves to wherever they're planted. Words do the same. Once they're planted, they start to grow roots and either fill you with hope or with fear. Being mindful of what you're speaking is a discipline that takes time; so does being aware of what seeds are being planted by others in your life. It's so important to know what seeds you're watering in your life, especially the seeds planted by others. Not all seeds bear good fruit. Let me share a story that I think will help explain what I am trying to say.

One day when I was about eight years old, mum and I had a fight in the car. Well, she yelled and I just listened. I don't do verbal fights well, I don't do them at all actually. I turn into a turtle trying to hide in its shell, which often angered mum even more! As her anger continued, she had many words to say. Some of them were very personal and caused a lot of pain. I don't remember the specific words spoken that day, but I remember how wounded I felt. As the car filled with silence, without me knowing, the devil started to place seeds of shame and guilt in my heart. He twisted her words and started planting seeds, "maybe if you weren't born, your mum wouldn't have become so sick and felt like she was failing all the time. Having a child creates a lot of pressure to marriages, maybe too much for your mum and dad. Maybe you were too much for them. Maybe that's why your dad left. It wasn't because of your mum, but because of you. Or maybe it was because of your mum but your mum is broken because of you. Having you was when it all started, so remove you and all the pain is removed".

Soon I was lost in a world of thoughts and in a mental prison that took years to break free of. Those seeds laid some pretty deep roots. Years later I found the courage to tell yell back to mum when she was using me as her person to dump her pain on, "well I am sorry I was ever born! Without me, you would be better". Talk about a high five moment for the devil. Little did he know, God was celebrating too. Now that the devil's lies had been exposed, God was letting the truth be told. Mum had no idea her words had impacted me so deeply, and they became seeds of incredible pain. Seeds are powerful. So are words.

Living a life well, with pain, is like flowers still blooming when surrounded by weeds. It's a seed that can either grow as hope soaked in expectation that God has a plan and a purpose, or it can be a seed of resentment and bitterness. Easier said than done, I know. God is able, that He is good, that He is kind, that He is just and that He is always in control.

The enemy is the master of deception, just ask Eve. As I mentioned before, he only had to slightly twist a sentence around for her to feel rejection and doubt. He's still doing the same with us today. Where we feel deep pain and anguish is where the devil finds his greatest joy. He has no desire to comfort you or be there for you, though it feels like he is on your side at times. He is a liar. Every moment of every day he is offering us a bite of the apple, just an innocent taste.

"He (the devil) has always been a murderer and a liar. There is nothing truthful about him. He speaks on his own, and everything he says is a lie. Not only is he a liar himself, but he is also the father of all lies" - John 8:44 CEV

There's not much difference between protecting your seed and resisting the devil. When a farmer protects his seeds, or anything valuable on the farm, measures are put in place. Our seeds aren't much different to the seeds a farmer has, except our seeds are more valuable. Our lives are the harvest. Our seeds are just as valuable, if not more. Our lives are the harvest. Chickens are kept safe from foxes and snakes, gates are shut to keep horses in, some seeds are planted in a greenhouse and some are protected by electric fencing to keep the predators out. 'Resisting' in the Oxford Dictionary means to strive against, oppose or offer opposition.

'All you need to say is simply "Yes" or "No"; anything beyond this comes from the evil one.' – Matt 5:37 NIV

21

Immeasurably more

13th September 2009 was my wedding day. It was an incredible day and there's nothing I would change, except one thing: my dress.

Every girl dreams of having her dress fitting for her wedding. The numerous try-ons, the laughter, the lunching after and glass of champagne to celebrate and I was no different. I had a beautiful fitting day, surrounded by lifelong friends, my mother-in-law and my step-mum. As much that was such a gift, nothing could fill the empty space my mum left that day.

I'm sure some didn't notice my unusual mood that day, and those that did assumed it was just because every little girl wants her mum. They were right, but there was another reason only my mum would understand, and now you will too. The mirror at that bridal fitting is one I hope I never see again. The day I wore my wedding dress for the first time, I wanted my mum to be there but she wasn't. She wasn't there to tell me not to look at my stomach when I first stepped out in front of the mirror. She wasn't there to remind me not to listen to another lie that my bloated stomach ruined how I looked. She wasn't there to help me see all the beautiful things about the dress and why this should be the one I pick. She wasn't there and I wasn't ready to do this battle alone. If she'd been there maybe she could've helped prevent the next series of events from happening.

As soon as I stepped out of the fitting room, I looked at my stomach and I let the mirror take over. I let what I saw become my reality and in doing so, assumed it was what everyone else could see too. I was in a fierce battle, but no one knew. My anorexia days were long in the past but some old thought patterns weren't, and it felt as those the battle was starting all over again. Only mum and I knew the true hold it had over me. On that day, wearing that dress, I gave volume to the enemy and I raised my white flag. Silently. As I voiced my concern over the dress highlighting my bloated stomach to one of the sales assistants, I was innocently encouraged, "you look beautiful and you're just being silly about your weight!". Explaining, or even justifying how I felt, almost felt harder than going through the internal battle.

The next fittings I had, I went by myself. I watched as girls, surrounded with their family and girlfriends, beamed and glowed as they tried on different dresses. In every other fitting room there was laughter and smiles; in mine, just tears. The only one who knew what I was feeling, who would've known, wasn't there.

Aside from helping me in this battle, I wanted to her to feel joy too. I wanted my mum to finally see the positive impact she had on my life. She always felt such shame and regret for those early years, ashamed her life had such a negative impact on my world for so long. In this moment, even with my own value being questioned, there was a reason to celebrate. Because of her love for me and in me, I had become a woman that could feel deeply loved by and trust an incredible man. Her dedication to me, her love for me, and the words of life she constantly spoke over me mattered and this moment was evident of that.

She had watched her little girl struggle for so long and for so much of her life, and now she was about to be a wife to a man who adored her. Life wasn't just about struggle anymore. How was it possible the same little girl who felt isolated, unattractive and unwanted, was now standing on a platform in a white dress feeling love, joy, peace and hope? The not so-little-girl finally felt what her mumma could see all along – a beautiful, wanted, celebrated, desired and attractive woman who could know joy as much as sorrow. Watching me that day would not have been easy for her though, as love had a steep cost attached to it for my mum.

She was divorced, had a handful of broken romantic relationships that followed and fractured family relationships. Just like my relationship with the mirror, she had a complicated one with love. I know that day would've made her happy though, she never wanted me to give up on love. I hope she was watching, with angels, on the day of my fitting and saw not only did I not give up on love, but I embraced it fully. Seeing her pain so openly, it made me actually fight harder for love in my own life. She had expressed many times she hoped I'd see marriage as a gift and something to run to, rather than from. Love makes so many things possible.

> *Today I shared a collection of our wedding photos on Facebook for the first time publicly; they weren't cropped or altered. Most girls share their wedding photos when they first get them; I hid mine. I still remember the day I received the email with all our beautiful wedding photos...I physically felt ill. I felt so disappointed. I seriously thought about destroying them. I didn't want to take them home to show my now husband. Not because of the quality of the photos from our treasured photographer but because of how I looked. I felt so upset for Craig that I'd ruined his wedding photos.*
>
> *I know most people would say I'm being silly, that they can't see it, that I'm crazy, etc... but for me, my bloated belly was huge. In my eyes, it was all people saw. It determined my worth and beauty. All of who I was seemed to be based on my non-flat belly. It's all I could see and did for the last ten years. I was angry I didn't wear tummy hiding underwear. I was angry I ate bread the night before. I was angry I didn't do enough sit ups in the lead up. Ten years later, today, sharing my photos was about freedom.*

> *I am loved so deeply by my best friend and husband, supported by an incredible group of close friends and family, and miraculously healed by a loving God through this journey. But there were some things still remaining that only I could change, some mindsets and habits. And for that, I am so very thankful for the F45 Challenge I just did. It wasn't about losing weight but gaining my self worth and loving my body, for the first time, in a healthy way without the guilt and lies.*
>
> *I wanted to know if I could restrict, test, give to and change my body without falling into old traps. I wanted how I felt to be my driving force, not a number on the scale. I wanted to learn how to respect and enjoy food, as well life. Each of the eight weeks tested me more than I thought it would but each week, new habits were formed and my mind started to heal.*
>
> *I truly believe God used this challenge to help break any final chains off. Now I can look at these photos and see love, joy and cherished memories instead of regret, self-hatred and disappointment.*
>
> JOURNAL ENTRY : 19th June 2019

We got married on 13th September 2009; it took me ten years to share our wedding photos. Ten years. I had shared some before but they were carefully chosen, slightly cropped and highly filtered. That day I was tired of hiding and worrying about what I wanted others to see. For so long, I wanted people to see a certain version of me. I wanted them to see everything but my pain and vulnerability. No one knew my pain; I hid it like a special piece of jewellery you only wear for special occasions. That day, I made a decision.

I knew the version of me I wanted people to see, but what were they actually seeing? I wanted them to see that life isn't beautiful because of the absence of pain, but because of what you do with it. If they saw my pain, maybe there'd wipe their hands of me. My pain led me to believe I was forgotten about, pushed to the side and didn't matter. I thought I was more of a headache to God than a blessing, and to anyone else for that matter. I truly believed I was burden and I didn't want to give people any more reason to be 'done with me'.

> **'To the fatherless he is a father. To the widow he is a champion friend. To the lonely he makes them part of a family. To the prisoners He leads into prosperity until they sing for joy. This is our Holy God in his Holy Place!' – Psalm 68:5-6 TPT**

If you've suffered abuse or neglect of your own earthly father, I can imagine this verse is pretty hard to read *and* believe. If you've lost your spouse or someone special, I *know* this verse is pretty hard for you to read *and* believe? If you're lonely, I *know* believing for a full and abundant life is pretty hard to believe. If you're poor and struggling, I *know* trusting God is the One who will lead you to prosperity almost insulting. Regardless of how we feel it is true. Be careful not to let the facts of your situation distract you from the truth. The truth is, God is good and able. God will never leave you. God adores you and God is faithful to His Word.

I'll never have all, if any of, the answers to why you've had to or will have to endure seasons of pain. When you get to this point, it becomes less about why and more about who. More about letting God's love shine into every conversation and question, allowing His truth to be known. I thought by protecting what people saw of me, I was keeping my pain under control. I truly thought I could enjoy more of life if I hid the ugly bits, but I was restricting it. When you keep something like this hidden it has power over you, you fight so hard to keep it hidden that the very chance some of it could be exposed has you living in fear and shame.

> **'O Lord, we have passed through your fire; like precious metal made pure, you've proved us, perfected us, and made us holy. Everyone will say, "Come and see the incredible things God has done; it will take your breath away! He multiplies miracles for his people!"' – Psalm 66:10 & 5 TPT**

> **'So, if you're serious about living this new resurrection life with Christ, act like it. Pursue the things over which Christ presides. Don't shuffle along, eyes to the ground, absorbed with the things right in front of you. Look up and be alert to what is going on around Christ – that's where the action is. See things from his perspective.' – Col 3:2 MSG**

I didn't want to hide anymore. What do others see now?

Hopefully a woman, regardless of whether she is in pain or not, who knows she is deeply and truly loved by her God. A woman who knows that while life can be far from perfect, God is perfect and, a woman whose armour may be a little dented but who is now ready for the battles that lie ahead. Hopefully, I can help others believe in their story too. Hopefully my story can be a fresh does of oxygen to their story and they won't let pain have the final say.

22

Be quiet fear

'The sun was high in the sky when Lot arrived at Zoar. Then God rained brimstone and fire down on Sodom and Gomorrah – a river of lava from God out of the sky! – and destroyed these cities and the entire plain and everyone who lived in the cities and everything that grew from the ground. But Lot's wife looked back and turned into a pillar of salt.' – Genesis 19:23-26 MSG

Do you know the story of Lot's wife?

She was a woman who looked back when God had told her not to. He was really serious about it and even turned her into a pillar of salt when she did look back. Thankfully, I've never heard of anyone else being turned into a pillar of salt for looking back. I do think there's a lesson in the story and God cares about what any of us look at.

I'm very curious by nature as well as logical, full of questions about things and often get lost in my own wonder and imagination. For me, I've found looking both forward and behind has benefited me greatly. It's the looking side to side that's been the problem for me. Whenever I've looked back, I've seen God where I couldn't see at the time and when I look forward, little drops of hope fall into the empty spaces that await me. Side to side though, well that's when my pain intensifies. Looking back and forward has nothing to do with anyone else but me, and God, but side to side invites everyone else in.

It's probably one of my husband's greatest frustrations with me, he gets really annoyed when I look sideways because he knows the damage comparison does to me. It often blinds me from seeing the good happening in my own life. Slowly I'm learning to look side to side less, and when I do, I'm also learning to celebrate the wins of others more than wishing they were my own. When I say slowly, I mean very slowly. It hasn't always been like this. Most times when I looked side to side, my life felt like it was I was stuck in a glass box while everyone elses world were racing past me at a lightning pace. It felt as though I was still in the starting blocks on a running track about the run the race called life, and yet not only had everyone started but had already done a few laps. As I mentioned earlier though, looking behind me and before me is where I have found the greatest benefit - so glad God doesn't turn me into a pillar of salt!

I love sports, generally all types except for a few (yes to motorsport, cricket, football and ice hockey, but no to soccer, field hockey and netball. Sorry to those that play those sports!). No matter if you're a sports lover like me or not, there's something all sporting coaches do called 'reviewing the game'. Reviewing the game means that before a team meets their opponent, they watch previous games involving the other team in the hope of finding any flaws or weaknesses in the games they either won or lost. The coaches, and often team captain, spend a large part of their time looking back and analysing each game with great detail. When they spend time reviewing past games, it's more than just watching a game, it's about learning from it and becoming stronger.

It takes time to do. They continually stop the game, write notes, press play, stop the game again and write more notes, and repeat this process over and over again. For me, this is why looking back, more specifically journalling, has been a benefit to me. It hasn't been about sitting and staying in my pain, it's about learning from that season and seeing God was faithful every single moment of every single day. I feel if looking back is going to have any benefit for you too, then it's has to be more than just putting a movie on and watching your past not-so-great decisions, moments of regret or pain with a big bowl of popcorn. Looking back, if not done with the right intention, just creates more pain. Just because I've found a benefit in looking back, doesn't mean I haven't always done it well.

I've looked back on my life, especially as I wrote this book, and been reminded of what has and hasn't been, and what it feels like I've missed out on. The problem most of us have with looking back is that you don't see what's right in front of you. This is why I think God wanted Lot's wife to stay looking forward and let go of what's been. There have been beautiful moments I've missed out on enjoying because privately, I was too focused on looking back. I've lost many Christmas days because part of me was looking behind me to see the days I could've fallen pregnant, and in the process missed the chance to fully enjoy moments with family and friends. Thinking about those past Christmas's and lost moments, I find myself cringing and ashamed that for too many years, I chose envy and sadness, rather than gratitude. Again, I think that's why God didn't want Lot's wife to look back.

Leaving your home, the community around you, your loved ones and starting with almost nothing is no small or easy thing. It can be hard to see all the beautiful things God's been working on behind the scenes, and that's ahead of you. Instead you only see what is no more. It was the same for Lot's wife. Did God know she would be focused on pain and anger, rather than hope and gratitude as He removed them? Did He know as she saw the city being destroyed right in front of her she wouldn't see what she had been saved from but rather what He did to the people she loved? I can imagine it would've been hard to make the choice to be grateful for what she'd been brought out of, and the new space God was now giving her, while so much was being lost. But that's where looking forward becomes the perfect partner to looking behind.

We all hear *that* voice that reminds us of what is behind us. The voice that reminds us why we're disqualified for doing or receiving anything amazing in our future. For some of us, it's louder than for others. For me personally *that* voice has felt like a rope tied around my arms to the side of my body, making it almost impossible to reach forward. We have a very real enemy who despises us and wants nothing good to happen for or to us. He hates that anything good could happen for us. When you hear the lies, lies he enjoys telling you so much by the way, it is so vitally important for you to remind him of what your future is! I didn't do this for a long time, and for a long time I became captive to the lies.

LIE #1 - 'Remember when you were fat and how bad you looked? Remember when you tried to be skinny and failed? Remember when you tried to be attractive and were single for all of your teenage years?'

LIE #2 - 'I can't believe that 'friend' at work spoke to you like that! Don't they know who you are?! They deserve to be unhappy and alone if that is how they treat you! When was the last time they gave you a compliment or recognition in a team meeting?'

LIE #3 - 'Another bill. You'll never get ahead. A life of abundance just isn't for you. Maybe God's unhappy with you. You were destined for hardship, nothing has really changed since your childhood and nothing will now.'

LIE #4 - 'Not pregnant again. Like it was going to happen anyway, never does. Never has before. Remember that month you really thought you were. Oh, how that hurt and then you had to do it all again only to be disappointed. Maybe that doctor was right. Where's this loving God now? Where's this miracle God now?'

LIE #5 - 'They cancelled your coffee date again! Why don't they value you like you value them? I remember them doing this last month.'

I became best friends with those lies and fear for many years. Maybe yours sound completely different. None of us know the specifics of what our future holds but if it involves Jesus, you can expect that it also involves increase in some capacity. At some point you probably have heard a lie that feels like a chain trying to turn you back around to look back at your pain. It's a learnt skill to look back and not be distracted by what had or hadn't been. It takes discipline to use it as way to help you do life better today an all the days after. You might not be able to tell the devil all the specific details of God's provision over your life, but you can tell him that you are blessed, and that you are dearly loved.

"A thief has only one thing in mind - he wants to steal, slaughter, and destroy. But I have come to *give you everything in abundance, more than you expect* - life in its fullness until you overflow" – John 10:10 TPT

This is your official permission to tell fear that if God is for you then no one (including him!) can stand and remain against you. Tell fear your God is the God of increase and the One who makes all things possible, no matter how impossible it looks, and miracles are His specialty. Tell fear God has not finished yet with your future but your done with listening to fear. When you remind fear of this, you're reminding yourself too, and in the process, moving your gaze to see God and all His splendor rather than looking behind you. Writing this chapter presented me with a decision to make…was I ready to really tell fear to be quiet? You do too.

Fear is often what makes out heads turn backwards, and even sideways, but very rarely forward. Fear fills your unseen days with questions of doubt and confusion, and reminds you of your lack, rather than the One will always provide for you. Fear will steal your peace every time, and make you despise your future. Fear puts more value on the mistakes you've made then the lessons you've learnt, and says you haven't and you can't. Fear doesn't want you to believe God says you it just hasn't happened yet, and fear wants you to truly believe you've missed out.

Fear is purely false evidence appearing real. In other words, lies.

This chapter is your turning point, like a cruise ship that turns around at its dock before heading out on it's next adventure. I honestly don't think you can go any further in the healing journey if you don't tell fear to be quiet, at least once. You'll be bound by indecision, I was. Turning, healing, changing all takes time, determination, focus, practice, and it doesn't happen straight away. If you have never seen a cruise ship turn, I recommend you Google it! It's not only impressive but is the perfect example of this moment.

The amount of time it takes for the ship to turn is quite a while, based on a lot of little movements and corrections. The captain and deckhands rely on many instruments to guide the ship in order to do it well. This turning point for you, is actually no different. Instead of relying on a GPS, God's given you something far better - Holy Spirit! He wants to help all of us know when to start turning, which way to turn so we're positioned to head to where the safe route is, when to hit top speed and when to prepare to slow down. If you're struggling to hear His voice, can I suggest maybe you need to turn the volume down on your own voice, and the voices of others, so that His voice can be heard.

You have a decision to make in this chapter – whether to let the Holy Spirit be your GPS of your life again or to let Siri continue to guide you without knowing you, loving you or having the best intentions for you. What is it going to be?

'By following His ways they will break the past bondage of their fickle fathers, who were a stubborn, rebellious generation and whose spirits strayed from the eternal God. They refused to love Him with

all their hearts. Take, for example, the sons of Ephraim. Though they were all equipped warriors, each with weapons, when the battle began they retreated and ran away in fear. They didn't really believe the promises of God; they refused to trust Him and move forward in faith. They forgot His wonderful works and the miracles of the past, even their exodus from Egypt, the epic miracle of His might. They forgot the glories of His power at the place of passing over. God split the sea wide open, and the waters stood at attention on either side as the people passed on through! By day the moving glory-cloud led them forward. And all through the night the fire-cloud stood as a sentry of light. In the days of desert dryness He split open the mighty rock, and the waters flowed like a river before their very eyes. He gave them all they wanted to drink from His living springs. Yet they kept their rebellion alive against God Most High, and their sins against God continued to be counted. In their hearts they tested God just to get what they wanted, asking for the food their hearts craved. Like spoiled children they grumbled against God, demanding He prove his love by saying, "Can't God: provide for us in this barren wilderness? Will He give us food, or will He only give us water? Where's our meal?"' – Psalm 78:8-20 TPT

23

In the middle

All courses need a starting point, and a choice. A choice to start and choice to keep going. At the start it's easy to feel strong and excited because you have a direction and you're focussed, and then there's the middle. The middle ground is a weird place to be. It's a place where you've made a decision to no longer be where you were, but the road ahead to where you want to be can seem too big, too long and just too much. Hello Holy Spirit, our personal GPS.

Anytime I go somewhere new, I religiously set my GPS in the car to make sure I take the correct turns when needed and I'm heading in the right direction. When it's just me, it's a peaceful experience and if I take a wrong turn, I know it's easily fixed. It's a different story when my husband and I travel together! You'll never see my husband and I on the show *The Amazing Race!,* ever, because we travel to a destinations very differently. When we get lost or take a wrong turn, I remain calm and even find a reason to laugh about it. My husband does not. He finds no humour in getting lost. Can you relate?

The funny thing is, we actually love to travel and go on road trips together. We are excited little kids when we know we're going on one. We choose a playlist, pack snacks and let the conversation flow. And then it happens, we take the wrong exit. Just as suddenly as we found ourselves somewhere unknown, so do we find the mood in the car between us. However, as soon as we arrive at our destination, my husband is fine. The stress instantly seems to fall instantly off him and he acts as if nothing happened. I on the other hand, am rattled by it all and find it hard to just turn the stress off. I can feel my anger and annoyance still bubbling away and it sometimes takes everything in me not to explode. My goodness, men and women are different!

Although my husband and I have had a few stressful car trips, we've had many more enjoyable ones. Some of the fondest road trip memories are travelling around Tasmania are in a car we hired for the week. Most days we had no plan for the day, and only took notice of where we were when we had to remember which road to come back to on our way home. We took little turns here and there only to find the cutest pubs, creeks and campsites. Some days we had a destination we needed to be at, and on those days we always allowed more time than suggested so we could allow for surprises.

I don't think life is not much different. It's a journey full of wrong turns, misread map coordinates, unplanned detours, and unknown accidents. I seem to be okay with detours and accidents as long as I know I'm still on the right path and I'll eventually get to my destination. It's when I have no idea where I am, or if I'm even heading the right way, that I start to panic. Hello middle ground.

> **'Oh, that you would follow me, walking my path! That you would choose not to be blind and stubborn in your ways. Oh, that you would listen to me, my heart. Allow me to subdue your enemies and feed you the best foods available. I promise you will be satisfied.'**
> **– Psalm 119**

Back to our road trips. On the days we needed to be at a destination during our time in Tasmania, we could've gone straight there but we choose to leave early so we could see everything along the way. There's no doubt a straight line will get you where you need to be faster and without distraction, but there's also a good chance you'll miss out on seeing all the beauty along the way. There have been so many times I nearly missed out on seeing some truly beautiful things. If my life was just one straight line, I don't know if I would've ever really felt or believed God was real. And He knew that.

With every kick and scream, in every tear and shout, He knew it was all for the good of our relationship. He knew I would know Him better. He knew for me to feel His love in a way I'd never before, and for me to lean into Him like I'd never before, I needed a zig zag line of direction. God knew that - it was me that took a while to understand the beauty of zig zag lines and the time spent in the middle ground was a blessing. I like to now think of middle ground as a place of holding time, a time God holds us close until we are ready to fly. Now I think that way, before, not so much! I threw some mighty good tantrums and declared not one part of it was fair.

I just wanted to be at my destination. I was sick of being held back and in the middle. I just wanted to be pregnant. I just wanted to be successful. I just wanted to be free. I wanted the prize without the effort or time it needed. Ashamedly, I fought God at every single detour, roadblock and delay. I now see it as the only way I was going to see the beauty in the pain and mess, the beauty along the way. It's an interesting thought. Just like on a road trip, has there been beauty along the way in each of my pain journeys? Has there been beauty along the way in yours you would've otherwise never seen if the prayer was simply answered?

When you're living in a season of unanswered prayer, or middle ground between what was and what is yet to be, it's easy to say He isn't present. To write this book, I've needed a lot of time. Almost three years officially. At first the time was a gift. As our world shut down because of the pandemic in 2019, my workplace like many others closed. All of a sudden I had endless days of no plans and free hours, so I started to write my book, well type it.

I'd actually already written it by hand before but it now needed to be put together and made real. It needed time and attention.

Every day, I sat and typed chapter after chapter until I had something that resembled a real book. I never thought my life would look as it was beginning to, and then I had the crazy thought – I want to do this as my job. I want to write and find a way to make words be a gift of hope and encouragement to people. A new road trip was starting to take shape, and it felt different to every other one this time. For once it wasn't me setting the course and marking the destination, I was following the map God was asking me to follow. There wasn't any more fighting or resistance. Finally I felt an ease come upon my days. Professional writers spend a lot of time alone developing ideas, scribbling thoughts and rewriting sentences. It seems crazy to think I'd choose a life of quiet and solitariness, when it was the one thing I couldn't run fast enough away from when I was younger, and yet there has been such peace in it.

As the world began to reopen, I went back to work like many others did. While a lot of things were the same I was no longer the same. I made the decision to quit my safe and dependable job. I had nothing else to step into other than my writing and I was scared. I didn't had very small amounts of savings and everything I had to learn from hours on Goggle or asking people I'd never met question after question. It has blossomed into a business that now creates inspirational candles based on God's truth, and so much more. Has it made millions of dollars? Not yet. I hope it's something I can make a living from and bring financial support to my family with, but that's up to God. I won't say it's been easy. There have been many days the loneliness has been overwhelming and I've had to dig deep to find creativity. This middle ground has tested me in many ways, especially my faith in God and what His asked me to do. But my resolve has never been stronger either. Where there would've been fear in the past, there's a sense of real peace.

Maybe you've been busy setting your own course because you think God isn't real, or you're tired of being in the middle. I get it, more than you may realise. I can tell you one thing for sure - God is listening and He does care. He is real and He has always been present. I haven't seen Him with my own eyes, but I have felt Him. I've seen Him in the people who have held me up and loved me along the way, and that's where the beauty in all of it is found.

If I had just been healed of my eating disorder, then I wouldn't know God is a miracle working God. When He showed me the vision of myself, I don't know if I was more shocked of what I saw or what He just did. But in the years and decades after that moment, moments where I struggle to understand if He can do anything miraculous, I remember that moment and I am encouraged again. There was beauty along the way. If my heart had just been healed after my parents' divorce, I wouldn't know God as a real Father and restorer of relationships. It took years for each layer to be peeled back and dealt with so I could then cherish each relationship, new and old, in my life. I had to learn how to be responsible with them, protect them and nurture them. There was beauty along the way.

If I'd just fallen pregnant when I first wanted all those years ago, my goodness I'd be a broken mess now. As each month and year passed, there's been new truths I've discovered, learnt and declared. In the time that's been vacant of a child, it's been filled with so much more. I've had the chance to really build my faith and my marriage. I've learnt why family is important and the values I want for mine as I watch others go before me. I found the gift of my purpose in the waiting and the beauty that lies within the middle. As painful as it is to write, there's been beauty along the way. My life is a bit more of a zig zag line rather than a straight one, but I've come to love those zig zags more than I'll ever love a straight line.

I'll leave you with this story that may help you understand what I am trying to say -

One night a man had a dream. He dreamed he was walking along the beach with the LORD. Across the sky flashed scenes from his life. For each scene he noticed two sets of footprints in the sand: one belonging to him, and the other to the LORD. When the last scene of his life flashed before him, he looked back at the footprints in the sand. He noticed that many times along the path of his life there was only one set of footprints. He also noticed that it happened at the very lowest and saddest times in his life. This really bothered him and he questioned the LORD about it:

"LORD, you said that once I decided to follow you, you'd walk with me all the way. But I have noticed that during the most troublesome times in my life, there is only one set of footprints. I don't understand why when I needed you most you would leave me." The LORD replied: "My son, my precious child, I love you and I would never leave you. During your times of trial and suffering, when you see only one set of footprints, it was then that I carried you."

FOOTPRINTS POEM | CAROLYN JOYCE CARTY

IV

A COURAGEOUS LIFE

Chapters twenty four - thirty one

24

Help!

"Hi dad, can you help me out? I have some car trouble and I'm stuck on the side of the road". Have you ever made a call like that? I have. Who do you call? Your husband, wife, friend, brother, sister, dad, mum or even neighbour?

No one likes being stuck or immobile. When you are stuck though, the call you make will have the biggest impact on how, when and where you move. It's important you call the right person when you're in trouble. If you don't make the right call to the right person, there'll be very little chance you'll get moving anytime soon. The situation can quickly become complicated and harder to resolve. You don't call your local pizza guys if you have a shower leak, so why would you call anyone else than God when you are in pain?

I wish someone explained this me that years ago, maybe I wouldn't have avoided picking up the phone to make a call for help. My problem wasn't who I called but that I dind't call anyone. I mistook being strong for being scared. Nothing has taken more strength from me than the first time I called for help, and every single time after. It's taken every bit of strength in me to fight the urge not to keep going, and instead pause for a moment. Why is calling for help so hard? For me, if I am honest, it was for two reasons. I had become very self reliant after spending years alone and caring for my mum. The other was I wasn't sure if whoever I called would be able to fix my problems instantly.

'That day when evening came, he said to his disciples, "Let us go over to the other side." Leaving the crowd behind, they took him along, just as he was, in the boat. There were also other boats with him. A furious squall came up, and the waves broke over the boat, so that it was nearly swamped. Jesus was in the stern, sleeping on a cushion. The disciples woke him and said to him, "Teacher, don't you care if we drown?" He got up, rebuked the wind and said to the waves, "Quiet! Be still!" Then the wind died down and it was completely calm. He said to his disciples, "Why are you so afraid? Do you still have no faith?" They were terrified and asked each other, "Who is this? Even the wind and the waves obey him!"' –Mark 4:35-41 NIV

"Teacher, is it nothing to you that we are going to drown?", the disciples asked. Who do you call when the seas are raging and you find yourself in a storm? Are you listening to the voice on the other end?

The disciples wanted a quick fix. Don't we all? Jesus knew He could calm the seas within seconds, or even prevent the storm from ever occurring, but there was a lesson to be learnt. One we are learning nearly 2000 years later. I touch on this a bit later but I wanted to highlight a different part of the story here. In this story, you can almost feel their fear jumping off the pages and their sense of urgency for Jesus to understand their predicament. Maybe they felt He wasn't actually who He said He was, or that He wasn't real. There have been days when I felt like He isn't real. Maybe they felt completely abandoned and alone. There have been numerous days when I felt like that too.

I too have had times where I couldn't shake the feeling that my prayers and whispers of hope, were lost amongst the noise of heaven. I was sure His ear was turned toward someone in greater need, someone doing better at life or dealing with their pain, or someone He simply loved more than me. But what I felt wasn't the truth, and it wasn't the truth for the disciples. Jesus wasn't, and to this day, isn't about the quick fix.

He's not a Band-Aid over a wound and He isn't a dolphin that commands blessings and miracles on our demand to entertain us. He wants to heal the wound completely, not just cover it. The disciples needed help with their faith and their assurance in who Jesus is. Jesus knew this would become their foundation in the years to follow when they were tested time and time again, for their faith and understanding of who God is. They didn't know at the time, but each of them actually needed this storm. They needed Jesus to use this moment to heal any last doubt they had, and to teach them how to ask for help in their future times of need. It's no different for you and me today. If we allow it, pain will never have the last say in our lives and neither will hard times. God uses it all to helps us see who He really is. It's actually for our advantage I think. Without the storm, the disciples wouldn't have learnt they could trust this man they claimed to believe was their Saviour.

'God is educating you; that's why you must never drop out. He's treating you as dear children. This trouble you're in isn't punishment; it's *training*, the normal experience of children. Only irresponsible parents leave children to fend for themselves. Would you prefer an irresponsible God? We respect our own parents for training and not spoiling us, so why not embrace God's training so we can truly *live*? While we were children, our parents did what *seemed* best to them. But God is doing what *is* best for us, training us to live God's holy best. At the time, discipline isn't much fun. It always feels like it's going against the grain. Later, of course, it pays off big-time, for it's the well-trained who find themselves mature in their relationship with God.' – Hebrews 12:-5-6 MSG

Calling for assistance, calling for help, is like making a call to hope, to believe, and to surrender again. Picking up the phone and making the right call to the right person, means you're allowing even just the smallest seed of hope to still be alive in your pain and circumstances. Don't ever underestimate the value of making a call, just make sure you're ready to listen when you do. Making the call for help is one thing, making yourself available and being accepting of the response is another.

When we used to have the old-fashioned phones, the handset was connected to a cord and that cord was connected to the each end of the phone. Even though our phones aren't connected by a cord anymore when you make a call, the handset still needs to be connected to a source in order for it to communicate with someone on the other end. If that handset wasn't connected to the source, it simply wouldn't work. There'd be no connection and the two people trying to communicate wouldn't be able to hear or speak to one another. Making a call to God is kind of the same. When you reach out to Him, you're instantly connected to Heaven. He never asks an angel to take a message because He is busy, and He never lets the call ring out.

I love the idea of my call being on speaker phone with all of heaven. Angels listening and silently putting their hand up so God will pick them to come down and help me. Phone calls for help used to feel like a waste of time until I started ringing the right number. Sometimes in the midst of pain you can be so desperate for answers that you start to listen to anyone and everyone. If you're not connected to the right source you'll get the wrong information or be misguided down a path that wasn't meant for you. It's okay to make a call for help, but remember, only pick up the phone that rings for you. What about when God calls you? Are you available?

Thanks to modern technology, our phones are no longer connected to a cord. They move with us everywhere we go, meaning we can be contacted at any time of day. Technology has also meant we have caller ID now too. When the phone rings I'm sure I'm not the only one who looks at a strange number and often sends it straight to voice mail. If it's a legit phone call, they will leave a message. Sometimes God calls us and we don't expect the

HELP!

call, it catches us off guard and we might be tempted to send it to voicemail to deal with later. Sometimes God is the one that calls us because He can see we need help, guidance and support. Answering a call means you give time out of your day, and make it a priority over something else.

God loves when we are His hands and feet to people, helping where and when we can. I mean He really loves it. Let me share this though - you don't have to be everyone's answer for help.

I feel into the trap of thinking I was available to Him and had made Him a priority because I was available to everyone else. The time I would've spent in prayer or reading my bible, I was giving to other people. I served in my church morning and night every Sunday, became a youth leader and said 'yes' to another ministry that kept me busy with people. I did the same thing when my husband began working as a FIFO (fly in fly out) worker. In the first couple of years, I said yes to every invite because no one wanted me to be alone. I didn't want to be alone either, I didn't want to relive those days of my childhood. The truth was I kept as busy as I could, diverting every call He made asking me to stop and sent His requests straight to voice mail. Soon I ran out of excuses not to answer His calls, and the expense of living this life was adding up. I started sending fewer calls to voice mail.

25

This is your journey

> 'At the crack of dawn on Sunday, the women came to the tomb carrying the burial spices they had prepared. They found the entrance stone rolled back from the tomb, so they walked in. But once inside, they couldn't find the body of the Master Jesus. They were puzzled, wondering what to make of this.' – Luke 24:1-4 MSG

The world had been told Jesus was dead and whatever they'd hoped for Him to accomplish was also dead. Prior to this moment though, these women had been told by Jesus Himself that He was going to rise again, and they forgot. Or maybe they just couldn't see how it was possible. I get that! They let the noise of the world drown out the very words Jesus had said to them personally. I do understand their doubt, I mean when you're dead you normally stay dead. Not with Jesus though. Not always anyway. I could imagine they felt so overwhelmed, confused and lost. Have you ever felt like that?

Ever felt like you're hungover from something unfortunate happening the day (or months) before, only to have to deal with something new the next day? I have. Before the day has begun, it feels like everything is too much and all I want to do is hide for the rest of the day. Maybe you've actually said the words, "I'm done". I have.

Every time I said those words it was based off the feeling I thought God had let go of me and the situation I so badly needed His touch upon. Every time I declared I was done holding onto hope, it wasn't God letting go but me. I was making a choice to no longer believe He was who He said He was. I allowed what others had to say to become my reality and my guide steps; it just seemed to be more realistic, make more sense and even hurt less. Every time I listened to anyone else instead of God, my pain only intensified. It just seemed too hard to believe He could do what He said He was able to do, I imagine much like the women who went to His tomb. Can you imagine the thoughts speeding through the women's minds when they approached the tomb?

'All you need to say is simply "Yes" or "No"; anything beyond this comes from the evil one.' - Matt 5:37 NIV

Until His death, a tomb represented death but now it represented life too. When the world said Jesus was dead and that He wasn't the Son of God, the women had to choose who they listened to. The women had to choose if they listened to what the world was saying or remember what Jesus had told them. That moment wasn't necessarily about bold declarations, it was simply about reminding themselves of what they knew to be true. It didn't make sense, it almost seemed impossible.

'Then, out of nowhere it seemed, two men, light cascading over them, stood there. The women were awestruck and bowed down in worship. The men said, "Why are you looking for the Living One in a cemetery? He is not here, but raised up. Remember how he told you when you were still back in Galilee that he had to be handed over to sinners, be killed on a cross, and in three days rise up?" Then they remembered Jesus' words.' – Luke 24:4-8 MSG

When it comes to Jesus things often don't make sense in our thinking but always, everything has life. He wanted to change the course a little.

'They left the tomb and broke the news of all this to the Eleven and the rest. Mary Magdalene, Joanna, Mary the mother of James, and the other women with them kept telling these things to the apostles, but the apostles didn't believe a word of it, thought they were making it all up.' – Luke 24:9-11 MSG

I used to think staying silent meant I was safe and nothing could be taken, I learnt quite the opposite is true. Saying nothing gives space for someone to speak. Saying nothing means that someone could be given the authority and glory rather than Jesus.

'The Lord is my best friend and my shepherd. I always have more than enough. He offers a resting place for me in His luxurious love. His tracks take me to an oasis of peace, the quiet brook of bliss. That's where He restores and revives my life. He opens pathways before me, and leads me along in His footsteps of righteousness so that I can bring honour to His name.' - Psalm 23:1-2 tpt

How quickly have you forgotten what Jesus has spoken over your life? It seemed almost daily for me at times.

"God, why am I not pregnant yet? Why? Have I missed it? Don't you know what happens as my body gets older? The doctors say it just can't be explained. The doctors say it just won't happen".

This morning, Mother's Day 2019, the Holy Spirit made sure I was not without. He highlighted Psalm 23:1, especially the opening lines 'The Lord is my shepherd – I will always have enough'. I used to always think, especially on days like today, that this meant I will get everything I want, or He will answer all my prayers just as I ask. But looking at it from the Passion Translation, I understand God's heart more. I will have more than enough because I have Him first. Not just my needs, but

He will be all I need. Whether that be a comforter, a healer, a provider, a friend, a restorer or just my peace in that moment – He will be it all.

Lord, even when Your path takes me through the valley of deepest darkness, fear will never conquer me, for You already have!

You remain close to me and lead me through it all the way. Your authority is my strength and my peace. The comfort of Your love takes away my fear. I'll never be lonely, for you are near. (vs 4)

There's no denial in this moment today is a hard day. I long for it not to be. I long for it not to be an avoided day in our marriage and with my family. A day we know exists but pretend it doesn't. A day we don't give the loss of me not having my mum and not being a mum, be outweighed but what might yet be. In these last 7yrs I haven't considered who God was in the mystery. That He was even there. I just thought what He wasn't and to me, that determined who He couldn't be.

I figured because my womb was empty, so were my hands and spirit. I never thought I could have a gap in my heart and yet, my spirit be overflowing. His goodness really does indeed follow me all my days.

JOURNAL ENTRY 12.05.19 – MOTHERS DAY

Everyone has had an opinion about how we should seek to become parents, and we've had lots of people give us their opinion hoping to help me grieve for mum. Some opinions were helpful and some weren't.

It happened. Move on. Get over it. Let it go. Shake it off. Don't worry about it. Stop thinking about it. You're better than that or them. Don't dwell on the past or what you can't change. It's done, there's nothing you can do. It's just life, don't let it weigh you down.

Do any of these sound familiar? Maybe you've only heard one of them, or maybe you've heard all of them. I've heard all of them over the years, and I can't say I've enjoyed hearing any of them. Not because it's not true or they're spoken out of love. Purely because it's one opinion from one point of view. Finding the right people is key is vital when processing fear, doubt and disappointment. People that will not just tell you what you want to hear or alternatively don't. But people who will love you and encourage you to seek God's opinion, and be the one you always listen to. How do you know you've found the right people? They won't be scared of your questions and or to get real with you. They'll be comfortable with the long moments of silence and big thoughts, and they'll always point you back to God and what He has to say over their own opinion.

Many people know my story, but seldom know the details. Only a few have held my hand as I walk through each season of pain, even less haven't been scared of my thoughts and wiped my tears. They know although it's messy, I'm safe and praying my way through it. They know I am hungry for God's truth over my life more than anything else. My words aren't brushed to the side or disregarded; they know I don't want to dwell in my sadness but for a moment I need to process the reality of my pain. Sometimes it just really hurts. They know I need to verbalise it, release it from my heart with someone who will love me at the end of it. When I miss mum the most, these are the people who are there. Their voice is the one I've come to trust.

In times when all I wanted to do was rebel and lie my way out of my mess, I've been truly blessed to have some friends who weren't scared about being real with me. Their words directed me back to God. It's okay for everyone to have an opinion, that isn't the issue. The issue, I found, was when I listened to all of those opinions rather than seek God's. It got me nowhere, but only trapped in more circles and being so unsure about anything. The atmosphere of my heart was not great at those times and my attitude towards God slowly crumbled. The answers aren't found in everyone's opinions, it's found in God's Word.

Just like a lemon cannot taste like a banana, God cannot be anything but good, kind, full of mercy and grace, loving and gentle. When you listen to the right source, your perspective starts to change. For too long I searched for the answers to all my questions from everyone but God. I asked friends, doctors, medical specialists, other people who'd struggled with fertility too, family and even Google. I let their opinions, so-called facts and points of view become my reality. I was in turmoil. I was so confused. Unsure if I should step left or right, I just became stuck. Eventually I went back to God and blocked everything else out for a while.

Some days I just stared at my bible, sometimes I read it. I want to be clear - it takes time and making it a habit. We might not choose the circumstances we find ourselves in, but we have full control over what we speak into our lives and who we listen to. Everything I ever needed to know, or want to know for my life, is found in the Bible. It's not always immediately clear, or what I want to hear and sometimes it takes time to understand, but His Word never fails. My Bible has every colour of ink through it, with notes scribbled everywhere and pages slightly folded over. From the moment I made my first call for help, I've found it in His Word.

In whatever you're facing, what voice are you listening to? Are you listening to the voices that say it can't be, won't be, shouldn't be? The crowd said Jesus was dead, oh but how wrong they were. If you're unsure what you feel you're hearing is from God, a good way to check is by what it gives you. If there is peace, it's probably God. If what is being spoken allows more confusion, anger, resentment, doubt, fear and anxiety to rise, there's a good chance it's not from God.

Remember this is YOUR journey...you get to choose who is part of it!

26

Finding your brave

When I began writing this book, I was under no illusion that pain was in my past. I really wanted it to be but deep down I knew it wasn't the case. What I wasn't ready for however, was the onslaught of things being brought back to my memory that I'd forgotten about and tried so hard never to think about again. God knew if I still had a reaction to them all these years later, it hadn't been dealt with. I'm going to tell you one thing I know for sure, there's no shame in the word *again*.

I've never jumped off a diving spring board but I'd like to! That doesn't mean I wouldn't be scared. I have a pretty good feeling once I got up there, I'd want to come straight back down. Finding your brave is a little like jumping off a diving board. First, you make the decision to do it. Then, you walk up each storey, trying to squash every negative thought and reason why you shouldn't be doing this out of your head, and then you stand on the board. Maybe you consider what type of jump you will do, how big will the splash be or how many people are watching. Do you jump or walk back down?

It's one thing to live in spite of pain, and it's another thing to still live a beautiful life in spite of it. When you get to the second decision, you get to a place where you respect your pain because of the worth it has in your life.

It's not always going to be easy to be happy when you're travelling through hard seasons of life. Discovering beauty in your life even in painful seasons means you realise it isn't just about you. You choose to keep living because you know the value your life holds for other people. In other words, you find your brave. Did you know your life and the way you manage your painful seasons impacts everyone around you?

"Don't you want kids?" "Why haven't you had kids yet?" "When are you give your parents grandchildren?" "You do know the time is running out, don't you?" "It won't be easy for you if you leave it too late" "Tick tock! There's an expiry date on your womb" "With each year, your eggs start to die" "All you need now is children and life would be just perfect"

That's a lot of questions and statements! They're just some of the most popular questions we have been asked over the years. Lots of questions and I haven't had one genuine answer I beleive. While each question has never been asked out of anything but love, they still hurt. Each time we were asked one of those questions/statement, it felt like someone kept poking on a bruise or open wound. Our patience was tested and at times we snapped.

Many years ago I walked into a shop after a stressful day.

Everything that could've gone wrong did that day. I woke up late, had no milk left in the fridge, my hair wasn't playing nice and I missed an appointment. I should have just gone home but I decided I wanted to do something for me. I headed to my favourite shopping centre and yup you guesses it, I couldn't find a park and I got angry all over again. To make it all that much worse, I was hungry. I went into a store, hungry & frustrated, and I hit my limit. The piece of clothing I wanted was sold out. The beautiful young girl at the counter was super helpful in trying to help me find something else and I snapped. I gave the shop assistant a healthy dose of attitude and took my bad day out on her. There was nothing beautiful about that. I acted out because I wanted to and felt I was justified to. Living our lives with pain is not much different. We can't live a beautiful life, even if we're in pain, if we're not doing beautiful things or saying kind words. You'll be happy to know I did apologise to her and tell her it's not her fault. We ended up having a laugh at my bad day! That day is the underlying message for this book - just because you're having a bad day doesn't mean everyone else has to as well.

I've been so blessed with how each person in my world took the time to share their pregnancy news with me. Each time their focus wasn't their reason for celebration but my reason for sadness. Some wrote letters or emails in preparation for their public announcement, some called or took me out to lunch so they can share their news privately. Each time they took such care because they didn't want me to feel any more pain. But what about the pain I have imposed on them?

Every time they had a reason to celebrate, it felt like it highlighted my sadness. I wish I could say my happiness for them overrode the sadness I felt for myself. I did my best to keep it hidden but I'm sure at times it was far from hidden. Each announcement hit me right in the middle of my heart, like a sniper in the distance hitting its mark. In the early years of handling this pain, I got angry and felt defeated and forgotten. I wish I didn't, but the truth was I let those words hurt me greatly. I envied my friend, desperate to be on the other side of the conversation we were having. My pain wasn't their fault. They were allowed to feel happiness and be on the receiving end of a miracle. Most of them had struggled to get to this very moment themselves, and so why would I want them to suffer for longer?

Living a beautiful life means you add colour to the lives around you, not add more black and grey. That lesson took me a long time to learn, and it took even more time for me to find the bravery to do so. As the years have passed, it's understandable that I've come to expect a negative symbol on a pregnancy test. My moments of hope, expectation and possibility stolen with one line. In those early years my courage was taken too. Not anymore.

It used to feel like a little game between me and the test, who could be the bravest for the longest.

Could I stay hopeful long enough before the line appears to enable another to appear? Could I pray a special prayer to make it work?

What if I closed my eyes, would that make a difference? I wasn't being brave at all, or living in a state of hope. I was scared and hopeless. Something I've learnt about living without hope is that you tend to focus on what isn't rather than what could be, and it's easier to push everything good and living away, just to make room for anger and frustration.

Hopelessness stole every one of my birthdays in my thirties. Before then I loved my birthday, my mum knew how to celebrate others well and it is something I inherited from her until I turned 30. Mum always thought about the person and the gift had to be something intentional, purposeful and bring a smile to their face. Everything about the birthday gift mattered – the wrapping, the writing in the card as well as the gift itself. Everyone deserved to feel special and unique one day a year. We weren't a mistake.

When our fertility journey began, I started to dread them. They became deadlines and death sentences of a dream, rather than a celebration of what is yet to be. They became lonely and painful. We moved our 'deadline' date multiple times in hope that if we pushed it back then there was a chance it could still happen. First it was at my 35th birthday, then my 37th, and then my 40th.

The morning I turned 35, I woke up early and took myself to sit on the beach by myself. My husband was away for work and I wanted to do this as a gift to myself. Five years prior to this day, we'd agreed that if I didn't fall pregnant by 35 well then that will be okay and we will have known we tried. it would be the line in the sand and we would get on with life. Never in my wildest dreams did we think it would take five years, let alone eight, then ten, and then never! At that five years mark it still hadn't happened and I wasn't ready to let go or 'be okay' with it. By now our friends were finding schools for their children and they all had seven seater 4WDs in the garage.

Each birthday I felt like I was becoming weaker and more fearful, being brave was definitely the last thing I wanted to be or felt like I could be.

I didn't think I could feel lonelier than what I have on some of my birthdays. I don't know if this fits here, but I feel it's important to say to anyone going through something similar. It's common and easy to get frustrated with our partners. To feel alone in the midst of a fertility battle, but please remember each of you is feel different things at different times. Maybe you feel they don't care they way you do, I promise you they do. For me, what I later realised was my husband was responsible with his pain in his own way. While I was still having my temper tantrum in the corner, he just got on with life. Walking hand in hand with your partner doesn't really work if one of you is ahead of the other. You're no longer side by side, but stretched out with big amounts of space in between. Living with your pain well doesn't just bless you, but it blesses your partner, or family and friends too. You align yourselves again and you walk in harmony with each other. The struggle doesn't necessarily become less, but the space between you reduces and you make each other stronger. Braver.

For me, I had to stop with the tantrums and make a conscious decision to be wise about how I walked the rest of this life out, with or without pain. There comes a time when you welcome discipline into your world, it's a key to finding your brave I feel. It is hard to describe what hopelessness *feels* like but I know what it *sounds* like. It's snappy and short. It's defensive and angry. It is very ugly and it blames everyone else. I used to think my life wasn't beautiful because of everyone else.

I thought everyone else asked too many questions, no one seemed to understand and everyone was insensitive. In honest truth, the issue wasn't them and their questions, it was how I reacted to it all. Just like how I reacted to the young shop assistant that day because of a bad day she had nothing to do with. I used to take no responsibility for my own happiness, it was easier to blame everyone and anyone else.

Take the example of a doctor hitting you on the knee. It's okay if you kick him back isn't it? The act of reaction or response isn't the problem, but more how we respond when the unexpected happens – good or bad. When Jesus was hit with a hammer how did He respond? His hit was with more than a rubber hammer though. His was brutal and intense. And yet with His final breath, He forgave and loved. Life is all a series of our reactions and responses to situations and questions being asked of us.

Don't discount how important your response is, especially to God.

When Mary was told by Gabriel she would be pregnant with a son while still being a virgin, her response mattered. I expand upon this in the last chapter but I want to touch on it here too. Months beforehand, her cousin's husband had a similar encounter but he had a very different response to the unexpected. They both encountered the same God and were given the same promise, but they responded very differently to one another. One response led to fruitfulness and joy, and one led to fear and doubt. Living a beautiful life meant I found my brave and ask God what beautiful life did He have for me. My bravery was no longer found in my own strength, but in God's. The God who is well able, who loves me and finishes what He starts.

'And I am certain that God, who began the good work within you, will continue his work until it is finally finished on the day when Christ Jesus returns.' – Philippians 1:6 NLT

The thing about being brave, I've found, is that it doesn't mean you don't feel scared or unsure at times. It's a decision to keep going past those feelings and thoughts. Being brave isn't just about saying you're brave, it's more about following through with steps to surrender what scares you, overwhelms you and unsettles you to God. Think of being brave like wearing a cape, and each morning you choose to wrap it around yourself. You can choose to leave it hanging on the hook by the door but that is no good to anyone. Not everyone will notice your cape or give you praise for doing something courageous. Does that really matter? Is that why you are wearing the cape? No! It's because when you say hello to courage, you do life better and fear has to go bother someone else for the day.

Being brave is praying again. It's hoping, trusting, loving, forgiving and being generous all over again. It's apologising and repenting, surrendering and listening again. It's about putting action to a word and do small things that make big impacts - like opening the bible again.

There is real power in seeing things from God's viewpoint, again. The reason I can write this book about a not just creating but living and fighting for my beautiful life is because I've learnt the value of my days are in the ones I haven't yet lived. I'm happy to share the lessons I've learnt & the truths hidden I've found in the days behind me, but not everything needs to be rehashed and not everything needs to be remembered. It can take me to places that I worked really hard to get out of and they aren't life giving anymore. The days I haven't lived yet, the days where I haven't been filled with God's breath to carry out His work are the days I hold dear. Those days are where the beauty really lies.

Being brave says yes I am weak, *but* God is not.

27

A courageous faith

You have two choices when it comes to dealing with your pain – come out swinging or run for cover. I think there's a time for both if I am honest, and I think both take a lot of courage to do. Facing something difficult head on is scary and often takes great strength. Knowing when to not fight, knowing when to take cover and protect yourself takes just as much strength at times.

I touched on the sport of boxing earlier and I want to talk about it a little more here. I personally don't watch a lot of boxing, I think I've only ever watched a whole match once in my life! In the matches I've caught glimpses of, there always seems to be one boxer that is always slightly more confident than the other. One is hungrier to win than the other, sometimes it's the underdog and sometimes it's the champion. Regardless, one always wants it more than the other. Despite what the odds say about them or how much support they have in the crowd, they come out swinging and give it all they've got.

As mentioned, there's a time to run for cover when you find yourself in painful seasons. Sometimes the fight isn't ours to fight, it's Gods and it's our time to take refuge in Him. I don't think He wants us to stay hiding though, and at some point, you have to come out swinging. There's a time when you decide enough is enough, and you step into the promises God has placed over your life. Despite the odds stacked against you, how confident the enemy seems and how impossible it looks, there's a point where you make a choice that you want something better. How bad do you want this situation to change?

No matter what your answer is to that, God's is, "badly!". His desire for us to live a beautifully abundant life is His motivation to step in the ring every day for us. I once heard it said that if you know who God is, His nature or character if you will, then you'll never question His motives. You can trust someone who you know only wants the best for you, just like a boxer trusts and listens to their coach and the suggestions they make. When you know who God is, praising Him becomes easier regardless of the valley you're in, possibly even enjoyable.

"Sing, barren woman, you who never bore a child; burst into song, shout for joy, you who were never in labor; because more are the children of the desolate woman than of her who has a husband," says the Lord. - Isaiah 54:1 NIV

For anyone who knows pain well, the suggestion to praise Him or even find it enjoyable to praise Him in the depth of a painful season probably seems completely absurd, confronting or even insulting. I thought the same when I first heard it. Driving to work one morning many years ago, angry and struggling to smile, I listened to a random podcast by Melissa Helser and Jonathan David when I heard them explain how this was possible. All I wanted to do was turn the volume down but I just physically couldn't do it. My spirit was hungry for breakthrough and my everything other desire just had to submit.

I remember my mind going into overdrive hearing them talk about understanding God, in an instant all I thought God was being smashed to pieces. From when I was a little girl, I had built God into Oz from Wizard of Oz like figure in my mind. In my mind He was an all-powerful being sitting on a throne somewhere far above us all, commanding orders in a booming and cold voice. I never considered Him close, if anything I always felt like He was removed. He was cold. He was clinical. He was orderly. I knew He loved us, but I envisioned His love like the love a really strict father gives to his children or even a school principal giving instructions to his pupils. I hadn't considered His nature was fun and relaxed, that it was fluid and that He was right beside me. I never stopped to consider His nature. I knew the name God, I knew about Him but I started to realise I never *knew* Him.

I've been in church for close to two decades, but it felt like I was discovering my faith for the first time. I was relearning what He could do, who He was and what He had done. There was no doubt in my mind He was the big guy with the final word on everything, but I never thought about His nature, His personality.

Let's go back for a moment and expand on the sentence I said at the start - sometimes the fight isn't ours to fight, it's Gods and it's our time to take refuge in Him. For the 40years of my life, it'd been a fight. It'd been hard work. There's been beautiful moments where His blessings have flowed freely and I've experienced unexplainable peace and joy, but there's been a lot of the opposite as well. When we tie this all together, the real highlighted truth that came to life for me was that I never thought about God being a fighter *for me*.

I never thought about Him entering the boxing ring every day so that I wouldn't have to, or at least less. I'd always thought of Him as the boxing match promoter, sitting in a corporate box watching on. Suddenly, I started to see what I'd missed my whole life: His nature. How? It wasn't anything more than taking a moment to see what was in front of me the whole time - His people. If you want to see God's nature, just look at the incredible people in this world.

Have you ever wondered how some people have the ability to listen really well? Have you ever wondered how some people have the ability to give and bless other people? Have you ever wondered how some people have the ability to pray really well? Have you ever wondered how some people have the gift of wisdom? Have you ever wondered how some people have the gift of encouragement? Have you ever wondered how some people have the gift of writing and drawing so people can connect with each other?

Spoiler alert : they got it from God. He is the best listener, the most generous person you'll ever meet, the one who gave us the gift of prayer and wisdom, He is the best encouragement and He is the most creative person that will ever live!

That's when I understood the value of 'yes' and 'amen' because I started to get to know Him. I was the boxer and He was my coach. Instead of being two people who didn't know one another, we were building an intimate relationship. Despite the knocks I was getting, I could say 'yes' and 'amen' to it all, and despite the amount of times I got knocked out, I found a reason to get back up again. I truly believe that's the atmosphere of Heaven. An attitude that says in spite of it all, in spite of how many people say it can't or won't happen, in spite of how long it's been and regardless of how much it's hurt…we say 'yes' and 'amen' to Him. When you know God, you know who He is and you can stand confident knowing He is with you in the battle.

> **'Fix my eyes on God – when my soul is in the dumps and I am on a diet of tears, I rehearse everything I know of You. Shouting praises and singing thanksgiving – celebrating God's feast! You promise me love all day. My life is your prayer. You are my God.'**
> **– Summary of Psalm 42 MSG**

When you come out swinging, you change your atmosphere. It changes your intentions, and decisions that follow. A world champion boxer doesn't just become a champion, no matter how much raw talent and grit they have, there's a time of preparation and discipline. It's the same with changing your atmosphere even when the pain is still alive and well. If you've ever been to an amazing party I can guarantee it didn't just happen. There's often weeks of planning to ensure every little detail is accounted for. No party planner seeks to find the oldest decorations for styling, the worst food for everyone to hate or a playlist that puts everyone to sleep. You remember a great party, they have a certain feel to them and their magic lingers long after the event is finished. Great parties don't just happen, they're initially created.

When my close friend moved in after mum left for America, the atmosphere started to change. We made an active decision to change the atmosphere and we took action. When it was the home my mum and I shared, some days it used to feel cold, dark and really lonely, and on other days it was the happiest place on earth. I remember the first day my bestie moved in, everything changed. We opened windows and blinds, changed the layout of the house and bought new furniture. Even the smell of the home changed, there was different perfumes and food being cooked. It felt like a new home with a new sound. There was more laughter than ever before, and definitely more chatting than ever before. The closest thing to what it felt like was as if someone had finally changed the radio station. I could've insisted the home stayed like it was, but something in me wanted something different. I have no other way to describe it than I was ready to fight for the first time in a long time.

'Give thanks to the Lord, for He is good, His love endures forever.' – Psalm 107:1

> *Yesterday, as I was making the bed I heard the words 'praise' & 'praise Him' so clearly. I was enjoying our home being quiet after a busy week at work, the last thing I wanted to do was make noise. But the words remained. Praise. I put some praise music on in the background and*

I returned to my domestic duties. I asked the Holy Spirit why that was so important. Right now in this moment, why did I need to put praise on? He must think just once, 'I wish she did have a question for everything!'. He told me that praise is a weapon. Praise is what changes the atmosphere and the devil hates it, more than I hate waiting to see our fertility situation change and other things have the touch of God over them. That's a lot! I can't make the sperm go to my eggs. I can't make my husband want to come to church all the time. I can't make someone come knocking on my door to offer me the chance to write for a job, or business be as seemingly successful as others.

I can't make a lot of things happen. But I can praise. I can change the atmosphere in my home from one of a defeated heart to a hopeful heart. I can add light where there would otherwise be darkness. Praise reminds my heart, my head, my spirit, and the devil who is in control. It reminds me what is possible, what He has done before and why my prayers matter.

It builds my faith and connects me to God. We start speaking the same language. I often am discouraged I can't hear God but I never stopped to consider that maybe we weren't communicating properly. I am speaking French and He is speaking Spanish. It's time we start communicating better.

JOURNAL ENTRY 18.11.18 - RIGHT LANGUAGE

'Let us come before Him with thanksgiving and praise, exhort Him with music and song. For the Lord is the great God, the great King above all gods.' – Psalm 95:2-3

For many years, I was so scared to come out swinging because it felt like it was another thing I was doing alone while God just watched on. It seemed too hard, and honestly it felt like the victory had already been robbed from me. For nearly two decades I had no fight in me. I cowered in the corner, hoping it'd all be over soon, taking each punch and blow as best as I could. I couldn't hear all of heaven yelling for me to stand up and that I wasn't alone. When you're cowered in the corner, you don't see anyone else. Your head is down and buried under your arms. If you can imagine the saddest love song, then imagine pressing repeat – that's what the atmosphere of my heart was. Your head is down and you are swallowed up by the darkness, just how the devil likes it. But when you make a decision to stand up and fight back, you see your corner is full of people cheering you on!

Was my life as hard as it seemed to me? Maybe not, but the thing about pain is it's personal. To me, every good thing felt like it had been or was being robed, held back or withdrawn from me even if it wasn't. I thought I was already defeated, I couldn't see any point in fighting. My attitude was my biggest obstacle.

Pain can't always be explained seen, held or really explained, it can only be felt. When you're cowered in the corner, the atmosphere within your heart and mind is different to when you decide to come out swinging. As I reflect back though, I wonder if I really was robbed of my ability or I let it be stolen, or gave it away even. Is it really robbery if you did nothing to prevent it from being stolen? Can you say your home was robbed, if you left all your doors unlocked and windows open?

Anyone going through a painful situation knows what it's like to no longer feel hope or joy, and the ability to believe and trust in anything good feels almost impossible. Rarely do you feel peace and the atmosphere in your heart is dark and dull. Want some good news? The atmosphere can always be changed! The atmosphere in your heart and mind is like finding the right playlist and pressing repeat on that playlist every day. Listening to a playlist that reminds you of God's truths and rehearsing the goodness of His love, not retelling the lies you've just broken free from. I've often wondered how actors can remember so many lines and do scenes so naturally. It isn't just because they are good at remembering things, for some it makes it easier, but mostly it's because they rehearse.

The real story each of us lives and tells, isn't the ones we show on social media or boast about at parties. It's the story we rehearse when we think no one is watching – the story we tell ourselves, listen to and read the 'lines' we practice when we are alone. None of us can change the weather, make miracles happen or answer prayers. What we do have is the ability to change the atmosphere of our heart, and the way we react to pain itself.

The days behind me are done, and now I have the choice to choose what atmosphere I create in the days ahead. So do you. If you have breath in your lungs and a beating heart, you are not dead. Not even spiritually. There's someone higher and bigger fighting for you, believing in you and championing for you. God has never left your corner and never will. Just because the volume on your prayers might be muted, and everything you do is a struggle doesn't mean you are dead; you are still alive. Don't let your life become your tomb. Will you come out from your corner and take a swing?

Then he (God) said to me, "Prophesy to these bones and say to them, 'Dry bones, hear the word of the Lord! This is what the Sovereign Lord says to these bones: I will make breath enter you, and you will come to life. - Exekiel 37:4-5

'Generous in love – God, give grace! Huge in mercy – wipe out my bad record. Scrub away my guilt, soak out my sins in your laundry. I know how bad I've been; my sins are staring me down. You're the One I've violated, and you've seen it all, seen the full extent of my evil. You have all the facts before you; whatever you decide about me is fair. I've been out of step with you for a long time, in the wrong since before I was born. What you're after is truth from the inside out. Enter me, then; conceive a new, true life.'
– Psalm 51:1-6 MSG

28

The birth of joy

Imagine that feeling when God finally answers. *When* not if. Let that soak in for a moment. WHEN. I've always thought that meant I got the answer I wanted. I never thought or allowed myself to consider that God might answer my prayers differently to what I'd expected. If I prayed for chocolate ice cream, I never considered I could get chocolate ice cream with chocolate chips or low-fat chocolate ice cream. I wanted plain, traditional ice cream and that's what I thought I would get. Not always. It seemed like a foreign idea that I could have joy *before* God answered my prayer.

The story of Job is a classic one of a life that was strongly tested. Bad thing after bad thing kept happening to him and he had no reason why. All he wanted was for his life to go back to normal; keep his wife, his family, his success and regain his health. He wanted what had been taken to be restored. I would too. He never considered that when he prayed for the madness and the destruction to stop, anything would be good again. He never imagined his later life would be blessed even more than his earlier life. We are all guilty of thinking that God will give us what we want, when we want, how we want it and where we want it based upon the scriptures we read and sermons we hear. Rarely have I heard stories or testimonies of God answering prayers exactly the way people wanted. With God, it's generally unusual, different, creative, and normally quite the opposite to what we were hoping for (just like in Job's story). His answer is more extravagant than we were hoping for, better timed than we could foresee and generally way more creative than we could've have imagined. But rarely exactly how we wanted.

> *The Bible is clear, He does always answer. If that is the case, then I truly should be able and need to discipline myself to rest in His ways while I wait. I have been so focused on the timing of the promise that the delay meant I looked at my God in a way that limited His power, His love, and His Sovereignty in my life. I truly didn't understand, and to be really honest with myself, still don't. I don't understand why my heart yearns for something so intensely when you'd think by now, I'd be over it. But maybe, it was in this very moment when it all settled in my heart and made sense, God could be released to do what only He can do.*
>
> JOURNAL ENTRY 14.10.2019 - WHEN GOD FINALLY ANSWERS

By now, you'll know I'm a deep thinker. Someone who ponders and someone who always thinks about many things; often all at once. What I'm not is someone who can see something that isn't there. I need a list, set of instructions or guide. I'm so amazed at some of the dishes TV chefs make within a 30-minute program from nothing. Amazed they can start with just an idea of the finished product in their head, partnered with the understanding of what food does and doesn't work well together, and make something 'simple'. It's the same with renovations of homes. Like millions of people in the world, I adore Chip and Jo from the TV show *Fixer Upper*. I love watching the process of them removing walls, adding walls, painting things black; and it always looking great!

I'm someone who can see the end result if I've seen it before, maybe in a magazine or a drawing, I'm an excellent copycat. God, however, has a great eye for the unseen. God sees all the finer details many of us miss. Most times, God isn't the one holding the tools, He's the one in the master design room making it all happen. Gifting people with the skills and trade expertise to carry out His master plans. He can see all the elements and work them together perfectly, *and* He trusts Himself. He knows He can do it, is good at it and has the confidence to execute it without asking anyone else.

> *I have approached life and my prayers TO God like my dad has with his building plans. I have designed a plan and then asked God to be my builder, my electrician, my plumber and my general handyman to make it all happen. But isn't it supposed to be the other way? Isn't he supposed to be the designer and the builder and I am just the worker? Isn't He the one that can see everything in an instant and who has the perfect plan? Can I tell the snow where to fall on the earth, tell the rain where to wet the ground, the tides to go up or down, the wind to blow in a direction or the sun to sit in the blue sky a little longer? Um, no. I cannot. He can. Thank you for this reminder Lord, thank you for the story of Job and your mercy to forgive.*
> JOURNAL ENTRY 12.10.2019 - SUBMITTING THE PLANS

It's become clear to me, that for a long time, I held the Almighty One accountable to *my* building plan. I had an idea of how life was supposed to look and play out, and I hadn't allowed for alterations or changes or even delays to happen. Just like Job. Job had a rough time for a while. He lost everything and everyone. He was the definition of brokenness. He had every reason to be mad and frustrated, and deeply discouraged. If you haven't read the story of Job, I encourage you to do so! Right towards the end of the story, Job did something truly powerful. He repented. He acknowledged who God is and he surrendered his plans. He surrendered his will and he let God be the builder again. He did what he was supposed to do, rest in God's truth and wait for more instruction.

Job faced some pretty full-on things and I think it would break most of us at some point. Resting would've been pretty hard to do and waiting would've been torture. When I re-read Job's story, I finally understood God's whisper to me all those years ago at the Colour Conference I was sobbing at.

It was time to be responsible with my pain starting to take on a whole new understanding.

'Trespassers can steal our fruit from off the vines, and *now* every wild beast comes breaking through our walls to ravage us' – Psalm 80:13 TPT

At some point, I just had to say NO. No more. It's easy to blame God for not being where we want Him to be. Job did exactly that and I have too. But what about God's instruction in the Bible where He instructs us to resist the devil and he will flee? Is it like waving a fly away from your food or is there more to it than that? I found in that moment of my journal that it required more than waving him off my life. I had to let gratitude be my weapon, my voice if you will. Learning how to be responsible with the pain you're facing means, like me, you get serious about the condition of your heart and life, and our response to God. It's a confronting thought. You can't control any other person's will, Lord knows we have all tried!, but we can control the condition of our hearts.

'No good tree bears bad fruit, nor does a bad tree bear good fruit. Each tree is recognized by its own fruit. People do not pick figs from thorn bushes, or grapes from briers. A good man brings good things out of the good stored up in his heart, and an evil man brings evil things out of the evil stored up in his heart. For the mouth speaks what the heart is full of.' – Luke 6:43-46 NIV

The birth of joy comes when we change our perspective, and a changed perspective comes from surrendering all our feelings and emotions to God. I remember one time when everything was a real struggle shortly after piecing this book together. Joy was the last thing I felt. I was angry and I was broken. I simply couldn't be grateful for anything. Around this time I received an order for 120 of my books. I should have been ecstatic but instead I was made it wasn't more. There was no joy. I had a choice to keep

THE BIRTH OF JOY

living this way or listen to my own advice. I went to my quiet place and I got out my journal. I wrote down everything that I was mad about, and I mean everything! I filled two pages without lifting my pen. Then I wrote what I was grateful for, honestly grateful for. I filled 3 lines. That's it. But it was my birth place of joy again.

I was tired of throwing tantrums and the weight of my anger was getting too much. I can tell you wholeheartedly that when you allow joy to come into your world, your life really does change.

29

Praise is your weapon

Your praise (gratitude/thankfulness) makes room for what you've been praying for, it's the red carpet to your prayers. I have yet another question for you, have you ever wondered where people received the gift of laughter from? This might seem like a strange question and the answer is pretty obvious, but it didn't stop me from wondering one day. Where did I get my gift of laughter from? Jesus.

Laughter is a gift from God, sent directly from heaven.

We talk about joy in church, but not so much the outworking of joy – praise and laughter! I like to wonder about what it would look like to see Jesus laughing and having a good chuckle. Does He prefer classic dad jokes, or the witty kind? Does His laugh have an audible sound and does He cry tears when He is laughing really hard? I have no idea if He actually laughs, but after living nearly half my life already, I've come the conclusion He must have some kind of humorous side. Life itself just makes you laugh sometimes which makes me I think there's a good chance Jesus loves a good joke. I think He also likes to relax, to be creative, to be kind and gentle, to share wisdom and to bless us.

In that same podcast I listened to many years ago on the way to work,

Melissa shared a question her brother-in-law asked of her while she was in the midst of some serious pain, 'Is this season producing fruit from you?'. He asked her, "Are you being kind and generous to those around you? Are you laughing and sharing joy? Do you still have hope? Is your faith making you unmovable? Are you displaying love in your words and actions? If the answer is yes, then you have a reason to praise Him".

It wasn't the Israelites' natural ability that broke each brick in the walls of Jericho foundation, but their obedience to praise Him. Joy does something to the atmosphere and it rattles the devil. How can we be happy, praise and have joy when we're in deep seasons of pain? We should feel defeated, rejected and broken.

I like my worship music at a volume where I can't hear the enemy – Daneila Raena

Prasie confuses the devil so much when we're producing fruit in the biggest fight of our lives! It makes no sense we can be joyful when we have every reason to be the opposite, and still bear good fruit in our lives. I'm sure the devil does everything he could to stop the praise coming out of the Israelites as they walked around those walls. In their minds as they marched, I'm sure the devil was reminding each Israelite how tired they were, how silly this seemed, how unfair God was being and if He is who He says He is why doesn't He just bring the walls down. I'm sure the devil would've been working overtime that week and yet it still didn't work. They kept praising, pushing past the lies and the doubts and kept being obedient. Joy does something to the atmosphere.

Have you ever been to a large sporting event? The praise and admiration the fans have for their teams is close to overwhelming and incomprehensible. You can feel the shouting, the stomping of feet and clapping of hands in your chest, it rattles the very chair you sit on sometimes. It breaks invisible walls and people show different sides of themselves, me included! Being joyful defies logic. The devil knows the power of praise and he'll do everything he can to stop it. Remember that day I shared the Holy Spirit asked me to put praise on, not worship but praise. This is why. He knew some walls needed to come down, He knew the enemy needed to be put back in his place. God wanted me remind it was time to roll out the red carpet for the goodness of what was to come. Praise different to worship.

True praise puts you front and centre on the front battle line, when you've made a decision to come out and fight, praise is your lions roar! Praise puts you in an attacking position and that's why it costs more because it's hard to do when you don't *feel like it*. I can put worship on at any point, no issue, but when I want to put praise on, it's battle time. When I've been in the midst of true deep, smothering, debilitating pain – worship has been my greatest comfort and a soothing blanket for my soul.

It didn't ask any more of me than I was willing to give in that moment. Praise is different; it's a fast-moving train moving with purpose and direction. There's an intensity to it. If you want to be part of what's happening with praise, you need to move fast like trying to jump onto that fast-moving train so you're not late for work. There's an energy that can't be explained or denied. "I don't feel like that up-tempo music, I think I need to just receive at the moment, I am not in the mood for happy clappy music, I am tired!", I've said to myself. Why does the devil fight me when I want to put praise on, but the resistance is less with worship?

The devil knows that when I start to praise, I'm about to attack. It becomes my weapon. There's nothing I love more than embarrassing him and making him look stupid. He's tried to take me out many times, and spent years teasing and tormenting me (and I allowed it!) He has tried to be on the attack but when praise comes on he knows it's time to run, time to hide. Don't be the one to not know the power praise has, because your enemy does and he's hoping you'll never realise. Praise declares who God is and reminds him of what is rightfully mine. Praise says NO to the enemy's plans.

Praise pushes the devil back to the dark, cold and miserable hole he crawled out from. Can you now see how the joy of my Lord will be your strength (Nehemiah 8:10)?

How can joy be turned into strength? How can praise not be one of your most powerful weapons? Joy is a strength that can tear down strongholds, bring light into a dark situation or turn a heaviness into a light burden. A weapon that can destroy every lie of Satan and keep you safe. None of this in the natural makes sense, but we operate in a different realm of reality and truth. We operate with the understanding that when you lay down the natural and tap into the supernatural workings of Jesus Christ, the unexplainable, the unshakable, the otherwise unmovable and unimaginable is normal. Praise is just another way to open yourself up to positive thinking.

'May these words of my mouth and this meditation of my heart be pleasing in your sight, Lord, my Rock and my Redeemer.' – Psalm 19:14

'Rejoice always, pray continually, give thanks in all circumstances; for this is God's will for you in Jesus Christ. Do not quench the Spirit'. – 1 Thessalonians 5:16-19

You name it, I've had every reason not to praise God. My mum and two aunties took their own life, my mum & I've struggled financially for most of my life, my health has been in jeopardy, my first business failed, my confidence has been shattered and my womb has remained empty – and yet I've always had Jesus. I've always had Him and He has always had me. That is the foundation for my praise.

Praise isn't about saying you're happy with the way life is right now, it goes further. It states regardless of the darkness you're in now, you have God. You know He's already worked it all out, and He not only has worked it out but done more than I could ever do (Ephesians 3:20). Praise aligns your words with heaven over your promises, and means you start to see things in a positive frame of mind. Our words truly are powerful. You've probably heard it said at some point that you what you rehearse is what you become, and praise is simply rehearsing the good things God has for you.

A social experiment by 'Bully A Plant' demonstrated the power of a positive word. Praise. For 30 days, students were invited to compliment or bully one of two identical plants. The students' comments were fed through speakers rigged into each enclosure, and a recording device then transmitted the messages to each plant. After 30 days, the plant that received compliments was healthy and thriving, while its insult-riddled counterpart was wilted and noticeably droopy.

Your pain is like that plant, and ultimately, so is your life. There are days I don't speak nicely to my 'plant' and it's evident. When I praise God, that very same plant comes alive. It's as though it glistens even! Despite it all, praise will always be the best response. Praise can be simply defined as taking notice of what God has done (or is going to do, or well able to do), keeping account and giving Him praise.

Take a moment to maybe look how far God has brought you. If that alone is your reason to praise despite it all, that's enough.

30

Prepare for what's next

'I start talking...' – Psalm 40:4-5 MSG

My husband and I are not ones to unpack our bags when we go on holidays. We unpack our toiletries and important items, but other than that we are happy to live for that week or so out of a suitcase. Halfway through our holiday we find ourselves repacking though, sorting through which clothes are clean and which are not. There's a point in each season of pain too, where you have to sort through what is helpful and not. Decide what you'll carry with you and what you'll leave behind. We all have a choice.

Every time, in all my different seasons of pain, I could've chosen to turn back and retrace the steps I'd already walked. I could've done it the same as before, or I could do some rearranging to keep moving forward. I don't know about you, but the very thought of walking back through all of that I've come from makes me ill, so does the thought of nothing changing and staying exactly where I am. Therefore, I was left with one option - to keep walking forward, walking through.

Marathon runners come to mind when I think of the wanting to give up and pushing through to what's next. Running 42 kilometres is not my idea of fun, give me a slide and waterpark with endless ice cream and cheese pizza any day over a marathon! The mental toll it must take to run so many kilometres is huge. When marathon runners hit a certain point, their bodies ache and they're beyond tired. They're depleted of almost everything and there's a moment where they probably want to give up.

How many times did they want to give up? How many times did they think they couldn't keep going? How many times did they then think – but I only have halfway to go now!

In that moment is where most of the damage has occurred for me. At the start, I was completely unaware of what awaited me and often found myself caught off guard. I was fully expectant the journey wouldn't take as long as it was, and I definitely wasn't prepared for what was next! When it stopped being easy and the cramps and fatigue set in, I began to wrestle with what little strength I had left. I bombared God with endless questions of why and when, instead of surrendering to Him and letting His peace, love and joy renew my strength. The very thought of taking another step made me more tired and unsettled, I doubted I could even do it. More often than not, resentment always tried to find a home in these moments, until I found the beauty in them. These moments turned into rest stations to catch my breath.

When you're here, whether it's in the middle or towards the end or even nor far from the start, everything seems to go slower. It's as if life is passing you by, that's how it feels for me anyway, and the slowness was just another thing that created more frustration. It can be the most precious part of the journey. At this very moment is where a beautiful exchange happens, the old is exchanged for the new. We are being prepared for what's next.

'He has given me a new song to sing.' – Psalm 40:3 NLT

I love playlists on Spotify, and more so I love to make my own! It's like the new way of making your very own mixed tap (it's what we did before

Spotify for anyone wondering what I'm talking about!). All the playlists I make are very specific. Some have been created to help me through my grief with mum, and actually still offer great support now on some hard days. There are some that build my hope and faith, others are safe places for me to unravel and some are just a reason to dance! Each has its time and place. In the moments where God is preparing me for what's next, the same song that helped my heart to heal when I thought I was alone, isn't the same song I am now declaring over my future days. Does that make sense?

Let me try it this way. There's a term called 'old fuel'. Old fuel is fuel that's no longer any good or will be of any benefit to the engine if used. If anything, old fuel can cause damage to the engine. Sometimes people are tempting to use old fuel when they break down or need to top up, but using old fuel can be very harmful as it can cause long lasting issues to the car's engine. Just like old fuel can be tempting to use, but crippling, when a car is broken down halfway through a road trip, so can't some old ways of thinking get you through the next leg of your journey.

At this very moment in whatever season and situation you're in, imagine right now Jesus is giving you a new song to sing for what's next. Think of it as a fresh tank of gas in your fuel tank. There's a moment where the brokenness of what hasn't been or alternatively, has been, doesn't matter anymore. Towards the end of my anorexic years, my song wasn't about why I wasn't eating anymore. That had been addressed and the next part of my journey was how do I heal from that. I had learn how to eat while managing the onslaught of thoughts raging in my head, and how to love my body even though it was beginning to look different. I was becoming aware of what my triggers were, and what my reactions to those triggers were. It was about being responsible with each obstacle that came my way to stop me from eating again.

It was no different in the middle of my ten-year pain after mum died, God gave me a new song of strength so I could courageously do life without her.

It isnt't about me feeling sorry for myself and denying it happened, or even that it didn't then or does now still hurt. I still miss her and my heart is still heavy but I have a new song to sing. And the same was in my fertility journey. There came I point where I had to move past not being pregnant. It wasn't about knowing why anymore, or being mad at myself (or God) for not doing enough. Instead it was about coming to a place of full surrender to His ways. It wasn't about being without or having lack in my life but instead, singing a song that keeps me hopeful and joyful.

I want to make some very clear before we continue, reaching this point isn't a distance thing. I don't believe being in here is like being exactly in the middle. You don't automatically have the same amount of time or distance to travel on the other side (thank goodness!). Just because I waited ten years to become pregnant, I don't think it means I have another ten to wait for God's goodness to flow from that season. I think being at this point is more of a mental thing than an actual logistical thing. It's a turning point, a decision, an exchange point. How many times has life not turned out how you wanted it to?

Maybe your marriage didn't work, your kids dropped out of school, you're distant from your family, your dream job stopped abruptly, you got really sick, or you haven't had the children you thought you would. In the below scripture Jesus gets it. He explains how the jar wasn't turning out how the potter wanted so he squashed it and started again. My goodness I have come to love the word *again*.

'This is the word that came to Jeremiah from the Lord: "Go down to the potter's house, and there I will give you my message." So I went down to the potter's house, and I saw him working at the wheel. But the pot he was shaping from the clay was marred in his hands; so the potter formed it into another pot, shaping it as seemed best to him. Then the word of the Lord came to me. He said, "Can I not do with you, Israel, as this potter does?" declares the Lord. "Like clay in the

> hand of the potter, so are you in my hand, Israel. If at any time I announce that a nation or kingdom is to be uprooted, torn down and destroyed, and if that nation I warned repents of its evil, then I will relent and not inflict on it the disaster I had planned. And if at another time I announce that a nation or kingdom is to be built up and planted, and if it does evil in my sight and does not obey me, then I will reconsider the good I had intended to do for it. "Now therefore say to the people of Judah and those living in Jerusalem, 'This is what the Lord says: Look! I am preparing a disaster for you and devising a plan against you. So turn from your evil ways, each one of you, and reform your ways and your actions.' But they will reply, 'It's no use. We will continue with our own plans; we will all follow the stubbornness of our evil hearts.' – Jeremiah 18:1-12 NIV

If *again* was to be a picture, I think this story in Jeremiah would be it. I used to hate the word *again*. I used to hate to pray *again*. I used to hate to hope *again*. I used to hate to forgive *again*. I used to hate to surrender my plans and dreams *again*.

Every time, I felt like I'd failed with what I'd been given, if anything at all. Every time, the devil loved to remind me what he thought *again* meant, and I believed him for a long time. My frustration, anger, resentment, lies and disappointment would grow. In those years it felt as though God kept letting me down, again and again. That He wasn't big enough to rise above whatever was standing in my way. The truth was and still is, He is big enough but I had reduced Him to a size that made Him small and unable. The very squashing of my dreams, that which upset me most, was the very blessing He was giving. Again was actually all about what was next.

> 'Satan's angel did his best to get me down; what he in fact did was push me to my knees. No danger then of walking around high and mighty! At first, I didn't think of it as a gift, and begged God to remove it. Three times I did that, and then he told me, "My grace is

enough; it's all you need. My strength comes into its own in your weakness". Once I heard that, I was glad to let it happen. I quit focusing on the handicap and began appreciating the gift. It was a case of Christ's strength moving in on my weakness.' – 2 Corinthians 12:7-10 MSG

I suppose to be really simple, preparing for what's next is a bit like brushing your teeth. If you don't brush your teeth, plaque will set in. Plaque is a hard substance, so hard a dentist often needs multiple utensils, even a drill, to remove it from our teeth. Plague can be hidden and even seem invisible, but regardless of that, it eats away and destroys your teeth. If plaque is not dealt with, holes and decay start and eventually the root of the tooth is attacked. When we are here I think God does a dental check-up on our pain.

He knows what's next and this where He is preparing us for it. Don't despise the fact that time feels like it is standing still or going slower than normal. Please don't despise the oasis of rest He is giving you before you have to get back on your way to your promise. At this very point of my pain, is where I felt Him do His deepest and purest work. Let Him remove the plaque – the pain, the resentment, the anger, the doubt, the frustration – that has found its way into my heart and begun to set in place. He is chipping away at the hardness so my heart can beat freely and my lips can sing a new song for my new journey.

Will you repack your bags differently to the way they were originally packed? Will you leave behind the things that make your journey heavier or harder than it needs to be? Will you let God take some of the heavy lifting and allow your load to be lighter?

31

Your future is waiting

It's not surprise to know that looking in the mirror for many years was an interesting experience. At times, I've seen myself as the beautifully created woman God took great care with. I see myself as fierce and confident, and I see the woman my husband seems to always see. In those moments, I feel safe to lean into and believe the words I've heard my husband say over me, about me and to me. For a moment, I even believe them and I feel the warmth of his words as they become my reality. In these moments it's easy to appreciate God's craftsmanship of me and easily confess He did indeed do a good job when creating me in His image. It isn't vanity, it's deep appreciation.

Then there's the days the woman looking back at me is someone I'd rather not see. Her nose is a funny shape, she has dark circles under her eyes, her hair is full of grey hairs and so on. I do everything I can to avoid seeing the reflection staring straight back at me. In those moments I try to look away, but as I start to turn my gaze away, my reflection is demanding my attention, desperate for me to see myself. The thing about looking in the mirror, there's usually no one else. No filters, no hashtags, no backdrops or fancy backgrounds – just me looking at me. Just you looking at you.

'Every single moment you are thinking of me! How precious and wonderful to consider that you cherish me constantly in your every thought' Psalm 139:17-18 TPT

"Mirror, mirror on the wall, who is the fairest of them all?"

We've all heard that line in the classic Disney movie, *Snow White*. Maybe like me, you've even said that to your mirror at home (come on be honest, you've said it at least once!). My question is, who gave 'the' mirror, any mirror, so much power over us? How has a single pane of mirrored glass become something so powerful in our lives, a way of measuring ourselves? For years I allowed the mirror to lie to me on a daily basis, and allowed the enemy to use it as his greatest weapon against me. That weapon nearly took my life. Nearly.

What if we, me included, took the power away from the mirror? What if I was the one who did the talking and told the mirror some home truths about myself, and my future?

Power is only truly effective if you know how to use it. When someone is trained to be a police officer, they're taught to be responsible with the weapons they're entrusted to use when needed. They're taught the damage it can cause if not used correctly, and how effective it can be when used as needed. Why is a mirror any different?

I truly wish someone had given me responsible mirror training before I was given one, or allowed me be in front of one. I wish someone had told me how to use it correctly, and the damage it can cause when used incorrectly. Some parents hold their children back a year in school because they know they aren't ready for what awaits them, I wish I'd been held back a little longer before being placed in front of a mirror. I was completely unprepared or ready for battle. I wish someone had told me I can let it have as much power over me as I allow.

What do I want to see when I look in the mirror?

I want to see a woman, who will have a thankful heart. Who will be thankful no matter the storm she faces or the pain she is in, the place she finds herself in or the path she is led on. I want to be a woman who sees past the physical and instead sees a woman who has faults but isn't limited or held back by them. Who sees a woman with pain and insecurity and who STILL stands declaring God's truth and reality. A woman who still chooses life.

JOURNAL ENTRY : date unknown

We spend our lives continually looking in the mirror and catching a reflection of who we want to see or tell ourselves we are. Constantly checking our outfits, hair, makeup, shoes and everything else. The truth is we are constantly looking at ourselves! Imagine if we just looked at ourselves in the mirror on Monday morning and didn't do it again until the following Monday. Mirrors are a blessing when we know how to use them. For someone who's spent a lot of time in front of a mirror, I've never really liked it. Why? Normally because I didn't have the courage to see myself.

I've mentioned many times already how I've found a lot of solace and comfort in being alone. I adore people and being around them, but time to myself is something I also deeply cherish. Admittedly there have been times I've enjoyed being along a little too much, it's always been a known place for me. I've found safety in hiding over the years, but that can be a dangerous place too. When you hide, you're isolated. There's no one else in that space – obviously, otherwise it wouldn't really be called hiding, would it?

One of the hardest sentences I've type in this book is, "I've definitely hidden from my husband". Well I've felt like I've hidden from him, but I after I gave him a copy of this to read before I published it, he told me even if I never put volume to all of my thoughts and feelings he knew. He knew I needed to do this my way, just as he needed to do it his way. He's known sometimes I just had to let the tears fall, I had to find something to laugh about to break the grief, and he's known when he had to let God hold me when he desperately wanted to. Somehow he knew I'd be okay either way. My husband's care for me has always gone above and beyond. He knows me better than I think he does, and I'm so grateful he's let me work through my pain my way, in my time.

I'm not proud of how I've always dealt with my pain over the years, or that I've hid from my husband. It isn't because I don't trust his love or capability to hold me. It was more that if I made my pain real, with our fertility journey, I made his real too. I thought if I hid my tears and only showed him my strength, I'd make it easier for him. Purposely, I've taken every pregnancy test alone, not because I didn't need him or want him there. I didn't want his hope to be crushed all over again, or for him to see how much it hurt me each time. I thought if restricted myself from falling into his arms, I could be the one to hold him up. But he was the one wanting to catch me. I've hidden my true feelings and thoughts about my fertility pain because I thought it would help him, and shield him. I've even tried to pretend this whole painful mess isn't real for me. But it is real, for both of us. It's very real, and sometimes it's been more real than anything else happening in our life. We just processed our pain differently.

It's not uncommon to hear stories about husbands struggling to understand the intensity of infertility for a woman and it's been no different for my husband and I over the years. For me, it's felt like a giant octopus in my life, not ours, but mine. From this one deep desire and pain, many little pains seem to have grown from it. Like the tentacles off the main body of an octopus, it reached into my work life, affected how I made every decision, and my relationships with friends and family. Holidays were put on hold in case I fell pregnant. Jobs weren't pursued in case I fell pregnant within the first month and lost the maternity benefits of my existing employment. Everything I ate and didn't eat was put under the microscope; maybe I ate the wrong food, I exercised too much or not enough, or maybe the wine or soft cheese I ate caused something to go wrong. Even though every test under the sun said my husband and I were (are still are!) physically perfect, nothing ever felt very perfect about any of it. For him however, it was just something that wasn't happening. We tried and it wasn't meant to be for us.

As a (very broad!) generalisation, men can tend to see things pragmatically and women can be more emotionally led. This can make dealing with things hard at times, especially when the man can't do anything to fix it or make it better. Although my husband loved me before we ever thought about having a family, as I do him, his heart still hurts when he sees a family on a night out bowling together; or a dad teaching a son to fish at the father's not-so-hidden fishing spot, he manages his heartache differently to me.

He made his desire to be a dad just another thing that he doesn't give much thought to anymore. For the whole ten years we struggled with this, I couldn't just put it in a category of 'not happening' like the old Ford pickup truck that sits in our backyard *we will* restore one day. Even though he never said it, I know he struggled at times to understand why I couldn't be okay with what we had rather than what we didn't. I can now.

I couldn't let go because, for me, I wanted it all. I wanted more and to be very honest, I wanted what everyone else had too. I wanted to see him hold his own child. I wanted to see his eyes filled with so much love as he looked at me as only a man can when they share the knowledge they created another life together. I wanted to see him teach our child how to ride a bike. I wanted him to see me as a mother. I wanted Him to see God had a plan all along and that He hears every prayer and catches every tear. I wanted our conversations to be more than just us. I wanted the sleepless nights, the full dinner table, the messy car and the snuggles in bed. I wanted it all. But they are big things to say and admit, so I hid it all.

The truth is not many saw, or will know of my husband's heartache, because his life doesn't reflect it. He doesn't hide it, but he doesn't tell everyone about it like me. He still chases dreams, is generous to anyone and finds the joy in life. One of the biggest compliments I can give him is that his life reflects his heart, not his pain. I thought by hiding my pain I was doing the same thing. Watching my husband do his side of this journey has taught me our life reflects what's on the inside, no matter who you are.

Some can put a filter over their heart, their words and actions. Some can pretend for a while, but ultimately our life will always show the true condition of our heart. Some people, like my husband, live life really well regardless of the pain inside their heart. Some people try to hide it all, like I did for a long time. Our future, as is yours, is waiting for you. There are better days ahead, and maybe more hard days too. Hiding all your feeling is only holding back your future, this I know well. I was so busy hiding everything, holding everything together, I had nothing left to give to my future. All my energy was being used to cover up everything I wasn't brave enough to share, and then I wrote this book. Nothing is hidden now!

No one truly knew about my life when I was a child. A few select friends saw parts of it, as well as my dad and my church family, but no one ever saw it all because I never told anyone. During my years of anorexia, I didn't tell anyone how hungry and scared I truly was. They saw me get skinny and sick but no one ever knew how broken I was inside. I didn't want them to feel more responsible for my pain. I wanted to be rescued so desperately, but no one could because no one ever knew.

When sadness hit my heart after mum left the country, and then left this world, I didn't tell anyone how sad I was and how lost I felt. I didn't ever tell anyone how lonely and sad I had been in case they thought I was crazy like they thought she was. Mental illness is hard for people to understand, and I knew how people saw my mum. How could I not, she knew how they saw her and that broke my heart. I heard the whispers and saw the looks, so did she. I learnt to hide what my heart was feeling from her as I watched her hide the pain and shame she felt.

I didn't want the same whispers about me or the same looks sent my way.

In my pain of not having a child or the life we'd hoped for, I found myself hiding again. Hiding from the very people who love me regardless of it all. Hiding from the very people who just wanted to be my shelter in the mess. Hiding only meant I was in living in darkness. Thankfully God knew where I was, and He wasn't content with me being hidden. His love was the very invitation to turn my pain into a beautiful reflection of His power and grace.

'Jesus called out to them, "Come, follow me, and I will show you how to fish for people!" And they left their nets at once and followed him.'
– Matt 4:19-20 NLT

Your life is a beautiful story, all of it, not just the good bits. If I disregarded the painful bits, the dark bits and the not so easily told bits, the book wouldn't be in your hands encouraging you right now. You may have hidden your past or what you have been feeling, but don't hide from your future. God has rolled out the red carpet and wants to put a spotlight on you. When the world celebrates you, it celebrates Him!

Don't choose to be alone. For some of us, there will be a large part of us that we will be alone in life BUT there will always be invitations to say yes to. It is a choice to push past what you feel and to believe what is real - remember there's fact and the truth! Your life has the potential to be a great story. How do you remain happy when you're surrounded by sadness? How can you still believe when nothing has happened? My prayer is that your eyes would be open to the precious people God has placed as the guards in your life, not to lock you up but the ones to unlock the gates and set you free.

V

A PROMISED LIFE

Chapters thirty two - forty

32

Miracles still happen

Just because I wasn't at the Superbowl in 1979 where the Steelers defeated the Cowboys, it doesn't mean it didn't happen. It's not much different with God's miracles. Just because I haven't received the miracle I've spent the last 10 years asking and praying for, doesn't mean God doesn't has run out of promises, or do them anymore. Earlier I shared the story of Moses mum, a complete act of surrender and trust. I want to touch on it again because I think her story fits well here too.

'Then she placed the child in it and put it among the reeds along the bank of the Nile.' – Exodus 2:3 NIV

I can only imagine the variety of emotions and thoughts going through Moses's mum's mind at this point. She had just put her baby boy into the Nile, and while the bible doesn't tell us God told her to do this, I think it's safe to assume He was still heavily involved. I have no doubt she prayed to God and asked for His help with this. When the time came for her to release her little baby into the river, I'm sure she felt grief like she'd never felt before and wondered if this was the right thing to do. I'm curious if she questioned if God really loved her like I feel I would've at that moment. Once she let go of that basket, it was all in God's hands. All the dreams she had of raising her boy, gone and in God's hands. All the memories she thought they'd make, gone and in God's hands. All the meals she thought they'd share, gone and in God's hands.

I wonder if she believed miracles still happened after this? Little did she know her story of trust was about to become one of the most amazing miracles to happen that we're still learning from over 2000 years later! She carried this child, she bonded with this child and she would've had dreams for this child. In one moment she was a mum, and in the next, she wasn't. But is that really true? Was she no longer a mother because she was no longer holding her baby? I don't believe so. I believe who she was still remained – she was a mother. She still had another child but even she didn't, she was still a mother. I don't think who we are changes because our external circumstances do, unless we allow it to. We have a choice to believe who we are.

"I have loved you with an everlasting love; therefore I have continued my faithfulness to you." - Jeremiah 31:3

What if I never become a mum? That used to be the hardest question I ever said out loud. I always believed it would happen until the moment I knew it wasn't going to. The truth of who I hasn't changed and the truth of who God is hasn't either. Just because I didn't get the miracle I wanted doesn't mean they don't still happen. Go to a hospital and tell me miracles don't happen! God is still God and I am still loved. God is still God and I am still seen. God is still God and I am still heard. God is still God and I am still valued. God is still God and I am still created for a purpose. God is still God and I am still able to accomplish so many things.

I still have a plan upon my life regardless of whether I ever became a mother or not, as do you. The reality is I will never feel life grow in my belly or sit in the bathroom, completely shocked while holding a positive pregnancy test and, our parents will never be grandparents.

I will also never......

Have the chance to buy baby clothes for myself as I've done for many friends over the years. Have a child to feed, to love, nurse and to hold. Know what true exhaustion feels like after many sleepless nights. Be able to tell you why it didn't happen for us but so easily for others. Know what it is like to wake up on Christmas morning or Easter Sunday with all of us in the bed feeling love explode over all of us. Know what it is like to look at a tiny human for hours and being lost in complete awe and wonder. Feel the bond that a husband and wife feel when they are responsible for little humans and I may never know what raw, intense stress feels like. Know what it is like to have a miracle celebrated at my own baby shower or see what the female human body can do at childbirth.

I simply will never know.

That doesn't mean I who I am dissolves too, or what my purpose is. When God leaves us seemingly empty handed we still always have something. What do you have? For me personally I have time, and lots of it. It's my choice how I use it. I used to spend my time poorly, believing that I was worthless and sitting around waiting for someone to wave their magic wand to make everything better. That all changed after an intense night of wrestling with God and myself, my time became a gift not a curse.

My time grew into a gift of writing. I've always written cards that are mini novels, sent long text messages and written in many, many journals. As time went on I got a little braver and started a social media page and a blog where I shared my thoughts and elements of my story. Some people make a big splash in the world, honestly I've been envious of that but I have learnt that God's plan is often better even if it's different. As my presence grew I realised something, everything we do has a ripple effect into other lives. I'm far from anyone famous, but the truth is I'm an influencer and so are you!

Hear me out! We influence people every day with our reactions to what happens to us and how we live every day. The time I would've had to raise children now goes into my writing, to my candle making and to my videos that I make to share my story so others find encouragement to live out theirs. I connect with many people each day, that can't happen unless you have the gift of time. My time has also meant I can be available where others can't - in my church, local volunteer groups, my family and friends who need extra help and support. I used to think I had nothing, or nothing left, if my promises weren't living and breathing in front of me. How wrong I was!

When Moses' mum let go of that basket, she would've never known what was next. The rest of this story is just miracle after miracle and definitely worth reading. Maybe for you it's not about being a mother and it's about being married, starting a business, writing a book, starting a health journey, or accomplishing a dream. Who we are is who we are, but that doesn't mean there it can't change because of painful times in our life. In my experience there's only been one way to make this easier than harder – surrender. Honest and real surrender like the one Moses' mum exampled for us. While there are so many powerful stories of surrender in the Bible, none stirs me like this one (oh, Daniel and the lions is a close second!).

Surrender is hard, no doubt about it. Moses' mum seemed to trust God so easily but I'm not sure I would've personally. A real thought of 'what now' stirs something deep within me. This incredibly brave woman didn't spend the rest of her days by the bank of the Nile crying (that we know of - as I would have done!), waiting and cursing the name of God. I'm sure she spent *some* time by those banks in deep grief, but at some point she had to get up. Her hands were empty but the truth was she was still a mother, and each of her days still had hours in them for her live out. It's a vulnerable place to be, and I think that's where God wants us sometimes. When our days are full and busy, it's easy to think we know who we are. We give ourselves, and allow other people to give us titles, but the title God gives us is the one that really matters.

Last night was pure turmoil, well at least it felt like it. Physically, emotionally and spiritually. It felt like an endless wrestle where I would catch my breath for a moment, only to be drawn back into the fight. It was real last night and it was intense. My mind was filled with rogue thoughts and dreams, my body was sweaty and unsettled, and my spirit oh so anxious. I'd love to say I came out victorious like Jacob did after his wrestle with God, but I didn't, well I don't think so anyway. I woke up this morning feeling defeated and deflated. How can you hear the voice of God only days before, so clear and confidently, only to be so lost so soon after? Even Jesus was tempted after He experienced the greatness of God upon Him, but it is still a significant wonder to me. Am I back at the start of it all again? Does the clock reset? Has God had enough of my failures and setbacks? When do I get the strength and ability to fight harder, better even? Is this who I am?

'Claire, God is not an accidental God. This morning wasn't about making you feel small and insignificant, quite the opposite. God was there with you last night. His heart was to bring you close again and soften your heart towards yourself.

The Israelites suffered because they didn't change, and they wanted God to do everything for them, all the time. They never got responsible with their situation, or their pain. They didn't have these stories to encourage them, like you do. Don't waste them. The continued to act like children. You won't break free of all that comes at you if you don't start to act differently and teach yourself to think differently. But you can't do any of that until you know who you are. When you know who you are, you don't despise the wrestle or the temptation. When you know who you are you are stronger in the fight and those questions you asked have already been answered.' – Holy Spirit

JOURNAL ENTRY 17.10.2019 – WHO YOU ARE

I still remember that night clearly. I'd never experienced anything like it but I'm thankful for it. I needed that night to wrestle away false beliefs of who I thought I was and be reminded of who He said I was. I remember waking up the following morning feeling like I had nothing left, but maybe that was the whole point and actually a gift. Prior to that morning, all my questions came from a place of me not knowing who I was.

Are you willing for your story to be His touch of truth and love to another? Have you considered that your gifts were formed in the fire of your battles?

Only after that night of wrestle and discomfort was I able to hear His voice clearly again. Even though I was in pain that day and have been in days after, the questions of His love for me had answers. The miracle my husband and I wanted so badly might not have come to fruition but that doesn't mean miracles still don't happen. Oh my goodness they do. In the absence of that miracle coming to life for us, many more miracles have been given space to bloom - this book is just one of them. When you know who you are, you begin to see life (all of it) as a wonderful opportunity to do things you might normally been too busy or blind to see.

"Consider it a sheer gift, friends, when tests and challenges come at you from all sides. You know that under pressure, your faith-life is forced into the open and shows its true colours. So don't try to get out of anything prematurely. Let it do its work so you become mature and well-developed, not deficient in any way. If you don't know what you're doing, pray to the Father. He loves to help. You'll get his help, and won't be condescended to when you ask for it." - James 2-5 MSG

Each day is full of wonder and miracles. Even the painful ones are gifts too.

They give you a chance to see how much bigger God is than anything you face and that's when joy starts to explode instead of just pain. When I truly understood who I was, there was finally room in my heart for more joy than anything else. Just like a garden has to be stripped and pruned during different seasons so new growth can occur, so is the same with our life.

MIRACLES STILL HAPPEN

We can too easily think God is shrinking our world in seasons of pain, when really He is making room for more than we could ever have dreamed about.

When I understood this my life became less about my world shrinking and instead seeing how much bigger it was becoming, I started not only seeing that miracles still happen but that I'm part of some of them! This has helped shorten the time it takes me to turn my pain into something that gives me joy and hope when I find myself in another season of pain and struggle. The truth is, my gardens weren't stripped and empty – they were just being prepared to bloom and be a harvest.

33

No shame in again

How many times have you made a new year's resolution or started a new diet? We all have and I'm sure we will make many more, again! Over the years, managing my pain has been like making new year's resolutions or starting a diet all over again.

I wish I could say I was completely free of pain as I wrote this book, but I am not and that is okay. I wish I could say I am an expert at managing it perfectly, but I am not and that is okay. I am, however, getting better at managing each new season of struggle and learning to live with pain with more hope and faith than the last. With every new challenge, setback, loss or failure, I've had to dust myself off and start back at chapter one all over, again.

It sounds strange I know but doing things over and over should be something I'm used to given where I live, Queensland. Let me explain. We flood a lot and it's something that happens almost every summer in some part of the state. Many homes built in the far north, and even in certain areas of our capital city, are built on stilts so they can be safe from the rising flood waters. Personally I've never had my house flood and hopefully never will, the images you see are heartbreaking. When the flood hits there's little you can do. As the waters rise, the house becomes filled with mud and mess.

As quickly as they rose, the water seems to go too but what it leaves behind doesn't go so quickly. After the water is gone what remains are the visible signs of where the muddied waters were. The clean-up is overwhelming to be blunt. So much damage and mess, and then there's the smell. Tropical not only means swaying palm trees, warm sunshine and long sandy beaches, but it also means lots of humidity. If the sight of muddied walls and furniture isn't enough to overwhelm you, the smell absolutely would. Our humid climate makes floods a really unpleasant time.

What astounds me when I watch this happen every year though, is the response of the residents to the flood. I've not heard one person interviewed rant about how unfair it was, they're sad and in shock, but not much room for blame. I've not heard one person being interviewed yell at the reporter to be more sensitive, if they do they never show it! There just doesn't seem to room or time for bitterness. Instead, there's a sense of appreciation. How can they be appreciative at a time like this? Because they prepared for it I think. They prepared for *again*. I really think preparation is vital. When you purchase a house, there are numerous checks done prior to the sale being finalised, including checks to see whether your home sits on a flood plain or not. Some of these residents knew the risks and prepared the best way they could to avoid the damage. For those who have been flooded before, they do everything they can to ensure they won't be flooded again. They add water pumps, raise the house, change how they live, and change where things are placed in the house. Sometimes it's not enough. Sometimes it floods again. You can imagine the sense of hopelessness and despair in these moments. It would feel as though everything is dead.

Again, they clean up. Again, they deal with so much damage and mess. Again, they move while their house is repaired. Again, there's that smell. Again, the carpet needs to be replaced and the walls repainted. Again, the electrical equipment needs to repaired and rewired. Again, they cry and wipe their tears. Again, they feel deflated and defeated. Again, they have to ask for help or spend money from their savings. Again. What's the alternative?

> **'And don't allow yourselves to be weary or disheartened in planting good seeds, for the season of reaping the wonderful harvest you've planted is coming!' – Galatians 6:9 TPT**

The alternative is living in a home that smells, is falling apart and is full of dirt. Doing all that again might seem too much, but not doing it has to be worse. A lot of the time we can't choose when or how pain enters our life, quick or slow, the choice you do have though, is whether it becomes your best friend. Will you allow it to be a permanent feature in your life, quietly shaping your responses to the situations we walk through and the relationships we build?

A long time ago, I decided I was allowed, and even deserved, a good life regardless of the pain that had been in my life. Pain wasn't my full stop, it was just a comma. My decision meant I wanted to honour the days ahead of me instead of glorifying the ones behind me. I wanted to live well despite my pain, and so did God!

I wanted to still be a good friend who could celebrate in the joys happening for others. I wanted to still reach out to my family and make myself available even when I didn't feel like it. I wanted my pain to help me to reach others, rather than just give volume to my own voice. The real change came when I matched those decisions with actions. I became passionate about making healthy life giving choices while in pain, choices that resulted in better things for my life. Some of those choices meant I had to learn who I could lean into and who I needed to keep at a distance. It's the same for your choices, they'll either build a home or tear one down. What choices are you making?

Have you ever hit 'repeat' on your favourite song? I love a good 90's boy band hit and have been guilty of hitting 'repeat' one too many times when they come up on my Spotify playlists! On a side note, I'm amazed that after nearly 20 years I can still remember the lyrics and what I was doing when I first heard the song. Anyone else?

Imagine if we hit *repeat* on God's Word, and on the truth of who we are again? Imagine if we hit *repeat* on God's promises by reminded ourselves of His promises, again? Imagine if we hit *repeat* on all the things we learnt along the way when we were stuck in the middle of our pain and practiced what we'd learnt, again? Every time I've done this, it's been a chance to learn something new or to be taken back to something I had forgotten.

There have been many times since I have recovered from anorexia where I forgot my value. I forgot that how much my body weighed didn't determine my worth, and in those moments I had to again ask Him to remind me again. This sometimes lasted months at a time. While I don't have the fondest memories of my wedding dress fittings, I'm thankful God used that time to heal wounds that still needed addressing. Looking in the mirror since has become less of a struggle because I learnt to repeat His Word over me. He formed all of us, knew us and loved us before we weighed a single gram. My weight doesn't determine how good God is to me, or how beautiful I am to anyone else.

Similarly, I had to learn how to surrender and trust Him each time my periods came, or after a new doctor's appointment. They've been the hardest by far, along with building my business. Those wounds took a long time to heal. It was a daily wrestle at times to choose to repeat (and believe) God's promises in spite of the reality I was in. Again, I chose to repeat God's love for myself, my husband and our dreams even when love felt like it was the furthest thing away from me at the time. Suddenly I found myself back at one of these opening chapters, again. Relearning how to bring God's Word back into my reality. Every time I hit repeat it took effort and intention, but the more I did it and the quicker I hit the repeat button the easier it got. Each time I did, I felt God pull me a little closer, my faith get a little stronger and my hope come alive again. It was hard to be appreciative for what I had when I felt like I had nothing at all, but the truth was, I had so much.

I've come to the belief that God often brings us back to a place where we've been before so no wound is left open and exposed. The Oxford Dictionary defines the word repeat as something to say, do, produce, or it's a thing told to oneself or a thing to occur again. I love that in the very definition of repeat, the word *again* is present. Honestly, I'd love to tell you that you won't have to hit repeat in life, but the truth is at some point you probably will.

I didn't think there'd be anymore after all I had gone through and yet then came the biggest of them all – loneliness. All the other battles have been seasons that have come and gone, but loneliness has been the one woven through all of them. There's a famous quote that I strongly believe - 'there's a definite difference between being alone and feeling lonely'. I've felt both each independently and both at the same time, by far loneliness is the worse of the two. As I shared in the opening chapters, I used to struggle with being alone and did everything I could to be with people...and then Covid hit!.

When the world went quiet because of Covid, loneliness and I had some time to look at each other straight in the eye. This when God asked me to write a little each day. As I wrote this book, I reflected and the healing began. I was still alone, but not lonely.

I was alone, but not abandoned or rejected. I was alone, but not cast aside or forgotten. I was alone, and peaceful because I was full of purpose and joy. I was alone, and I knew my God. I was discovering and finding God in it all. I took the time all over again to find out who He was and in turn I found who I was. Whatever your pain is now or has been, it will never truly be gone from your life until deal with it. If you're wondering why it keeps hanging around or you can't seem to shake it, maybe it's because it's still hindering and holding you back. If it's still causing you, and maybe others, pain then God wants to free you of it. It may really hurt to do so, but so worth it.

Again, you may need to forgive. Again, you may need to surrender. Again, you may need to ask for help. Again, you may need to pray. Again, you may need to cry. Again, you may need to apologise.

'My old identity has been co-crucified with Messiah and no longer lives; *for the nails of his cross crucified me with him.* **And now the essence of this new life is no longer mine, for the Anointed One lives his life through me –** *we live in union as one*! **My new life is empowered by the faith of the Son of God who loves me so much that he gave himself for me and dispenses his life into mine!' – Galatians 2:20 TPT**

God is still good. He is still just and fair. His love never fails. His Word never returns void and His ways are always better than our own. His will is for each of us to prosper. None of our pain can ever trump God. Never. He is bigger than any mess you find yourself in and if I can come out the other side of my stuff, you can too. He cares about everything that happens in your life, the big and small things. He wants good and beautiful things for you, He doesn't punish you or push aside to make someone elses life better. Ever.

'If God gives such attention to the appearance of wildflowers – most of which are never even seen – don't you think he'll attend to you, take pride in you, do his best for you?' – Matt 6:30 MSG

I am not one of the lucky ones, nor am I more or less loved than someone else. I simply made a decision to deal with every tear better than the last one, and learnt what thoughts to entertain and what ones to stop listening to.

I became stronger in who I truly am because of God. My story isn't any more special than yours, or more significant. Nobody's story is considered beautiful because of the clothes you wear when you tell it or the successes you have to show for it. It's beautiful because of how you live it and the light that shines from you in spite of it.. The good and the bad, and the in-between. The beauty lies in the 'again' moments, where people can connect to you and be encouraged that it is okay for them to try again. Until I take my last breath, my story hasn't yet been fully told. Neither has yours. You will make a difference in someone's world because of how you live yours.

34

Get your hopes up, again

"When God made his promise to Abraham, He backed it all the way, putting His own reputation on the line. He said, "I promise that I'll bless you with everything I have—bless and bless and bless!" Abraham stuck it out and got everything that had been promised to him. When people make promises, they guarantee them by appeal to some authority above them so that if there is any question that they'll make good on the promise, the authority will back them up. When God wanted to guarantee his promises, he gave his word, a rock-solid guarantee—God can't break his word. And because his word cannot change, the promise is likewise unchangeable." - Hebrews 6:13-18 MSG

If reading that doesn't get your hopes up, again, I'm not sure what will to be honest.

For one of our wedding anniversaries, my husband and I went on a hot air balloon ride. I never realised how big they were until I was standing next to ours reading to jump in! They seemed to take forever to fill and be raised of the ground. Once you were up floating in the sky, you knew it only took something small to cause you to come crashing down pretty quickly. Hope has felt a little like a hot air balloon to me, forever to build up and comes crashing down so quickly. It's a strange thing really, it takes forever to build up and yet in an instant can be taken away.

Hope is a word that evokes so much feeling and it's hard to describe. For you, maybe it fills you with excitement. For me, it's starting to fill me with more excitement, but for a long time, it was a word I avoided the same way I avoid anchovies. I wonder if it's possible to feel neutral about this word? A little bit excited and a little bit fearful. Can one be in the same space as the other? Furthermore, should life have *some* expectations but not be lived according to them? So many questions!

When I explored the definitions of expectation and hope, there was a similar theme summed up in three words - *regard as likely*. Hope and expectations are often described as a state of wanting, hoping, dreaming, believing and trusting for more. When it's put like that, you can't help but look forward. You can't help but have a little…hope and expectation. I don't have the answers to the above questions, just my opinion based on my life experiences. I think there's a time when you need to set expectations and there's a time where expectations can cause more damage than any benefit. Like anything in life, expectations can be a good thing and a not so good thing. I'm constantly learning the key to expectations is how you manage them, and understanding the difference between good expectations and ones that can be harmful.

There is a view that the best way to avoid making the wrong decision or a mistake even, is just to not do it. This book nearly didn't become real. I know it's not perfect, some sentences aren't structurally correct and some words might be misplaced or misspelt. I don't expect that I will have the same opinion on some things as I did when I wrote it ten years on. Instead of not doing this at all, I changed my expectations. I didn't publish this book expecting to sell 1 million copies. I do hope that it helps people choose to live a beautiful life. My hope is that this book is the light you need, that you use my story for your own benefit and that it reinforces your sense of worth and value. If I have any expectation with this book, it's that God will not be limited by short comings.

I appreciate the theory behind not setting expectations for some. Arguably, if you keep the bar low you'll never be disappointed. You'll never have a reason to doubt yourself or even beat yourself up, again. You'll never have your hopes crushed and courage dented. Life may even be more enjoyable if you're not living up to a measured standard of achievement that you may not reach. True and that's one train of thought. I agree there is validity to some of those statements, maybe you do too or maybe you strongly disagree. Let's keep going. If you're somebody who has dealt with some level of pain or disappointment, then I imagine you definitely do. I've set many expectations for myself and my life, and felt completely defeated when I've missed them. I didn't even come close to some. If my expectations were a dart board to illustrate, my dart didn't even reach the board but instead fell to the ground!

We've all missed the mark. We've all had our hopes come crashing to the ground. The condition of your mind is the tool that will help you become responsible with your pain, and the life you're left when you miss the mark. In doing some research for this chapter, hoping to wow you with some incredible insight from business coaches and world influencers, I was genuinely shocked to find anything encouraging about expectations. Every quote I found was about preparing you to come up short.

There was very limited quotes or material I found that was positive and hopeful. The general message seemed to be 'reach for the stars but you'll probably land on the moon so be okay with that'. If I am honest with you, I've never been okay with that. I found myself silently arguing with these quotes and wondering if there is another perspective or whether I'm the odd one out to be not agreeing with this train of thought. So, I asked God about His thoughts about expectations and it seems He didn't agree either.

'Now to Him who is able to do immeasurably more than all we ask or imagine, according to His power that is at work within us.' – Ephesians 3:20 NIV

'That's why I don't think there's any comparison between the present hard times and the coming good times. The created world itself can hardly wait for what's coming next. Everything in creation is being more or less held back. God reins it in until both creation and all the creatures are ready and can be released at the same moment into the glorious times ahead. Meanwhile, the joyful anticipation *(expectation)* deepens.' – Romans 8:18-20 MSG

'In the morning, Lord, you hear my voice; in the morning I lay my requests before you and wait expectantly.' – Psalm 5:3 NIV

'Now a man who was lame from birth was being carried to the temple gate called Beautiful, where he was put every day to beg from those going into the temple courts. When he saw Peter and John about to enter, he asked them for money. Peter looked straight at him, as did John. Then Peter said, "Look at us!" So the man gave them his attention, expecting to get something from them.' – Acts 3:3-5 NIV

Have you been on a long journey with your pain or does the one your on now feel like it might be a long one? If so, like me, maybe you've started to expect pain and even disappointment. Maybe hope is the very last thing you thought you'd ever do, again. I became someone who expected to fall short, not be invited or seen, and not achieve what I'd hoped to. It seemed impossible to not expect disappointment, it was all I seemed to feel for many months at a time. Time after time I asked myself, "How do I expect God to move and give us the gift of a child (or bless my business, or bring breakthrough, etc) when all we have to show for our expectation is tears and emptiness?". Maybe you can relate to this.

The truth was I was saying one thing and believing another though. I caught myself one day saying, "I am hoping this might be our month to fall pregnant, but expecting not to be". Hope and expectations fighting with doubt and unbelief. What my mouth was saying was different to what my heart was believing. For every step I was taking forward, I was instantly following it with another step backwards - never making any ground or moving anywhere. Just stuck and defeated - and so the cycle continued for many years.

The very thing that helped me break free and actually get my hopes up again was forgiveness. Forgiving myself, my family and friends, strangers and very much so, God. Forgiveness made surrendering my plans and desires, for His will to be done actually possible. Forgiveness granted me something I wasn't expecting, the gift of patience in the wait. Eventually my heart softened and my mindset changed, but it took time. Time for the effects of anger, resentment and frustration to wear off, just like a hit of anesthetic.

In 2019, God asked me to get my hopes up again. It was a big ask as I'd just come to a place in my life where I wasn't working towards anything or praying for a specific need. I felt like I was just floating in the sea, and then God said "it's time to swim again". Only a loving God can do that.

He asked me to expect more than just pain from life again. Years prior, I remember being offended when He asked me the same question. With new understanding and with a healthy dose of maturity in my faith, I traded my offense for gratitude. Pain is now something I appreciate, don't necessarily like however. I appreciate pain because it led to moments like the ones I just shared, moments where my heart was remolded and shaped by His love. When our expectations line up to His Word, His will and His plans we will never, and can never be disappointed.

Pain has helped me become a wife who expectantly prays for her husband. Pain has helped me become a daughter who expectantly prays for her family.

Pain has helped me become a daughter who expectantly prays for herself. Pain has helped me become a friend who expectantly prays for she loves. Pain has helped me to get my hopes up again and pray. Pain has helped me see the value in prayer, *and* to pray until she sees God move in this life, full of expectation will move at the right time in the right way.

> **'There's a way that looks harmless enough; look again – it leads straight to hell.' – Proverbs 16:25 MSG**

Even in our pain and even when our hopes or expectations fall short, God can still be glorified, if we allow it. Expectations are part of our relationship with God, we just need to be careful where we place them on people.

Could there be more than what you've known for so long? I believe so. I believe it's safe to expect more from Him. Maybe you are weary. Maybe you are worn out. Maybe you are out of breath. Maybe your faith seems too faint to move any mountains. Maybe. But one thing is for sure, you are not dead. Disappointment can feel like a deep sleep. God is asking you to wake up and emerge from your deep state of sleep.

> **'We wait in hope *(expectation)* for the Lord; He is our help and our shield.' – Psalm 33:20**

> **'There's absolutely nothing His power cannot accomplish, and He has infinite understanding of everything.' – Psalm 147:5 TPT**

35

It's okay to ask, again

'A thief has only one thing in mind— he wants to steal, slaughter, and destroy. But I have come to give you everything in abundance, more than you expect - life in its fullness until you overflow!' – John 10:10 TPT

'They'll help you live a long, long time, a long life lived full and well... Your body will glow with health, your very bones will vibrate with life! Honour God with everything you own; give him the first and the best. Your barns will burst, your wine vats will brim over.'
– First part of Proverbs 3 MSG

God hasn't just given us a life, He gave us life abundantly, holding nothing back.

I know it can be a real challenge to expect anything good can happen in life when there hasn't been much good or everything has felt like a constant struggle. Sometimes that's where the abundance starts – aligning your thoughts to God's and pushing past what you feel. I know from experience, that no good thing will come from a mindset where expectations have been built on a false truth, a truth that doesn't match with the Word of God. You will never achieve anything good, significant or grand if your mindset is full of false truths that you believe - you're not smart enough, it will fail, someone else is doing it better, no one will support this, and so on. All that happens is your trap yourself into a mental prison where there's only rejection, doubt and self fear to be friends with.

Hallmark movies, especially Christmas ones, are renowned for having perfect families where the children grow up watching their parents have a special love and want it for themselves. It's amazing how men always seem surprised by how much we love a good love story, mine included. I'm addicted to Hallmark romance movies, even if it is way too obvious how it's going to end, but I did have to stop watching them for a while. I started to measure my own reality against the perfection of a scripted movie that aimed for perfection. I thought my marriage wasn't good enough, I needed more friends, my life wasn't good enough, where I lived wasn't nice enough and the list went on!

These movies that I love so much highlight what we all want but cant have - perfection. What caught me most of guard was how these innocent movies highlight the impact of my parents' divorce, the lack of finance while growing up, and a trail of unanswered prayers and brokenness from my own decisions. I didn't realise until after watching another one of these movies and feeling worse than when I started that all those things left me with a mindset of not expecting anything more than what I had. Asking for anything more just seemed like such a big thing and I never knew why, until then. My husband and I were dating for six years before getting engaged, we wanted to be sure. Getting married wasn't the issue for either of us; it was how it would end was. For me, I just thought it would end in divorce like it had for my parents. It had almost become factual, there was no emotion to it.

'But I have come to give you everything in abundance, more than you expect - life in its fullness until you overflow!'- John 10:10

A marriage that ends in divorce isn't one that is abundant, or more than anything I ever expected or lived to the fullest and overflowing. Fortunately, God had a plan to show me He didn't just want me to give me a marriage that lasted for a period of time. He wanted me to have a marriage that was full and balanced and equal, that was rich in love and trust. He wanted me to know my value and worth in my marriage, and for all those things to felt by my husband too. He too came from a divorced home and neither of us wanted to live it again. Our expectation of marriage wasn't something terrible, but it wasn't great. Fortunately for us, God isn't scared of our hesitations and reservations. God is a creative God and uses everything in our lives to get our attention, it's just up to us if we see it.

One night in our dating years, while my husband and I were swing dancing, God took me on my own private dance. To give you some understanding of what type of dancing…we enjoy 50's and swing dancing. Craig is amazing and has a unique ability to make me look better than I am. There are often many older couples at the places we dance, and every now and then a cheeky gentleman asks for my hand to dance, while giving my husband a wink. This one night, God asked for my hand to dance (we didn't actually dance!). As we floated around the floor, He told me to look over at a couple who must have been in their late 80's/early 90's. They looked so sweet as they held each other and slowly shuffled along the dance floor in their own world. They smiled at each other and stayed close the whole time. Each move they took seemed effortless and in perfect harmony. It was as though I was watching a happily-ever-after right in front me, but this was better than any Disney princess movie I'd seen before. That's when God whispered, "I've given you a happily-ever-after too!". Suddenly I wasn't watching a beautiful couple in their later years, but I saw Craig and I dancing…happily ever after.

Day after day, week after week, and month after month I was reminded of that vision, and there was a choice in it. A choice to believe God's Word over my life rather than the expectations I had held onto for so long. I've found old expectations like to come back every now and then as if to see if you're still not only believing God's truth for you but if you're bold enough to ask for it. Maybe again. Subtle little lies and thoughts come to our minds, each time giving us the choice to align our life to the hope we'd placed in God, again. For me, it was the opportunity to fix my thoughts on His Word, write out His promises, and ask for what was rightfully mine. Again. You might have to too.

Will you continue to agree with the expectations you placed over your own life built off your past pain OR will you say 'yes' to more of what God wants for your life?

The second choice is the one I would recommend you make. Be warned though, if you choose the second it will take trust. Sometimes more than you've ever used before. Trusting the process is hard. We aren't fortunate to see our whole life laid out in front of us like a Monopoly board with all the pieces in front of us. There are so many stories in the Bible, especially in the New Testament, that tells us Jesus didn't do the expected miracle right away. He rarely did anything expected really. He didn't just feed the 5000 people without the disciples needing to ask first. They had to learn to ask and then trust Him. If they wanted more, they had to not only ask, but expect and more importantly, trust for more. He needed their trust to show them they already had what they needed in Him. On that day when there were 5000 hungry people, I wonder if they really expected Him to do something? Or did they hope He would, but deep down not think anything was possible? Time and time again, He shows us this pattern.

In another story, when the raging storm came and nearly killed all who were in the boat with Jesus, He could have prevented it from the very beginning. Jesus never was, and never will be, caught off guard like they were. If Jesus had not allowed storm to happen they wouldn't have had the chance to believe, and to trust. To build their hope and expectations in Jesus's name, not their idol gods or false mindsets. I bet Paul wished He could've had his the trust He was trying to tell the rest of ship to have reinforced another way rather than being shipwrecked and bitten by 2 snakes! Sometimes we're the vessel for others to build hope and expectation of more.

Then there's Mary and Martha in John's Gospel, their response would've been mine I think. If God had just come when they asked, everything would have been okay. But He didn't, He came when He knew the time was right. I'm not sure if it was a lack of trust on their part, as much as it was a lack of expecting more. No one had raised anyone from the dead before (that I know of), it just wasn't possible. They knew Jesus could heal, but they didn't know He could bring the dead to life – yet. What they also didn't know was their story was part of a process and plan that involved more than just them. If Jesus had gone straight away, we wouldn't be learning from it over 2000 years later. Jesus knew Lazarus needed to be dead so Mary and Martha could understand who Jesus is, and ultimately so we knew who He is.

Bringing Lazarus back to life was the last big miracle the disciples and the general public saw before Jesus was crucified. The disciples had seen so much in their time with Jesus and yet they still doubted Him most times. My goodness I constantly feel like I am learning from the disciples, slowly. They struggled to understand much of what He said and how anything different to what they had seen before was possible.

> *God didn't You just see my periods come again – why couldn't you do something? Why won't You do something? Anything. My business is just closed. Mum isn't here. God don't You see?! When will you finally do something? Can't you see all hope is gone. Dead. There's no undoing it. How do you expect me to dream, to hope, when the tomb is wedged shut!?*
> JOURNAL ENTRY 18.11.18 TRUST THE PROCESS

This journal entry reminded me there's always been another in the fire. Life isn't a book where it flows perfectly from one chapter to another. It is messy and sometimes just when you think you're at the end of a painful season, you find yourself right back at chapter three facing something new, or maybe familiar. When you know you're not alone you heal quicker. You learn to get your hopes up again and you learn to ask for what is rightfully yours, again.

'But even now I know that God will give you whatever' – John 11:22 NLT

Even though we're nearing the end of the book and the journal entry I've used in this chapter would suggest I've learnt nothing from the start, the truth is, this is where it matters most. The first time I wrote something like this, it took months and even years to get past it. I still have these moments but the time the pain lasts is less. Sometimes it's still day and sometimes it's hours, minutes and even seconds now. All God has shown me, taught me and told me comes rushing in like a flood. My prayer of desperation and confusion quickly turns into hope and assurance. I now understand I can't just ask for something to happen, and not align my words to God's Word. Once I ask, it's a choice to agree to the expectation. It has always been and always will be a choice, an invitation.

Asking means our expectation is anchored in a decision to believe in who God is and what He can do. Honestly, it's just another physical act of surrender. Not in my might but by His might and power. Expecting more of God means saying 'no' to fear, uncertainty, and anxiety. When we do that, it leaves an open space for Him to be bigger in our eyes.

> **'Trust God from the bottom of your heart; don't try to figure out everything on your own. Listen for God's voice in everything you do, everywhere you go; He's the one who will keep you on track. Don't assume that you know it all. Run to God! Run from evil! Your body will glow with health, your very bones will vibrate with life! Honour God with everything you own; give Him the first and the best. Your barns will burst, your wine vats will brim over.**

IT'S OKAY TO ASK, AGAIN

But don't, dear friend, resent God's discipline; don't sulk under His loving correction. It's the child He loves that God corrects; a father's delight is behind all this.' – Proverbs 3:5-12 MSG

36

It's okay to receive, again

I think that expectation, in God's language, is just another word for hope. Since we've just finished talking about hope and asking for more, it seems only fitting we talk about the piece to the triangle – expectation.

> **'Don't fret or worry. Instead of worrying, pray. Let petitions and praises shape your worries into prayers, letting God know your concerns. Before you know it, a sense of God's wholeness, everything coming together for good, will come and settle you down. It's wonderful what happens when Christ displaces worry at the centre of your life.' – Philippians 4:6 MSG**

I love a cuddle from my husband and a kiss on the forehead. I've often wondered if heaven gives out kisses. As mentioned in the previous chapter, I love a good romantic comedy. I'll trade any romantic comedy for a really good cry any day! I adore love stories, most of my friends hate it when I pick a movie because they know they'll need extra chocolate at the end of it. These movies are my not-so-secret indulgence. I won't pay money to see a movie that scares me out of my skin, but I will pay money only to end up crying. Go figure!?

Like my Hallmark movies, the ending is normally pretty predictable and has the same underlining theme - guy fights for the girl and guy gets the girl. I'm sure most boyfriends and husbands hate these movies because they're full of the things girls want guys to do, but guys don't always do. Every girl wants their boyfriend, husband or fiance to be just like the gorgeous lead in the movie. In the movie, all of his gestures are perfect, there's one thing they always do - the classic kiss on the forehead to remind the girl she is safe and loved. It gets me every time! There's a sense of ownership (in a healthy way!) and protection in it. Every girl knows that feeling, resting your head under the chin of their man and just being all theirs. You can visibly see the girl melt as she receives a forehead kiss, it's one of the best feelings! Hallmark has got nothing on God though!

'Nevertheless, blessed be our God forever and ever. Amen. Faithful is our King.' – Psalm 89:52

Imagine God, the best dad in the world, coming over to you for no reason and giving you a kiss on the forehead. Embracing you as only He could. Then, imagine if all of heaven came and kissed you on the head too! You actually don't have to imagine it because that love surrounds you every single day. When you know you're deeply loved, there's a sense of rest upon your days. When you know you're deeply loved, you can lay down all your struggle and pain, because someone's got you.

It's in that very moment of pure love and acceptance, every bit of pain is absorbed into His love. That is how gentle and kind God is. I used to be so upset when God would take things away from me, leave mountains unmoved or hold things back. It felt like He was enjoying it, when really He was making room for more, something different. He was taking away things, or withholding, that had the potential to cause more pain, while giving me a kiss on my forehead. If that isn't the definition of a beautiful exchange, I am not sure what is.

I was awake early this morning with the thought that the horrifically beautiful story of Jesus' death on the cross is also the same story that sits in line with our hopes and dreams. For the people of Israel, the way Jesus entered their world and did what He did wasn't what they expected or even hoped for. He didn't fit the profile picture they had imagined or/and He didn't come in demolishing every evil enemy as they thought He would. They made their minds up on what it should all be like based on what they had seen and experienced before. They never expected to see anything different. They didn't make room for that. They hadn't made room for God to do the impossible, the yet unseen and the yet unfelt. Are we the same today? Well I am. When God doesn't answer the way we expect, we mourn. Well I do. I sulk even. Just like His followers did for the days after His death, I can so easily be believing that they thought it was all over. That feeling of it's all done, it's all over and there are no more chances, is all too familiar. In their mourning, they actually celebrated! He was defeated. Now that is a convicting thought! But the prayer was still in motion, they just hadn't moved to the next scene yet. God was still working. He is still working now. In my life. In my mourning of what hasn't been, am I celebrating that He can't do anything? Am I celebrating He is a God of cannot, will nots and does not instead of just haven't yet? Where is my hope? My expectation?
    JOURNAL ENTRY 21.04.19 - THE CROSS

"Now, because of You Lord, I will lie down in peace and sleep comes at once, for no matter what happened, I will live unafraid." - Psalm 4:8
TPT

I love the idea of living unafraid. Bravery and courage aren't words I would use to describe myself, others definitely, but not me. Bravery makes me think of someone who is single minded and focussed, unmoved even. If overthinking was a sport, I'd have a few Olympic gold medals by now. I don't see or hear about brave people overthinking every decision or option available to them, being double minded or too scared to try something. I am sure they have their moments. I hope they do because it gives me hope that if they have are scared and unsure at times, then maybe I could be brave after all. I don't believe being afraid is the sin or the problem, I think the problem and what God is concerned about, is when you live from a place of fear. When fear dictates your decisions, when it stops you from trying and when it tells you you're never good enough. When I lived from this place, doubt and fear, I had no belief I was able to receive anything more than what I had. I simply didn't expect anything good to happen, therefore if it did, I'd push it away.

"Now, because of You Lord, I will lie down in peace and sleep comes at once, for no matter what happened, I will live unafraid."

For a few moments, let's pull apart this scripture. When you lie down, you often close your eyes. We all rest in different ways - some listen to music, read or pray. I do all three. In that state of rest and expectation is where you can start to allow yourself to dream. It seems easier and there's less struggle to fight back or wrestle away dreams when you're laying down. I feel like I need to be honest here. The thing about asking is, you might not always receive, well receive what you were asking for or hoping. Each time I have rested or laid down, my heart feels lighter and fuller, fresh dreams come alive as well as hope, and my expectation is bolstered again. That's when you can live, live a life unafraid because you have rested and been made new.

'At each and every sunrise you will hear my voice as I prepare my *sacrifice of* prayer to you. Every morning I lay out the pieces of my life on the altar and wait *for your fire to fall upon my heart*' – Psalm 5:3 TPT

Nothing has been more powerful for me than receiving a kiss from heaven, it's always been a moment of transformation for me.

STANDING WELL

I love there are many 'forehead kiss' moments in our life; we don't just get one or two. The very nature of God is about increase. Just spend some time reading any story in the Bible where God truly moved, and you'll see no story ends with any lacking or holding back. There might've been moments where those things were part of the story, but when God is involved, it always ends better than we could have asked or expected. Always. The only person holding Him back in our eyes is us. Each of these moments, are moments of more. More of what? More love than any of us have ever experienced before. More forgiveness than any of us deserve or have felt before. More blessings than any of us have been given before.

When a mother smothers a child and kisses them all over, it's the child who you see squirming and trying to wriggle away from her embrace. A mother never has a quota of kisses she can give out, her kisses and love is endless. Between the mother and the child, it's the child who is the one that pulls away. It's the child that says they've had enough. God's love for us is exactly the same. He is a big God and His love is big enough for us. His love is always ready to be poured out. Always. Think of your time in a shower. When the shower is on, the water keeps pouring until you turn it off. The shower can't turn itself off or determine when it thinks you've had enough water, that is up to us. Have you ever been in the shower and stood to the side, trying not to get too wet because the water isn't hot enough yet? This example of being in the shower is a great way to think of how you receive God's love. How many times have you turned the tap to God's love off?

Maybe you've turned it back on wanting more after a bad day. Been there! When you say 'yes' to Him, He never holds back. Sure, it might look different to what you would have done or expected but His love pours freely and without restraint. He never thinks you've had enough for the day. He doesn't tell you He is busy when you need some reassurance. Even when we stand to the side, trying to hide because of shame and guilt, His love still falls upon us even if it is just a sprinkle. So often we are the ones that pull away. And we are the ones that limit what we think He can do, limit what we receive.

> **'Then he said, "Take the arrows," and the king took them. Elisha told him, "Strike the ground."He struck the ground three time and stopped. But the man of God was angry with him and said, "You should have struck the ground five or six times. Then you would have struck down Aram until you had put an end to it. But now you will down Aram only three times' - 2 Kings 3:18-19 NIV**

The old testament can hard reading sometimes, everyone seems to be so angry and fierce! All joking aside, I never really understood this passage of scripture until I heard it preached at church one Sunday. So often we're the ones who limit what we receive, not God, and this scripture is a great example of that.

I resonate with the king so much, he didn't know what he could ask for *and* what God was able to do. I too have been scared to ask, or expect more, in fear I'll be left empty handed or simply denied. I never realised how much impact my childhood had on my thinking until I opened my first business and started our fertility journey. In my first business I was just happy to receive what anyone was willing to give me, this along with a few other reasons is why it didn't work. I didn't value myself. I didn't value God or the value He had over my life. It wasn't much different when asking for a child. I often didn't feel I had the right to ask, let alone expect the prayer to be answered.

A defeated mindset will always leave you empty handed, not because of God but because of yourself. I am not saying that to be cruel, I am saying that because I lived with that very mindset for close to 40 years. When prayers were answered or blessings came, nothing was good enough. In the silence, bitterness and resentment grew while gratitude faded away.

In my mind, being quiet means to be removed.

If you can't speak up and have your say then you aren't part of the solution. It means to be non-active, meek and mild. Dead even. How do you remain silent in the Lord but remain alive and full of life? Full of expectation to receive more? Once the mouth is shut, it is too easy to keep it shut. I've been thinking about what I've been saying of late. Often in the workplace my character and intentions can be questioned, even to the point where I question myself.

I've just finished reading 'The Heavenly Man' and I have been deeply impacted. What a story! I sat there so many times unsure if I could have walked through what he did and still say God loves me. Still stay faithful to the course. He never let fear stop him from receiving. The one thing that hit more initially was his first fast. Yes, he refused to eat and drink, but he refused to speak as well. He didn't speak because he didn't want to interrupt God's promise, burden his heart more and to have rest. Maybe when I don't have the words, that is actually God's gift to me?

Perhaps it is God's way of protecting me from making my heart heavier, hurting other people and being even more discouraged? Maybe His love isn't always in the form of the warm and fuzzies but maybe it's in the gift of practicality? Maybe when I think I am dead; I am actually more alive than ever before?

JOURNAL ENTRY 13.4.2019 BE QUIET, BE ALIVE

If you are not feeling God's love is it because He turned the tap off or because you did?

37

Keep praying

Does a prayer have to be spoken or can it be written?
　Does it have to be known by others?
　Does it have go for a certain period of time?
　Does it have to follow a certain script and format?
　Can it be sung instead of spoken?

I think prayer can be all those things. I personally think prayer is most powerful when they're heard. The idea of what prayer is and how it should be done is different for you and me. We are facing different situations, leading us to have different reason for praying. If you're treating your prayers like a shopping list, however, from experience I will say it only leads to disappointment. I know because I did it for so many years. When a child doesn't get a treat when they go shopping with their parent/s, they often throw a tantrum. Ever thrown a tantrum as an adult, it's not so funny! I was no different when I went 'life shopping' with God, except then I called it prayer.

My faith was dependent on what He gave me from my list, and even what He didn't. I treated healings, breakthroughs and miracles like they were items I wanted from the latest catalogue from heaven. I circled the things I wanted and told God all about why I thought I needed them, and deserved them!

I've even told God I'd pay the cost of express shipping in hope that my waiting could be less than any time before. I missed the whole point for so long. Even if prayer was a shopping list we could write and give to God, there would be no point as He already knows what is on the list! It shouldn't come as any surprise that I wasn't given my shopping list desires. His 'no' wasn't because He was mad or angry with me, or that He wanted me to lack any good thing. Quite the opposite, actually. He wanted to give me more than I ever imagined, and He wanted relationship with me. He wants that with you too!

'The serpent was the shrewdest of all the wild animals the Lord God had made. One day he asked the woman, "Did God really say you must not eat the fruit from any of the trees in the garden?". "Of course we may eat fruit from the trees in the garden," the woman replied. "It's only the fruit from the tree in the middle of the garden that we are not allowed to eat. God said, 'You must not eat it or even touch it; if you do, you will die.'"' – Genesis 3:1-3 NLT

God's 'no' isn't always easy to hear, let alone understand. Why would any loving father say 'no' to their child? It doesn't add up. It doesn't make sense why someone who loves you, and can do something about the pain you're in, do nothing to stop the tears from falling. The devil knows this very point is something that causes us great confusion and I'm sure this is one of the reasons he twisted God's words around to deceive Eve. The devil knew if he could get Eve so caught up and focused on God's 'no' then she wouldn't see everything He had said 'yes' to. One taste of the forbidden fruit would never have come close to how sweet the rest of God's blessings would've been for Adam and Eve. Nowhere close. I think He still says 'no' today for the same reasons.

He loves us so much and He knows what's best for us, even when we don't see it or understand. No father would let his child eat a candy every night just before bed after they'd brushed their teeth, the child's tooth would fall out and a life of suffering the child would ensue if he said 'yes'.

What does this all have to do with prayer? Soon I found out prayer, and the joy of prayer, wasn't about the 'yes' or 'no'. God could've given me everything I've ever wanted in my moments of demanding, but He knew I still wouldn't have been satisfied. Just as it was true then, it still is now: His true desire is to have relationship with me. He wanted it for me then and wants me now, to experience the joy of what living in true, deep relationship with my Father, my Creator, my God feels like. Living in harmony and unity with Him will be more than any gift of prayer answered. His 'no' is never about me missing out. Soon I found out prayer, and the joy of prayer, wasn't just about me receiving an answer to my prayer.

Prayer wasn't about what was in my hands after a successful shopping trip, or about giving God a lists of things I wanted and then waiting for delivery. Prayer wasn't sitting on my Father's knee once a year and listing off all the things I think I deserve based on how good or bad I was. It definitely wasn't about bargaining with Him and doing a trade, 'if you give me this one thing God, I promise I will tithe every week'.

'And did you know that your cousin Elizabeth conceived a son, old as she is? Everyone called her barren, and here she is six months pregnant! Nothing, you see, is impossible with God.' – Luke 1:36 MSG

Who said it? Who are you letting have the final say over your pain, your life and over your prayers? Jesus is the one who has the control, so can I encourage you to give Him the final say. How you view your pain will ultimately determine how you pray. When you know who you are praying to, it changes everything. Your prayers become less about the problem and more about the One who has never lost a battle or can do all things. When

I go to my doctor and tell him about my sickness, but I go to him because I want his knowledge and help. I trust he'll have the answer to help me. I know who he is, what he is trained to do and that he help me with my sickness. We have had a patient/doctor relationship for years, so I trust his word. Why can't it be the same with God?

Prayer with God will always be about relationship. A relationship based upon two people talking and engaging in conversation, listening and sharing together. But who is the other person in the relationship for you? Have you spent time with God to know who He really is? In order to trust what He says, and go to Him with all things, you need to know who He is. Remember the journal entry I shared earlier – 'Respecting the Pain'? Well, it can be applied here too. Let's read it again, this time with a different filter.

> *Imagine if we truly knew who dwelled in us? Imagine if we really knew whose name we said when we prayed? Imagine if we really believed what we said? Imagine if. This thought has really hit me this morning.*
>
> *Would more of my prayers be answered? Would my life be dramatically different? Would the lives around me be different? Would my relationship with Him be different? Would it be what I imagined? Would I still be frustrated and confused and juggling my pain with my faith?*
>
> *Maybe. Imagine if, I woke up to the reality and the true understanding of who He was – I believe then, those questions wouldn't matter because I would be awoken to who I am because of who He is in me.'*
> JOURNAL ENTRY 31.07.2019 - IMAGINE IF

When we know who God is, just like our doctor, we can trust Him to listen to us and help us. Having a relationship with God involves time together. Time together outside of church, connect groups, podcasts and other people. Young couples need to spend a lot of time alone in order to get to know one another and learn to trust one another. They need to have conversations where it's just the two of them. Group dates are fun and provide a way of getting to know how one another acts around their friends, but a relationship is built when quality time is spent together.

I know this question might seem random at this point, but have you ever had a sports injury?

I've had a few, including the classic rolled ankle and fractured wrist, however, things took a significant turn when I had to have multiple surgeries on my wrist a few years ago. The result of the surgeries meant I'd have limited movement permanently in my left wrist. Ironically, the restriction allows the wrist to actually move better and means I can live 'normally' without pain medication or a wrist guard. I'm nothing like an elite athlete, but my surgeries meant I could understand what it meant to still move even when injured. An injured athlete doesn't stop training completely, instead they go about their training differently. Their capacity has changed but it doesn't mean they don't give their all anymore. Living life with pain is the very same. After my surgeries, I had to approach my fitness training differently. I couldn't do the same exercises as I used to, I had to change my approach.

When I started to go back to the gym it took time to lift certain weights and trust my body, trust it was capable of doing what it used to. My capacity had changed, and in some ways for the better. I found I could do some things better than I could before, and my belief in myself was greater. Living through a painful season is like knowing you have an injury you have to be aware of. You're aware of what will make your injury worse and delay your healing.

Again what does this have to do with prayer? Being injured doesn't mean you stop, you just rest. When you do start to move again, there's a chance you move differently. And when you're injured you really understand the importance of prayer, but sometimes your injury means your prayers sound a little different too. Prayer is vital when dealing with your pain. It brings you closer to God, and Him closer to you. Prayer draws a line in the sand,

and is the only tool that will help you and me live a life well. Especially when pain is front and centre in a season of our lives.

Prayer sometimes is simply saying 'no' to believing the lies the enemy is trying to trick you with. A prayer of 'no' leads to a beautiful prayer of 'yes' to God, every time. He hasn't finished working in your life, and He is not withholding from you because you haven't been good enough. He adores you. Prayer is about listening to one voice alone, and allowing yourself to believe in His name again.

'So let God work his will in you. Yell a loud *no* to the Devil and watch him make himself scarce. Say a quiet *yes* to God and he'll be there in no time. Quit dabbling in sin. Purify your inner life. Quit playing the field. Hit bottom, and cry your eyes out. The fun and games are over.
Get serious, really serious. Get down on your knees before the Master; it's the only way you'll get on your feet.' – James 4:7-10 MSG

38

Peace lives here now

"'Would you like to get well?' 'I can't sir,' the sick man replied 'for I have no one to help me into the pool when the water is stirred up. While I am trying to get in there (not by our power but by His!) someone else gets in there, ahead of me.' 'Stand up, pick up your mat and walk'" – John 5:6-8 MSG

I don't like camping. It doesn't make any sense to me – packing everything up only to unpack when you get there, pack back up to go home, only to unpack when you get home, clean and repack everything again ready for next time. That's more work than in a normal week of work. I'm exhausted just typing about it. But as much as I don't like camping, I have become very good at it. I've camped in my pain for weeks, months and even years at a time. Declared, "I'm not moving" and found every excuse to stay. As I started to prepare for this chapter, I was reminded of the blind Bartimaeus story in the Bible and would love us to pull it apart and study it.

'Then they came to Jericho. As Jesus and his disciples, together with a large crowd, were leaving the city, a blind man, Bartimaeus (which means "son of Timaeus"), was sitting by the roadside begging. When he heard that it was Jesus of Nazareth, he began to shout, "Jesus, Son

of David, have mercy on me!". Many rebuked him and told him to be quiet, but he shouted all the more, "Son of David, have mercy on me!". Jesus stopped and said, "Call him." So, they called to the blind man, "Cheer up! On your feet! He's calling you.". Throwing his cloak aside, he jumped to his feet and came to Jesus. "What do you want me to do for you?" Jesus asked him. The blind man said, "Rabbi, I want to see.". "Go," said Jesus, "your faith has healed you." Immediately he received his sight and followed Jesus along the road.' – Mark 10:46-52 NIV

He was blind and he had his place in society. I'm sure we can all relate to that; we all have our titles and places in society.

You're not a mother. You lost a mother. You are married. You are single. You are a citizen of the country you live in. You are travelling through. You didn't finish school. You didn't go to university. You are rich. You are poor. You are sick. You are healthy, and the list goes on.

All these labels mean you fit somewhere in life, and in society, but they also mean you don't fit somewhere else. Bartimaeus was disqualified from having the right to speak up because of his title given to him. Bartimaeus was expected to be quiet and set up a home in the reality of his pain. Some thought he should've been appreciative for what he was given, he should've wanted or been hoping for anything more. At every moment of this story I imagine his mind was a battlefield and his heart was under constant attack. The devil is patient, and he was quite happy to wait this out. Like a snake that wraps itself around it's prey, slowly taking each breathe, the devil was slowly squeezing Bartimaeus's life out of him. The devil spent years investing in this man, belittling him and slowly breaking him down until he gave up.

"He can't heal you! He's not talking to you, it's for someone else! If He really cared, He'd come to you! What if everyone is right and you are stripped of your mat and robe?"

"Why bother?", was a question I asked myself many times. Why should I bother to hope or expect for more? Why should I bother to try when history has shown me nothing different will happen? I was so comfortable with who I was with pain, I never considered who I could be without it. I can imagine Bartimaeus had years like this too.

Imagine how mad the devil was when he realised Bartimaeus wasn't ready to give up just yet?!

Bartimaeus could've let each lie get louder and louder, to the point it almost drowned out God's love for him. Bartimaeus wasn't interested in tantrums and justification anymore. And neither is Jesus. It's time it didn't matter to us either. Bartimaeus had lived with what his life was for so long you wouldn't blame him for starting to become comfortable with it, familiar with it even. Maybe even safe with it. But he wasn't. One day he'd enough, and he decided to move. He wasn't a young man when his path crossed Jesus. Day in and day out, he put on his designated robe and settled into his mat, and place in society. Society had given him a mark and a place, little did they know that when Jesus comes knocking, it's moving day!

Remember what I said about God's voice being one that drowns out everything else? Regardless of what was being shouted at him, God's voice and truth was louder.

"What do you want me to do for you?" Jesus asked him.

Bartimaeus finally discovered his identity wasn't in his pain, on the mat or in the robe he was given. It was in God. I love that Jesus didn't come to him and make it as easy as He could have. Bartimaeus had to make the choice and do some of the work. He had to choose to leave what was familiar and push past the resistance. That in itself is a battle. In the story, it feels like it all happened within minutes, and maybe it did, but to Bartimaeus I can imagine it felt like a lifetime. The thoughts he would've had to battle just to shout out loud at the start, the doubt and the unbelief would have been real. His first move wasn't physical, it was mental.

It was a decision that enough was enough. He wanted to change his address and he wanted more than what society had said he was worthy of having. I can imagine there was a period of time where he had to adjust to his new normal. He could finally see, he could finally be part of society and he had a full life to live ahead of him. This story has been something that I've become all too familiar with. I've been so encouraged by this story many times, each time reminding to get off my mat and put it in the storage cupboard.

I wish I didn't have to admit this, but I've also gone back to the storage cupboard and pulled the mat out, sat down and sulked more times than I'd like to admit. Just like Bartimaeus, Jesus was calling me to Him, His promise, His breakthrough. Unfortunately, I didn't understand this back then and I stepped back because of the crowds. I allowed the noise of everyone else to soften my courage to trust Him. The devil doesn't care about any of us, he just cares about keeping us as far away from God as possible. At any point, any of those thoughts could have been justified and been what Bartimaeus chose to believe. I am so glad he didn't; his story is still teaching many of us today!

"Be quiet" some of the people yelled back at him.' – Mark 10:48 NLT

The thing with God's voice is when you hear it, everything else goes dull and out of focus. Every other lie goes dim and it propels you forward. His Word gives you the ability to trust. I think Bartimaeus should be known as brave Bartimaeus, he is to me anyway. I would put Ruth in here too but that's for another time. When you've travelled, partnered, learnt to live with, or journeyed with pain for a long time, you feel like you're safe there. It gradually starts to be a familiar place because you know it so well. You know what to do and how to control your emotions when you are in the most intense parts of it. I suppose you could say it's like knowing how to do life with pain lingering in the background, like a day-old headache that won't go away.

My husband hates when I get a headache, I hate it too, but it he really hates it. He hates seeing me in pain and discomfort, and he hates not being able to fix it. He hates how my headaches hold me captive and the drugs I take to fight them off. They're less frequent than what they used to be, but when they hit, we both know about it. It stops any momentum I have for the day. When they come, though, I know what to do and how to deal with them. The same can be said for the other pains in my life; they just aren't as easily made to go away with a tablet and glass of water.

When my mum died, I thought I was okay. After all the life we'd done together, I thought I'd prepared myself enough for what happened. I know now only part of me was prepared. I was prepared for the fact it was her choice, but I wasn't prepared for when, how, and where it all happened. I wasn't prepared that it would actually happen.

In 2018, June 17th marked ten years since my dad sat me down to tell me what had happened. In reality, it took me ten years to heal. That day, the decade anniversary, was a day I closed the door on the pain of shame and regret I had carried for ten years. I didn't close my heart to the love I still had for her and the memories I cherished; I simply let go of the pain that came with losing a mum as a young woman. It no longer formed my identity and no longer held captive my dreams of being a mum without her here.

Since that anniversary, the pain has remained well behaved and controlled for the most part. Sometimes it has not. When it doesn't, they're hard days. It demands all my attention, and no matter what I try to do to calm it down, nothing works. That's when I realised that this pain, the one of losing my mother, was no attached to a new pain - my heartache over not being able to fall pregnant. I felt I deserved the right to linger in my self-pity a little longer. Years went by as I moved between what was no longer and what is yet to be, a woman without a mum and a woman who wasn't a mum. I found a place to camp, set up my tent and I was not moving. It almost gave me comfort knowing I was settled somewhere, I belonged somewhere. I just made the pain of not being a mum a place I wasn't moving from!

Throughout this book you probably keep noticing I referencing a child throwing a tantrum. That's because when we don't live well with our pain, we are like children throwing our very own tantrum! I've been that child through the years, especially at this point. Just like a child in the heat of a tantrum, I was no longer listening to anything anyone was saying. I was just shouting because I could and in that moment it made me feel better! Not even the pain of someone's else story quietened me. When someone was brave enough to share their story and struggle similar to mine, I'd tell them about my pain in waiting and how much longer it had been. I simply shouted over the top of them, and I am truly ashamed of those times.

"I promise you we've prayed every prayer and it just doesn't work for us" "We've tried and it doesn't make sense!" "The doctor say we can't" "We're too old now and we've missed out chance!" "We don't have enough money"

Equally, I'm ashamed of the years I wasted building my own story instead of letting God's story for my life be told. My pain and battle wounds became my bragging rights. I never considered God had a different story for me, or a different title over my name and life. Unlike Bartimaeus who was given his title without his approval, I gave myself my own titles which dictated the story I believed about myself.

I was the girl who went to church on her own. I was the girl who lost a mum, and furthermore to suicide. I was the girl who came from a divorced home. I was the girl who lost her childhood and knew what living with the bare minimum meant. I was the girl who battled anorexia. And now, on top of all that, I was girl without a child. In the midst of my tantrum, I couldn't hear what God was speaking over me.

The story of what wasn't became louder than what could be, might be, and what I hoped, would be. I was the girl who is a survivor. I was the girl who knew how deeply she was loved and because of that, I was able to pour love upon others and help others see how deeply they were loved. I was the girl who had a beautiful marriage. I was the girl who was planted in church where I was safe even when storms hit.

Your reality might be all of those things, none or some of those things, but that doesn't mean God is done. Bartimaeus was blind, not dead. Your story may be dry and with limited light, but it's not dead. Bartimaeus was old, he didn't have any money, the doctors couldn't help and I'm sure he thought he'd prayed every prayer available. Nothing changed his situation. Until Jesus came and his normal changed. He now had a new normal.

Where there was rejection, there was now peace.
   Where there was fear, there was now peace.
   Where there was hurt, there was now peace.
   Where there was anxiety, there was now peace.

We all have mats we are roll out and sit on, I surely did for many years. Here's the thing, the devil gives mats and Jesus gives red carpet. Mats are places where pain becomes the star attraction and it eats away at your life. Red carpets lead you to the unknown and open spaces only God can fill. Bartimaeus didn't just get off his mat, but he stepped onto the red carpet for his life. The day he moved, was the day his life truly began and peace began to be his constant companion.

Will you move off your mat and let peace live where pain once did?

39

Someone needs your story

I love movies and books about real life stories! Not crime ones, the ones that are full of hope and encouragement. The ones where people had massive mountains in their path and they climbed them anyway. The stories that defy logic and inspire you to do something special with your life. Oh man, I love those stories. I love these stories because they aren't free from struggles or fierce storms, but actually celebrate them almost. Why has Anthony Robins, Oprah Winfrey and Joyce Meyer sold so many books? Because they're written from a place of mountain tops. What are some of the great stories that come to mind for you?

For me, it's a wide mix of business people and everyday people. In recent times I've come to love Eddie Myeltt, Jamie Kern Lima and Gary Vee, but I also love the stories of Kevin Hart, Heidi Baker, Richard Branson, Jenn Johnson, and Jennifer Hudson. Their stories inspire me and leave me with many questions for my own life. Here's the thing, by the time they tell their story they're on the top of the mountain that tried to crush them. For years and years I was told to write a book, problem was I was nowhere near my mountain top. I measured the value of my story against others instead of trusting that sometimes God uses seasons in the valley to be the greatest stories to be told.

In late 2021 I entered a business competition my local Christian radio station was holding. I entered with honestly no expectation I would win but decided to enter anyway. As months went on, I forgot about it completely. It was Tuesday afternoon, almost six months since I entered and the phone rang. Previous to this phone call, I literally had been asking God if I'd heard Him wrong and that I was done struggling to make this business work. Every day felt like I was in the valley and every time I looked up, my mountain top seemed to get further away and harder to reach. That phone call was a life raft moment. Within seconds I was live on radio being told I'd won their business competition – talk about a mountain top moment. It felt as though someone had just picked me up in a helicopter and placed me straight on top of my mountain top. I couldn't wipe the smile off for days. As the excitement grew, a strange thing happened. My business got quieter and things got harder. Yup. I had my very own ad running on the radio reaching nearly 70 000 people a week who were my target audience, and my business was quieter than before. Radio silence actually. Instantly I was back in my valley. Fast forward to the end of the six month prize, and there was no mountain top moment. I was still only getting a few orders come through every week on a good week, and not much seemed to change. I will be very honest with you and say my faith took a big hit after that. I was mad. Deflated, annoyed, scared and everything else.

I've come to learn there are people who are amazing mountain top story tellers, and there are some that amazing valley story tellers. I am a valley story teller, and I've come to be okay with that. I want to be very clear, I am not playing the victim. Far from it. Maybe Paul can explain what I mean better.

"I want you to know how glad I am that it's me sitting here in this jail and not you. There's a lot of suffering to be entered into in this world—the kind of suffering Christ takes on. I welcome the chance to take my share in the church's part of that suffering. When I became a servant in this church, I experienced this suffering as a

sheer gift, God's way of helping me serve you, laying out the whole truth. This mystery has been kept in the dark for a long time, but now it's out in the open. God wanted everyone, not just Jews, to know this rich and glorious secret inside and out, regardless of their background, regardless of their religious standing. The mystery in a nutshell is just this: Christ is in you, so therefore you can look forward to sharing in God's glory. It's that simple. That is the substance of our Message. We preach *Christ*, warning people not to add to the Message. We teach in a spirit of profound common sense so that we can bring each person to maturity. To be mature is to be basic. Christ! No more, no less. That's what I'm working so hard at day after day, year after year, doing my best with the energy God so generously gives me." - Colossians 1:24-29 MSG

I've come to love my story and see what it has to offer people, I think I got it from my dad. My dad has done well for himself in business, and he shared a time where he was talking with a friend of his who had also done well in business. My dad's success came from doing it the hard way. There was no lucky break, just lots of hours, endless stress and living between almost going bankrupt and the great moments where it all works! Fortunately he finished with all working out very well and I'm so glad it did, he deserves it. However, his friend got lucky break after lucky break. My dad knows how to sit with people in business who want to give up and walk them out of the valley. My dad's friend can't. There's no understanding, empathy or skills to pass onto someone in the valley. But his story is a great mountain story, it inspires you and gives you hope. There are mountain top story tellers and valley story tellers.

There are not many people who had the gift like I have or even my dad, yes gift. A gift to walk through many valleys and still be standing. My story is richer because of each my valley's. I may not know what extreme success looks or feels like, or what it's like to have miracle prayers answered, yet, but I know my story still holds worth. I think of my story as one that's like offering someone else walking through their valley a cool drink and place to rest while they regain their strength.

Someone who knew about valleys and mountain tops well was Abraham!

His story feels like just as he climbs one mountain, he is back down the other side and into a new a valley. His story has so much value, it's a story many can identify with and learn from – myself included. One thing many know about him is that he had to wait a long time to be a father. A really long time! Just when I imagine he and his wife Sarah were about to give up all hope, God's promise came alive. They had a son! I envision they rightfully soaked in every moment of being parents for the first time. Talk about a mountain top moment! I imagine he expected life to be pretty good from that point on, given that life hadn't been necessarily easy up until that point. And then God said it's time to climb an *actual* mountain and leave his heart there too, his son.

That's a lot to ask of anyone, but even more so given how long Abraham and Sarah had waited for this blessing. Honestly, I'm not so sure I would've been as obedient as Moses and Sarah (the bible doesn't tell us of her reaction to this request. Did she know?), I would hope I would've but I just don't know. The story tells us God saved Isaac and blessed Abraham for his obedience. I'm not so sure either of the men loved mountains after that but I am sure they loved the story they could tell from it!

That story would've brought so much encouragement to everyone they encountered all the days after. A story that's been personally lived has so much more value than one not. Please hear me, I am not disregarding mountain tops. Not at all. Mountain top stories hold just as much as value as valley ones. Mountain tops stories are often like ropes that pull people out of their valleys and act as life rafts when people don't think they can hold on a minute longer. Standing on top of any mountain (or indoor rock climbing platform), no matter the size, is a beautiful feeling and one that needs to celebrated. Life suddenly seems achievable in that moment, manageable even. Mountain tops are not just places of celebration and rest, but platforms of transformation and encounter too.

When you're on your next mountain top, savour the moments and linger a little. In every movie or TV show I've seen where someone climbs a mountain, they never rush straight back down. They stand and catch their breath. They look around and often down, amazed at where they are compared with where they started. They look out onto the horizon and consider their next mountain, but before they do, they linger and soak it all in. I feel God is asking the same of us when we are the top of each of our mountains. Maybe you never expected to reach the top. In those moments, He's inviting us to sit with Him before embarking on the rest of our journey.

He's giving us time to reflect, appreciate and rest. Your story isn't just about the mountain tops you stand on, or the one you hope to get to, but it's about the valleys too. The valleys are the very foundations in which mountains sit on. Let that sit for a moment. This book has primarily been about the valley's I've walked through and ones you might be able to connect with. These last few chapters are about mountain tops. In my days I've discovered God's work of transformation starts often when we are in the valley, and with every step forward we make our way out and up to our very own mountain top. There'll be another valley and another mountain top, but the next valley you walk through will be different because you are different. You've learnt things you didn't know before and you're better equipped. After each mountain we have a choice before we embark on our next – to be the same person we were when we first started, or use what we have learnt from this climb and do the next better. The reality is that euphoric moment is what gives us the strength to walk through another valley.

I was ready to give up on the beautiful business God has given me because I was tired, felt defeated and a little lost. I wondered why it felt so hard when others had just seemingly easy success. Then the phone rang. My mountain top moment lasted a week and then I was back in the valley. If it wasn't for the brief moment on top of the mountain, I wouldn't have shown up every day to do what God asked me. He knew I needed some fresh air, a fresh perspective from a different point of view and to see my story was still being written.

One of the editors of this book said this to me when I was complaining about being back in the valley, "Claire, your story of withstanding is one that is rarely told. It's easy to tell your story when everything has fallen into place and life is good. It's easy to tell people to pray and keep praying until your miracle comes. It's easy to believe God is good and make good choices. It's easy when you're on the mountain top, not so much when you're in the valley. You refuse to turn your back on God even though anyone would say you have every right to. You refuse to stop holding on, trusting, believing and giving Him your days just because you're in the valley. That is a story that needs to be told. That is a story that will be the reason people choose to hold on one more day. Mountain top story are incredible, my valley stories are the one that are real"

Someone needs your story.

Someone needs your story to know they will be okay, just like you were, and they too can trust in God's love, maybe for the first time or maybe all over again. Someone needs your story to hope, again, and pray, again. Your story gives someone hope their their own mountain top is close, and that if someone else survived, they have a chance too.

[Jesus said,] "I have told you these things, so that in me you may have peace. In this world you will have trouble. But take heart! I have overcome the world." – John 16:33 NIV

A life without pain isn't real, with or without God.

Each one of us at some point will face situations that take all of our courage and strength to overcome. Jesus's life wasn't free of pain, humiliation and hurt. His life still was beautiful regardless, and in fact, His pain is what connects us to Him. If He just floated through life we wouldn't be able to go to Him and bare our heart. He knows pain, He lived it and watched others struggle with it. His story is richer and more relatable because of pain, not the exclusion of it. The whole point of this book is to help you see there is still extraordinary beauty in your life, even though it might have been painted with seasons of pain. You are not disqualified, if anything you are now even more qualified.

Your story gives you a seat at a table you might not have been welcomed to otherwise. Why? Because you know how it feels to walk through the valley and stand on the mountain tops. You know God is faithful and you know He is worth holding onto. *Your story will* tell others to expect fruitfulness from hard seasons, and help people believe healing from pain, not be exempt from it. Your story tell others to expect to have help in times of hardships, and that to expect God to still be a good God when surrounded by darkness. Your story will tell others to expect Him to still be able when everything seems impossible. Imagine if you didn't read my story, now imagine if no one knows your story!

There's no doubt there'll be more pain in life, maybe more confusion and doubt, and maybe there'll be other prayers that may go seemingly unanswered. There might be more tears, along with the joy. Maybe. It doesn't really matter how many 'maybes' you or I have, because we know someone needs all of it to help them find their story. My story used to be about the pain in my life, now it's about saying thanks for the lessons pain and helping God use it all to make my story one that can help another.

'Because as for me, (I expect that when) I call upon the name of the Lord to save me (not anything else like a book, my own self, google search or friend – but God alone!), (I expect) He will save me. Every morning I will move my soul towards Him (in expectation that He will see me, and hear me!). Every evening I will explain my need to Him (because I expect Him to care enough to matter to Him). Every waking hour I will worship only Him, (in expectation) He will hear and respond to my cry.'
Psalm 55:16-17

JOURNAL ENTRY MAYBE...BUT MY EXPECTATION | 24.10.2018

40

Standing Well

"Stand up straight" "Shoulders back, tummy in" "Stop slouching"

It takes effort to stand well. No one else makes you stand well but you. Your parents, teacher or loved ones might influence your decision, but no one can make you stand a certain way but you. You might not have asked to be in the painful season you find yourself in, but you do have a choice how you stand in it. I know it hurts and know it's probably unfair, but that doesn't mean you can't stand well. You can't love others well and still have a beautiful life. As mentioned in the previous chapter, I didn't think my story had much value and really wrestled with its purpose. To be really honest, some of my hesitation was from the fact I didn't want to relive some of the memories I had chosen to forget, or cause people to hurt any more than they already had healed from. However, the value of anyone's story, including my own, isn't in what tried to knock you down, but how and why you still stand.

I was invited to a Saturday brunch in 2021 to celebrate Mother's Day. I'd made over 300 candles for church to gift every mother with the following morning, and my dear friend wanted to honour me and make a space for me. This year was especially tough given the recent death of my second aunty brought up a lot of old memories about mum. After the brunch and when everyone had left, myself and few other women stayed to clean up.

I think we did more laughing and talking than washing up! My book title came up in discussion and my friend stopped washing up, tuned to me and said this….

"Claire, I like the title but don't love it. It's not the truth. Yes you are still standing after all the different seasons of pain you have endured but more than that, you are standing well. There's a difference between still standing and standing well. Still standing makes me think of a rock against the waves (representing hard seasons that come against you), and standing well makes me think of seaweed. The seaweed is no less strong just because it swerves and sways, if anything it's stronger BECAUSE it does that. Its foundations never move but it stays soft and open. A rock, however, is hard and sharp. It hurts other people if it comes to close (stubbing your toe) and if the wave pushes hard enough, the rock can always move. It's roots aren't bedded in a deep foundation. We can choose to be a rock or seaweed when wave after wave comes. There's no glory in just or still standing if your heart is hard and you're unkind to others. Anyone can become bitter and angry at God, and everyone else. It's hard to be the seaweed. To still move when God asks you to, forgive when you don't want to and see sunshine on rainy days. You my friend are seaweed".

I wanted to end this book not with more stories of what I have endured, I am actually glad to say I don't have many more!, or even too many more of my own thoughts. Instead I wanted to pull apart of story that tells of two people from the bible who was still standing and one that chooses to stand well. It's my hope you find your own way to stand well in whatever trial or season of struggle you are in. We have no idea when life is going to take a turn for the worst, but we have been given the gift of wisdom to know how to react when they come. The bible is such a sweet gift that almost give us the gift of hindsight, giving us teachings to learn from so we don't actually have to live out the lessons. Sometimes we still need to do that too.

The story of still standing

'But the angel reassured him, "Don't fear, Zachariah. Your prayer has been heard. Elizabeth, your wife, will bear a son by you. You are to name him John. You're going to leap like a gazelle for joy, and not only you—many will delight in his birth. He'll achieve great stature with God.' – Luke 1:13-15

The response of a rock

'Zachariah said to the angel, "Do you expect me to believe this? I'm an old man and my wife is an old woman."' – Luke 1:18

We don't know much about Zachariah and his wife Elizabeth's heart about being parents, except that when they became parents it all seemed too late. I often wonder if it was something they longed for deeply like Abraham and Sarah, or was this caught them completely off guard. If it mattered, I'm sure God would've mentioned it but what mattered in this chapter is the response to God. Zachariah's response is one that's confronting because I am sure at some point, you've been there just like I have. The story doesn't tell us if the angel appeared to Elizabeth too or if her husband somehow told her, or if she just found out the old fashioned way. What the story does tell us is her response.

'It wasn't long before his wife, Elizabeth, conceived. She went off by herself for five months, relishing her pregnancy. "So, this is how God acts to remedy my unfortunate condition!" she said.' – Luke 1:24-25

Elizabeth removed herself, from her husband and her friends, and anything familiar.

That is a bold move, some would say a power move even. I love her trust in God was bolder than any fear she felt. She knew this was a miracle and she wanted to protect it. She didn't make it happen on her own, and she recognised her part to play in it. Although the glory wasn't for her, we are still talking about her obedience today, and her wisdom to look after the promises God gives. While Elizabeth spent time soaking in God's gift of peace and love, her husband stayed angry and doubtful. His response created a divide between himself and God, and everyone he held dear.

God knew the only way He could help Zachariah become responsible with managing his pain and disbelief, as well God's promise, was to make him unable to do anything but trust Him and be quiet.

'But the angel said, "I am Gabriel, the sentinel of God, sent especially to bring you this glad news. But because you won't believe me, you'll be unable to say a word until the day of your son's birth. Every word I've spoken to you will come true on time – *God's* **time."' – Luke 1:19-20**

'Zachariah's mouth was now open, his tongue loose, and he was talking, praising God!' – Luke 1:64

God was aware that Zachariah's ability to praise was based solely on Him performing for him.

God wanted more. More for Zachariah because He knew how much it would bless Zachariah. The ability to praise when nothing seems will always bear good fruit. Zachariah had spent his life telling himself and others how good God was, and now he had a chance to put into action and he chose not to. Zachariah had to learn that his response mattered. While all this was happening for Zachariah and Elizabeth, the greatest story was unfolding for Elizabeth's cousin Mary. She wasn't even married and possibly not even thinking about children when the angel Gabriel appeared to her. In my mind, she had a greater reason to question what was about to happen, more than Zachariah. He at least was married and had been possibly waiting for a child. Mary though, was nowhere close to that being her reality. Her response stirs me every time:

The story of standing well

'**She was thoroughly shaken, wondering what was behind a greeting like that. But the angel assured her, "Mary, you have nothing to fear. God has a surprise for you: You will become pregnant and give birth to a son and call his name Jesus." – Luke 1:29-33**

The response of seaweed

'**And Mary said, "Yes, I see it all now: I'm the Lord's maid, ready to serve. Let it be with me just as you say" Mary didn't waste a minute. She got up and travelled to a town in Judah in the hill country, straight to Zachariah's house, and greeted Elizabeth.'**
– Luke 1:38-39

She didn't waste a minute. I've wasted many minutes, many hours and many days questioning God. Wondering if He really spoke and what I feel to do, is really what He is asking me. But Mary just said 'yes'. She would have so much weight on her mind after that encounter, along with so many questions.

What was everyone going to say and think? How did this even become possible? What would Joseph say or feel? Would he stay or leave? Why was she chosen? Would she be a good mum? Did she know how to be a mum?

Have you ever been there? Mary knew her response mattered though. So she too removed herself and joined Elizabeth. Both these women knew the power of a response and managing their pain was the key to standing well. While they had an incredible joy, their hearts were heavy with so much to consider. Mary had an outside world ready to judge her and Elizabeth was separated from her husband, a husband she couldn't even communicate with. They knew they had to keep strong and protect their blessing. Now wasn't a time for disbelief and doubt. Now was a time for wisdom and faith.

The pain Mary endured nearly 30 years later, as she watched her son be crucified and tortured, would've been truly heartbreaking. Luke 1 tells us about when she first carried Jesus and those few short months are what I believe set her up to not just survive, but live well. God knew the incredible joy she would feel as she gave birth to Jesus, but He also knew the depth of her sadness many years later. Mary's response isn't recorded, but we know she was there with Him as He was crucified. And yet, after all the pain she had endured, she still chose to say 'yes' to God again.

'They (the disciples) agreed they were in this for good, completely together in prayer, the women included. Also Jesus' mother, Mary, and his brothers.' – Acts 1:14 MSG

After the death of Jesus, Mary would have been completely justified to turn her back on God and His Kingdom. But then Jesus rose after three days. He again did the unimaginable, and unthinkable and incomprehensible. Her response mattered as much then as it did some 30 years before. Bad things in life will happen and we will experience great joy and great pain. God never promised we wouldn't suffer and giving your life to Him doesn't make you untouchable. But it doesn't make following Him any less worth it. So where do we go from here? That is a question only you can answer, and ask God. I've been pretty raw with you in this book, and it's my pleasure to share my story with you.

I ask that you allow yourself to be raw with someone in your world, and share your story with them. Put into practice all the things we have spoken about in this book and find your own way through your seasons of pain. Maybe you aren't ready to share your story out loud. That's okay. Start with God first.

Maybe you don't know Him and feel like you can talk to Him yet. Well, that's the easy bit. Once you let Him into your world, it can only get brighter! If you want to know who this God is I've been talking about and you want to meet Him, then simply say this prayer. Don't just say it though, mean it, and be ready for your world to change, and be ready to do the work. Remember, God isn't a genie in a bottle. He wants a relationship with you, meaning you both have to make the effort.

If you are willing and ready to have your healing start, say this prayer:

Lord Jesus, I have turned my back on you for too long. When you have outstretched your hand to me, I have walked away. I'm so sorry. Thank you for you being so patient with me. I know that I am a sinner and that I cannot save myself. I no longer choose to walk away from you, but instead invite you into every part of my heart, my body and life. By faith I gratefully receive your gift of salvation and am ready to trust you as my Lord and Saviour. Thank you, Lord Jesus, for coming to earth just for me. Thank you for saying yes to dying on the cross for me and my sins. I believe you are the Son of God and that you indeed rose from the dead on the third day. Thank you taking the weight of all my sins and wrongdoings, and in return giving me the gift of eternal life. I believe your words are true. Come into my heart, Lord Jesus, and be my Saviour. Amen.

Congratulations!
Welcome to the family, I am so excited for your future!

He adores you so much and I promise you all of heaven is celebrating right now! I can imagine you are full of questions, and there is nothing wrong with that. Find yourself a local church to go to, ask your questions with the pastor and go treat yourself to a Bible – it will be the best purchase you ever make!

For those of you who already know Him, this is your invitation to trust Him. Maybe more or maybe again.

He is bigger than any mess you find yourself in. If I can come out the other end of my stuff, you can too! I hope that with every new and old pain you face, that you don't run. I hope you find the bravery to say your pain is real and give yourself time to grieve for it. That bravery will help you find the right people to be your tribe and be the right people to help you to look in the mirror, reminding yourself of who you really are. But most of all, I hope you treasure your life and see it as beautiful. That you never doubt your creation, worth or value. And that you come to a place where you see your pain as a gift instead of a curse.

I pray this book helps you see God is always be bigger than your pain, and that pain doesn't have the right to have the final say over your life - only God does. Don't let what you feel and see but the truth you hold onto. Get connected to Godly loving people who will catch your thoughts and be a safe place to be honest. Lean into God and give Him all you've got, even if it's just a whisper and may love always find a way to rule your world.

Don't worry about tomorrow, just do today and God will do the rest.

All my love & prayers,
   Claire

(I'd love to hear your story, maybe if this book helped and the beauty you've found in your life again! Please feel free to contact me via any of my socials, or email. I'd love to include you in my prayers too, if you're needing someone to be your strength in your battle then just give me hola. It would be my honour to do so.)

Epilogue

"Thank you mum"

Your love for me was something I don't think I ever fully understood, cherished and protected. It felt overwhelming at times. But know I know how precious it was, it never faded.

You weren't perfect and this book was never about celebrating your flaws, quite the opposite. This book was about discovering the value in your story and using to help another, I know that's what you would have wanted. Yes we fought and yes our honesty with one another was raw and intense at times, but the love that bonded us was never in question. Never. It was messy and imperfect, but isn't love exactly that. It doesn't fit in a perfect box and it doesn't always look or feel like we think it should. This book is real because of your love. So you deserve the biggest thank you of all!

Thank you for teaching me about love and the relationship between life and love, not just with your words but with your actions. And lack of them at times. You never held your love captive to how I did life. Your love made me the woman I am today. It held me through some very hard and dark days. It saved me more times than I can say to you. It taught me how to love others without restriction.

Your love for me broke chains from generations before, of sadness and of pain. My life was the start of something new for our family because your love was so fierce. You wanted my life to matter.

EPILOGUE

Your love was like a lioness who protected her cub. You never wanted me to feel the depths of the pain and sadness you had felt.

I wish I appreciated your love more when I had it available to me. I have learnt to be responsible with my pain, my life and my heart because of you. It is my pleasure to finish a life of love you started, and to keep writing the pages you didn't have the chance to finish yourself.

You'll always be remembered for your red lipstick, white leather boots, colourful shirts, infectious smiles, warm hugs and generosity. You were the best listener and you always made sure everyone's needs were met before your own. You loved the water, a glass of french champagne, fresh seafood and dressing up.

I love you mum and I miss you more.

About the Author

Words by Claire Roberts begun on the Gold Coast back in 2020 as a *blog to encourage women* with *bible verses* and offer *free daily devotionals.*

Claire has lived on the Gold Coast for most of her life, completing all her education the big city by the sea. She loves spending her weekends out on the water with her husband of 14 years, often on SUP and eating fish'n'chips afterwards, reading a book by the pool. Her friends know her best for her love of water slides, cheese pizza, her choice in Hallmark romantic movies and always having an analogy or two.

* Claire became a Christian when I was in grade 3 but really committed my life and choices to Jesus in my mid teenage years. Her favourite translations are the TPT, NIV and MSG.

* She's a natural blonde, kind of. Officially she has dark blonde hair with a little help to keep it be more golden than it naturally is.

* She only discovered what I wanted to do in life when she was 38 years old. Since then she's written 7 Christian books and one devotional for women.

* She hasn't been able to be a mother.

* She's a friend you can never get rid of! Most of her friendships from 5 years up to 20 or more.

* She's petrified of birds!

One thing Claire is incredibly passionate about is writing and sharing her story, as well as celebrating the stories of others. She created **Words by Claire Roberts** to celebrate the gift of words, using them to carefully create Christian books, candles with biblical encouragement and other faith based resources like devotionals and affirmation cards.

You can connect with me on:
- https://wordsbyclaireroberts.com
- https://www.facebook.com/wordsbyclairerberts
- https://www.instagram.com/wordsbyclairerberts

www.ingramcontent.com/pod-product-compliance
Lightning Source LLC
Chambersburg PA
CBHW010244010526
44107CB00063B/2680